Sustainability in Hospitality

SUSTAINABILITY IN HOSPITALITY

Vikas Choudhary

CENTRUM PRESS
NEW DELHI-110002 (INDIA)

CENTRUM PRESS
H.O.: 4360/4, Ansari Road, Daryaganj,
New Delhi-110002 (India)
Tel: 23278000, 23261597, 23255577, 23286875
B.O.: No. 1015, Ist Main Road, BSK IIIrd Stage,
IIIrd Phase, IIIrd Block, Bengaluru-560085 (INDIA)
Tel: 080-41723429
Email: centrumpress@gmail.com
Visit us at: www.centrumpress.com

Sustainability in Hospitality

First Edition, 2013

ISBN 978-93-81460-25-2

PRINTED IN INDIA

Printed at Balaji Offset, Delhi.

Contents

Preface

The Sustainable Development concept is not the dream of some political party that disdains capitalism and considers it to be evil. Nor is it the consequence of the delusion of people who determined that this world would be better of if we were going back to our natural roots and resources. SD is definitely geared toward profitability and the future. Without profit it seems obvious that no business would be sustainable.

The goal of Sustainable Development is clearly to secure economic development, social equity, and environmental protection. As much as they could work in harmony, these goals sometimes work against each other. The rapid development of good living, travel, and the consumer society has often resulted in less protection to the environment and to some groups of the world population.

The players who have signed on for Sustainable Development include governments, non-government organizations, corporations, and high-profile individuals ranging from the Prince of Wales to Bill Gates The timing is excellent for media coverage of Sustainable Development initiatives. Concerns about global warming and oil prices mean that most media outlets. are seeking stories about strategies to counteract these issues, and Sustainable Development is an excellent such strategy. Media representatives (whether old-line media or web-based sources) must know about your values and understand the difference between your hotel's stance and that of your competitors. As demonstrated by the press release at the outset of this report, promptly share news of your actions and prompt clients to choose your hotel. As I said above, at the moment, Sustainable Development remains a unique selling point (USP) for a hotel. This will not always be true, because one of the underlying ideas is to spread the strategy, including to competitors. The fact that it is a novelty to include such an ambitious program in the strategy of a single unit makes it easier to communicate and prove that "One can make a difference!"

In the last two decades the concern for environment has raised spreading awareness among all. This is the result of terms like "Ozone depletion", "Greenhouse effect" and "Acid rain", coming to surface and the increase in the level of awareness all over (Walker, 2000). As people are becoming more aware of the environmental damage caused by regular business activities, it has become increasingly clear that the hotel industry, due to its very specific function, operating characteristics and services provided, consumes substantial quantities of energy, water and non-durable products. The resulting environmental impacts of hotel facilities are thus characteristically greater than those caused by other types of buildings of similar size. Although concern for the environment can affect customers' choice, the current economic climate and sector downturn would suggest that price and value for money would be the overriding factors. Hoteliers can schedule high investment projects later when they have confidence in and have established benefits from earlier environmental actions." Green" is seldom the over-riding determinant of product or brand choice but just another benefit or attribute that adds value, usually a 'feel good' factor to the overall product". Customers patronise hotels that have adapted green practices though not compromising on service or product quality. Consumers would prefer to use lodging that follows these practices but are not willing to pay extra for these services.

This book provides deep insight to various dimensions of issues relating to development of this subject.

—Author

1

Introduction

The Costs and Benefits of Tourism

As the largest industry in the world, tourism has the potential to help deal with the key issues facing many parts of the globe and therefore can be seen as a positive and negative force. If the costs and benefits of tourism are understood from the outset, strengths and opportunities can be maximized while weaknesses and threats can be minimized.

Each tourism planning situation will be different in terms of its tourism characteristics. The costs and benefits of tourism will vary in each destination, and these can change over time, depending on tourism and other activities in the local and regional context.

Tourism can be Seen as having the following Benefits and Costs:

Economic Benefits:

- Tourism generates local employment, both directly in the tourism sector and in various support and resourcesm anagemenst ectors.
- Tourism stimulates profitable domestic industries-hotels and other lodging facilities, restaurants and other food services, transportation systems, handicrafts, and guide services.
- Tourism generates foreign exchange for the country and injects capital and new money into the local economy.

- Tourism diversifies the local economy, particularly in rural areas where agricultural employment may be sporadic or insufficient.
- Increased tax revenues from tourists can be reaped if a local sales tax is added to the provincial and federal taxes already in place.
- Employment opportunities will be created in the business communities due to the influx of tourists who will need goods and services.
- Increased entrepreneurial opportunities will provide goods and services not already available in the community and create new tourist products.
- Improved road systems and infrastructure can be financed through tourism attractions.

Economic Costs

- The jobs created through tourism may be low paying and require few skills.
- Inflated prices may result from local businesses attempting to raise profits or cover the cost of extra employees.
- Inflated property values may occur if the community becomes a tourist 'hot spot'. This will result in higher property taxes that may be unfavourable for local residents.
- If tourism is seasonal at a destination, so too will be the injection of income into the community.
- Health service provision and police services can increase during the tourist season at the expense of the local tax base.
- Affordability and availability of staff housing can be problematic.

Social Benefits:

- The quality of life of a community can be enhanced by economic diversification through tourism, following the principles of sustainable development.
- Tourism creates recreational and cultural facilities that can be used by local communities as well as domestic and international visitors.

- Public spaces may be developed and enhanced through tourism activity.
- Tourism enhances local community esteem and provides the opportunity for greater understanding and communication among peoples of diverse backgrounds.

Social Costs

- Rapid tourism growth can result in the inability to meet the capacities of local amenities and institutions; quality of amenity services can be diminished by over-use.
- Litter, vandalism, and crime are concerns associated with tourism development that will be the responsibility of the community.
- Tourism can bring overcrowding and traffic congestion. Congestion can result in the perception of inconvenience by the residents, which is interpreted as a negative impact on their quality of life.
- Foreigners bring with them material wealth and apparent freedom.

Young members of the host community are particularly susceptible to these economic expectations that tourists bring. The result can be a complete disruption of the traditional way of life in the community.

An increase in crime may result from tourism. The community structure may change (including community bonds, demographics, and institutions). The authenticity of the social and cultural environment can be changed. Organized events for tourists based on local social behaviour and culture can become distorted in their authenticity, which may not be a valid representation of the local environment. Lifestyles may be disrupted beyond levels acceptable to the host community.

Cultural Benefits

- Tourism can enhancel ocal cultural awarenessb, ut eventually might distort it.
- Tourism can generate income to help pay for preservation of archaeological sites, historic buildings, and districts.

- Despite many criticisms about alteration of cultures to unacceptable levels, the sharing of cultural knowledge and experience can be beneficial for both the hosts and the guests at tourist destinations, and could result in the revival of local traditions and crafts.

Cultural Costs

- Youth in the community could begin to emulate the speech and attire of tourists..Loss and damage to historic sites may occur through tourism development and pressures.
- Long-term damage to cultural traditions, and erosion of cultural values, resulting in cultural contamination beyond the level acceptable to the host destination.

Environmental Benefits

Nature tourism encourages productive use of lands that are marginal for agriculture, enabling large tracts to remain covered in natural vegetation..

Parks and nature preserves may be created, and ecological preservation supported as a necessity for nature-based tourism. Improved waste management can be achieved. Increased awareness and concern for the environment may develop.

Environmental Costs

- Negative changes in the physical integrity of the area may occur.
- Rapid development, over development, and overcrowding can forever change the physical environment and ecosystem of an area.
- Litter, erosion, overtaxed sewage, a and waste management systems may occur.
- Sensitive areas and habitat may be lost.
- Degradation of parks and preserves through over-use and poor management ay result.
- Excessive waste may be generated.
- Water and air pollution may occur.
- Wear and tear on infrastructure is accelerated.

The Basis of Sustainable Tourism

Over the past two decadest, he inter-relatedness fall earth systems and human systems has become abundantly clear. We have clearly understood that no human action ever occurs in total isolation from other natural systems, and we have appreciated the reality that humans are dependent on the earth's limited resources. We have realized the fundamental importance of somehow finding ways to live within the carrying capacity of the earth. Over the last twenty years, the global community has been primed for some fundamental changes, including a search for "sustainable development" that is based on new modes of resource allocation and accounting, new attitudes toward the preservation of environmental integrity, and new ways of making decisions in all sectors. Among the imperatives that promote and enhance the vision of sustainable futures, including that of a sustainable future for tourism, are the following:

- prudent use of the earth's resources within the limits of the planet's carrying capacity; devolution of top-down decision-making responsibilities and capabilities to a broader range of the destination's stakeholders; the abatement of poverty and gender inequalities, and respect for fundamental human rights;
- enhancement of the quality of life through improved health care, shelter, nutrition, and access to education and income-generating skills;
- preservation of biodiversity and life support systems for all natural habitats; and
- preservation of indigenous knowledge and ways of living, and respect for the spiritual and cultural traditions of different people. In fulfilling these imperatives, governments and other societal agents must struggle to find an appropriate balance between different, sometimes apparently conflicting needs and value systems. Sustainable development must meet three fundamental and equal objectives, namely:
- economic: production of goods and services (the overriding criterion in fulfilling this objective is efficiency);

- environmental: conservation and prudent management of natural resources (the overriding criterion is the preservation of biodiversity and maintenance of ecological integrity); and
- social: the maintenance and enhancement of the quality of life (equity is the main consideration in meeting this objective) and inter-generational, as well as intra-generational equity in the distribution of wealth.

Achieving sustainable tourism development requires that the private sector and the public sector cooperate as partners in working toward a sustainable society. Making decisions about sustainable tourism development also requires that governments work within a broader framework than may have been used traditionally, working toward decisions that are:

- longer-term: to better anticipate and prevent problems;
- multi-sectoral: to include the full range of functions of the tourism environment;
- ecosystem based: to recognize the cumulative and synergistic effects of actions;
- wider: to recognize the impacts of their actions on other sectors, regions, and communities;
- deeper: to recognize that the causes and consequences of the problems they seek to solve may involve others and other institutions; and
- full-cycle: to consider the full context of resource use from initial extraction to end use.

Individual tourist resource management decisions will have to be taken with increased understanding of all these dimensions if the goal of sustainable futures is to be attained.

Achieving sustainable futures requires the development of appropriate tourism on a continuum where growth decisions, development viewpoints and sustainability issues are balanced with environment and economy. In order to achieve profitability and environmental sustainability in the tourism industry, the tourism industry as a whole must take a different approach to planning and development.

Relationships

We can examine the interdependent relationships between tourism and the environment in terms of the interaction of the visitor, the place, and the host community, using the framework of the tourism system described in Section I. These three elements interact with each other and are affected by external influences. The relationships are essentially two way and can be either positive or negative.

In ten Ds of visitors, we are aware of the range of impacts that growing numbers of visitors and their growing demands have on the places and host communities where tourism opportunities exist, and we know that an increasing number of visitors are searching for higher quality and more satisfying experiences. These trends can bring positive results if there is appropriate and sustainable tourism development in order that the health and well-being of visitors and local residents is ensured, so that communication, education, awareness, and understanding grow from tourism opportunities provided by a community and its location. If tourism is poorly managed, negative results-such as scarred landscapes from overuse, crowding, and traffic problems-will reduce the quality of the tourism experience and quite possibly lead to a hostile and/or exploitative host community.

The concept of sustainability can be interpreted in a number of ways, for example, as a philosophy, as a set of principles and/or values to guide development, or as criteria or tests for determining sustainability. Sustainability is possible only if tourism resources (natural, human-made or cultural) can be maintained over time. The idea of stewardship/trusteeship-to hold the resources of a country in trust for future generations and the responsibility to pass them on in good condition-is applicable here. This means that we want to achieve a situation that can be maintained without depleting the resource, cheating the visitor or exploiting the local population. Achieving sustainability (economic, political, social, cultural, and environmental) requires an ability to accept and accommodate change. It implies, also, that mechanisms are in place to mediate between different interests, which mayor may not be true in any particular setting or situation.

In general, the terminology associated with sustainable tourism is inconsistent and frequently confusing. In spite of this variability in terminology, various actors, and interests have attempted to define their perspectives on goals, practices, effects, and expectations of tourism.

Principles for Sustainable Tourism

Many destinations are now pursuing strategies that aim to ensure a sensitive approach when dealing with tourism. Many of these strategies are based on a formal expression of principles for sustainable tourism. Planners and others can use these principles as basic guidelines when attempting to incorporate the broad vision of sustainability into local policies and practices.

The list of principles provided below are important for destinations and organizations that wish to be guided by the ethic of sustainable and responsible tourism.

Residents of a community must maintain control of tourism development by being involved in setting a community tourism vision, identifying the resources to be maintained and enhanced, and developing goals and strategies for tourism development and management. Equally important, community residents must participate in the implementation of strategies as well as the operation of the tourism infrastructure, services, and facilities.

A tourism initiative should be developed with the help of broad-based stakeholder input. Tourism development must provide quality employment. The provision of fulfilling jobs has to be seen as an integral part of any tourism development. Part of the process of achieving quality employment is to ensure that, as much as possible, the tourism infrastructure (hotels, restaurants, shops, etc.) is developed and managed by local people.

Experience has demonstrated that the provision of education and training for local residents and access to financing for local businesses and entrepreneurs are central to this type of policy. Broad-based distribution of the benefits of tourism must occur at the tourism destination. Local linkages and resident participation in the planning, development, and operation of tourism resources and services will help to ensure that a more equitable distribution of benefits will occur among residents, visitors, and other service providers.

Sustainable tourism development has to provide for intergenerational equity. Equitable distribution of the costs and benefits of tourism development must take place among present and future generations. To be fair to future generations of tourists and the travel industry, society should strive to leave a resource base no less than the one we have inherited. Sustainable tourism development must, therefore, avoid resource allocation actions that are irreversible.

A long-ten D planning horizon needs to be adopted by businesses and destination tourism organizations to ensure that destinations are not used for short-ten D gain and then abandoned as visitor tastes and business interests move elsewhere. A longer-ten D horizon encourages the use of proactive strategies to ensure destination sustainability and the establishment of local linkages over time.

Hannony is required between the needs of a visitor, the place, and the community. This is facilitated by broad stakeholder support with a proper balance between economic, social, cultural, and human objectives, and a recognition of the importance of cooperation among government, the host communities, and the tourism industry, and the non-profit organizations involved in community development and environmental protection.

Tourism strategies and plans must be linked with a broader set of initiatives and economic development plans. A need exists for more coordination at both policy and action levels among the various agencies involved and among different levels of government. This is particularly relevant to tourism and environmental policies. Service provisions such as transportation, parking, and water and sewer capacities must also be considered in conjunction with tourism plans and developments. Cooperation among attractions, businesses, and tourism operators is essential given that one business or operation can be directly affected by the performance or quality of another.

There is a definite need for impact assessment of tourism development proposals. The capacity of sites must be considered, including physical, natural, social, and cultural limits and development should be compatible with local and environmental limits. Plans and operations should be evaluated regularly with adjustments as required. Guidelines have to be established for tourism operations, including requirements for impact assessment. There should be codes of practice established for tourism at all levels-national, regional and local. There is also a need to develop indicators and threshold limits for measuring the impacts and success of local tourism ventures. Protection and monitoring strategies are essential if communities are to protect the resources that form the basis of their tourism product.

Tourism planning must move away from a traditional growth-oriented model to one that focuses on opportunities for employment, income and improved local well-being while ensuring that development decisions reflect the full value of the natural and cultural environments. The management and use of public goods such as water, air, and common lands should include accountability on behalf of the users to ensure that these resources are not abused.

Sustainable tourism development requires the establishment of education and training programmes to improve public understanding and enhance business, vocational and professional skills.

Sustainable tourism development involves promoting appropriate uses and activities that draw from and reinforce landscape character, sense of place, community identity and site opportunity. These activities and uses should aim to provide a quality tourism experience that satisfies visitors while adhering to the other principles of sustainable tourism.

The scale and type of tourism facilities must reflect the limits of acceptable use that resources can tolerate. Small-scale, low impact facilities and services should be encouraged, for example, through financing and other incentives.

The tourism process must also ensure that heritage and natural resources are maintained and enhanced using internationally acceptable criteria and standards.

Sustainable tourism marketing should include the provision of a high quality tourist experience which adheres to the other principles outlined above, and whose promotion should be a responsible and an ethical reflection of the destination's tourism attractions and services.

These principles are ambitious, and it is fair to say very difficult to achieve so that tourism developments that will always adhere to all of these principles. However, these principles must be seen as targets for all tourism planning.

Strategic Integrated Sustainable Tourism Planning

The nature of sustainable tourism development requires a process of planning and management that brings together a series of interests and concerns in a sustainable and strategic form of planning and development. Tourism planning continues to be contentious and somewhat nebulous, because most government officials and tourism industry practitioners harbour their own definitions and parameters of the task. By its very nature, planning is multi-dimensional and is purposely integrative. Even in the less complex circumstances of some Asian and Pacific countries at early phases of tourism development, it is necessary for those with the responsibility to oversee-or administer tourism planning in the public interest to be cognizant of two special dimensions: strategic planning and integrated planning.

Need for Integrated Tourism Planning

Although there is evidence that some tourism destinations have been developed without conscious, strategic and integrated planning, many of them have experienced unforeseen consequences that have led to their deterioration.

(a) *The need for planning:* Some managers and decision-makers argue that we are overwhelmed with plans and planning processes. Others argue that we require more regulation and planning in order to ensure that the goals of sustainable tourism can be met. There are others who maintain that we require less planning and possibly less regulation. There is no right answer to the level of planning that a particular situation calls for and clearly every societal context will determine what is appropriate. Similarly, though sustainable tourism calls for a high level of local involvement in planning and developing tourism, the amount and quality of resident participation will vary depending on the cultural and political factors in the destination. It is obviously useless to develop a sophisticated planning system if there is no political or community support for it. In these cases, one might first have to create an appropriate setting or structure for a planning process that avoids the failures of past planning practices.

(b) *The failures of traditional planning:* Many people are sceptical about the effectiveness of planning. They see it as a waste of time since most plans never see the light of day and end up on a shelf. In many cases, planning in the past has tended to be very much based on developing regulatory procedures as opposed to creating suitable mechanisms for achieving the goals and objectives developed within the planning process. The failure of traditional and rational approaches to planning can be attributed to a number of factors as discussed below.

(i) Lack of flexibility : The logical, rational approach to planning, it has been argued, has made plans far too rigorous and unable to adapt to changing conditions. Unless the external environment is perceived to be quite static, a detailed stepwise approach that is rigorously adhered to could make it very difficult for the organization or destination to create an optimal fit between its resources and the forces influencing tourism in its setting. A dynamic approach as provided through strategic planning principles enables a dynamic planning process, better able to adapt to changes.

(ii) Lack of strategic thinking and vision : A major criticism has been launched against traditional, rational planning approaches by some researchers who argue that such plans lack leadership vision in the process of formulating strategies. The inclusion of "strategic vision" by leaders and decision-makers (not technical planning experts) ensures that the plan is not merely an operational plan, but provides direction and concepts for achieving the organizations broad goals and interests.

(iii) Ineffective top-down planning : Planning by the destination's planning officials or by retaining planning experts from outside the destination results in a plan which is unable to effectively represent the diverse opinions, needs and attitudes of a range of tourism stakeholders. The chances of successful implementation of such a top-down plan is further inhibited by the lack of community support and involvement in the process, particularly in political systems where residents seek greater participation in the decision making of their community direction.

(iv) Poor linking of formulation and implementation : Another major impediment to planning has been the inability to link formulation of the plan to the outcomes of implementation so as to ensure accountability and to measure the success of the planning exercise. The lack of clear, easy to implement actions and responsibilities to ensure accountability for carrying out the actions, has been a deterrent to effective implementation. A clearly deemed relationship between the planning and implementation of action steps must be present to ensure effective delivery of both the tourism experience and the sustainability of the destination's assets and resources.

(c) *Strategic tourism planning-an action planning approach:* A strategic planning approach is essential for sustainable tourism, whereby the disparate planning and development activities related to tourism are linked to an overall, broad strategic tourism plan to provide an integrated framework for directing tourism.

Strategic planning seeks an optimal fit between the system and its environment. Hence, it:

- Residents is long-term;
- contains vision;

- specifies goals (ends);
- specifies major actions (means) to achieve goals;
- specifies the major resource allocations to arrive at (ways);
- is dynamic, flexible and adaptable;
- ensures that formulation and implementation of the strategic plan are not discrete, but linked closely through constant monitoring, environmental scanning, evaluation and adjustment; and
- is not a linear process (e.g., constant environmental scanning occurs throughout the process to enable proactive response and adjustment; monitoring can start as soon as target indicators and levels are established to provide base line information).

A strategic approach to a sustainable community tourism plan also requires:

- close coordination with local and regional legislative and political
- structures; community participation and support;
- a new role for planners as educators and providers of technical expertise, but not solely plan designers; the plan is designed
- primarily by those who have a stake in the outcome;
- an innovative and inclusive organizational structure for joint planning; a learning community that is informed, educated and aware;
- applying the principles of sustainable tourism development to ensure the long-term sustainability of the ecology, the local economy and the sociocultural values of the host community, while distributing the benefits equitably among the stakeholders.

The nature of strategic tourism plans: Sustainable tourism planning requires a strategic planning approach, which seeks an optimal fit between the system and its environment through the creation of a long-term direction (vision), goals and strategies for the allocation of resources and monitoring impacts, and detailed action plans. This is achieved through dynamic, flexible and adaptable planning, where:

- The fomulation and implementation are closely linked through constant environmental scanning, monitoring, evaluation and adjustment of the strategic plan.
- The plan is created by a broad and diverse group of actors (stakeholders) whose needs, attitudes and values are closely reflected in the plan's philosophy, vision and contents.
- There is a clear recognition of the interdependence among the various components of the plan, which is considered in the creation and implementation of goals and strategies.
- Planning approaches span a broad spectrum, ranging from a rational, lockstep approach all the way to strategic, broad-based plans.

Despite this proliferation, a good plan generally contains the following elements and action steps:

- Vision and/or mission statement
- Situation (issues) analysis
- Strategic goals
- Strategies.

Implementation of strategies (measurable objectives and detailed action plans) Monitoring and evaluation of implementation strategies and action plans Adjusting the strategic and operational plans based on information feedback from evaluation and constant scanning of the external environment.

Strategic planning principles: Strategic tourism planning requires careful consideration of the goals and principles of sustainable tourism. Some of the goals and principles that should be considered in tourism planning are:

Economic

- Development which takes into account the full costs and benefits of the alternatives and decision embarked upon, from an overall economic and social perspective.

- Broad-based distribution of benefits among all stakeholders..Provision of a quality visitor experience that is compatible with the destination's goals and values.
- Ensure that fiscal costs of infrastructure provision and marketing do not outweigh the benefits (for example, residents may end up paying higher taxes to subsidize tourism development but may not benefit from improved income, social services, use of or access to the publicly constructed infrastructure, education and training opportunities, etc.

Social

- Steady employment avoids the underemployment and unemployment associated with seasonal hiring for peak tourism periods.
- Better employment opportunities than the low pay positions typically associated with tourism services.
- Quality jobs that encourage the use of local knowledge, skills and traditions, and offer a sense of fulfilment and satisfaction to the residents.
- Improved standard of living and equitable distribution of benefits within (and between) generations in the present and future.

Ecological

- Maintenance of essential ecological processes, biological diversity and non-renewable resources for future generations (through preservation or conservation strategies).
- Planning at a scale and pace that enables effective and ongoing monitoring and mitigation of long-term impacts.
- Full-cost accounting of environmental resources in cost-benefit analyses.
- An environmental and cumulative impact that analyses important prerequisites to development, and environmental management systems needs to be implemented by businesses and organizations.

Cultural

- Tourist activities and behaviours should be respectful of cultural activities, sites and values.
- Designs should be compatible with national and local heritage and character and should foster the community's identity or sense of place.

Tourist types and activities should match the needs and expectations of the local people, with protection of sensitive and indigenous cultures against any adverse impact.

Political

- Compatibility between overall economic development goals of regional and community interests and tourism goals.
- Integration of plans and planning with other relevant community and regional plans and processes.
- Balance top-down planning with resident input and participation in planning and development.

(d) Strategic tourism planning-an action process

The major steps in a strategic planning process for tourism for a community-based destination is outlined in the figure that follows. Note that while the steps appear sequential, the process is an iterative one, with feedback loops connecting the various stages. It is also important to note that this is a recommended process-each nation/destination may need to tailor this process to suit its own requirements, norms and values.

Means of Achieving Strategic Action Oriented Integrated Tourism Policy

Tourism planning can operate at many levels:

- The individual site. (Examples include a beach, heritage site, park or theme park.)
- The destination. (In some cases the site and the destination may be the same, but usually it refers to the larger geographical setting where the site is situated.)

- A region within a country. (This can be a geographic or political boundary or it can be based on tourism attraction factors.)
- The nation. (Especially true in the case of smaller island countries.)
- Several countries. (A good example is the area around the Mekong River that is being presented as a theme-related destination involving several countries.)

There can be little argument that there should be integration within each of the levels and across all levels, so as to achieve balance, aesthetic harmony, cooperation, confidence (for investment), efficiency, identity, sensitivity and most importantly sustainability.

These aspirations of integration can be achieved through preparation of a tourism policy, which is a policy for tourism following a systematic process.

Developing a Tourism Policy

Policies can help guide a government and other stakeholders' programmes of action and provide a frame of reference for the tourism industry's actions. If we are to achieve sustainable tourism, it is always preferable that a set of tourism policies be developed either as a set of distinct tourism objectives or better still that all levels and areas of policy formation integrate tourism directives in their decision-making process.

Such a Policy should

- provide a set of guidelines for the actions of all stakeholders;
- specify the broad objectives to be achieved;
- specify action plans; and
- identify areas of responsibility and power for policy implementation.

Tourism objectives should be the product of stakeholder participation and recognize the complexity of tourism development and management. It is rare where there will be a classic policy development process. Political priorities, power realities, economic development requirements and industry pressures will very much influence what occurs in the policy development process. Ideally at least, the role that tourism should play in the overall national as well as regional development should be clearly articulated and understood. Only then can other areas of public and private development reflect tourism objectives and priorities. The officials responsible for economic development, environmental protection and tourism are just examples where the policy and decision-making areas of activity meet or should meet.

Each objective should be tested for its general applicability and contribution to broad objectives related to overall sustainable development with specific attention to:

- energy and water conservation;
- employment;
- economic growth;
- infrastructure plans;
- enviromnental and resource conservation;
- urban and rural revitalization;
- heritage conservation;
- consumer protection;
- community welfare; business creation.

A commitment to the achievement of a satisfactory tourism policy requires a set of objectives that focus on the following issues:

Economic

It is necessary to optimize the contribution of tourism and recreation to economic prosperity, full employment, regional economic development, and improved international balance of payments.

Sociocultural

It is essential to contribute to the personal growth and education of the population and encourage their 'appreciation of the local geography, history, and ethnic diversity. Social policy should also seek to avoid activities that have the potential to undennine or denigrate the social and cultural values and resources of the area and its traditions and lifestyles.

Market Development Oriented

Policies must encourage the free entry of foreign visitors, while balancing this goal with the need to monitor persons and goods entering the country with laws protecting public health.

Resource Protection and Conservation

Policies must protect and preserve the historical and cultural foundations as a living part of community life and development and to ensure future generations an opportunity to enjoy the rich heritage of the area.

These policies will also ensure the compatibility of tourism, recreational, and activity policies with other broader interests in energy development and conservation, environmental protection, and judicious use of natural resources.

Human Resource Development

It is important to ensure that tourism has an adequate supply of professionally-trained skilled and managerial staff to meet future needs. Human resource policies should also ensure that the education and training programmes and materials are available to meet the needs of tourism.

Government Operations Concerns

Policies must help to coordinate government activities related to tourism while allowing the public sector to take a leadership role by supporting the needs of tourists, residents and tourism businesses with appropriate legislation and administration. Most countries will have developed their own style of policy-making. It is important that the policy for tourism be consistent in its general aim and orientation and be readily integrated with other policy areas.

Lateral (with other policy areas) and vertical (internal) linkages must be integrated. A policy process progresses to strategies plans, programmes, legislation and regulations. It is important that each stage at any level (national/regional/local) be carefully integrated laterally and vertically.

Developing the Tourism Plan

There is no single model of tourism plan or one process. There are many variations in content, style, approach and emphasis, and some possibilities are identified here.

Alternative plan approaches: A master plan is the principal instrument of planning for tourism. Such a plan may be comprehensive and wide-ranging, or it may focus on one or a combination of:

- physical/environmental issues;
- economic issues;
- promotion and marketing;
- conservation (of environment or heritage resources);
- sociocultural issues;
- investment;
- human resources development.

On a temporal scale, the master plan may focus on a short-term time scale (five years, perhaps to coincide with the cycles of the national economic strategy), or it may focus on an indeterminate scale with indications of preferred end-states or achievements, not associated with particular time periods.

Other differences in approach may cover:

- attitudes to spontaneous development (strict or flexible planning);
- degree of incentives and technical assistance;
- apportionment of benefits;
- integration with tourism-related activities;
- certainty of site prescription;
- supervision;
- regulation and strategy support.

An important element in any tourism plan is the degree to which it is integrated with the nationwide or region-wide economic, welfare and physical development plan.

Tourism plans prepared in recent years, and those to be prepared, should include specific reference to:

- ecological sustainability;
- environmental conservation;
- heritage (built environment) and cultural heritage conservation;
- sustainable development of heritage resources.

Content: For any particular nation, the plan could adopt a particular focus, perhaps for only one of the review phases. However, a generalized prospectus of contents would include:

- the institutional or organizational framework, setting out:
- the principal organizations;
- the principal responsibilities;
- the legislative framework;
- the roles and functions of the private and public sectors.
- the principal plan elements, such as:
- infrastructure;
- facilities and services;
- visitor attractions.
- development implications-economic, environmental, and sociocultural;
- the principal means of securing implementation, including:
- financing and investment;
- incentives;
- marketing;
- promotion;
- tourism information systems;
- tourism awareness programmes;
- human resources development.

The plan of any nation may refer to regional cooperation in the various aspects of tourism planning and development, and the contribution which can be made to the regional circumstances.

In some cases, the emphasis of the plan may direct the considerations away from the physical dimensions of the tourism development. This would be unfortunate, because no matter what form the development takes, the tourism experience of the visitor will take place in a region, in a destination, at a site. Therefore, it is important that these particular aspects of tourism planning are given due attention.

The form and structure of physical plan elements: Tourism planning may focus on the nation, the region, a destination, or a site. Integration of all these will achieve the most satisfactory outcome. In the context of physical development, tourism planning at any level can be conducted with attention to spatial form and structure.

Regional: There are various operational issues linked to the principal detenninants of regional form and structure. Experimentation is ongoing, but there are some constant principles. The basic options include:

- using existing developments as magnets and regional control factors;
- creating new developments;
- creating a hierarchical network of tourism destinations by devising a balanced strategy;
- developing a region-wide strategy, eliminating those areas that have little tourism potential, devising a destination-focused strategy, devising a tour or circuit strategy; and
- developing a strategy of complementary tourism destinations, with each destination specializing in focus or market segment.

The basic fond and Structural Patterns include:

- concentration of tourism development:
- major resorts;
- tourism destination areas; and
- base camps on the threshold of a tourism region.
- gateways or points of entry into the destination areas.

Variants on this basic spatial formula exist in tourism planning literature and in many case studies worldwide. The dilemma for the Asian and Pacific region is to reinterpret the land-based concepts of regional form and structure into a region specific idiom.

Destination Area: The destination area contains the critical mass of resources, facilities and amenities that contribute to the satisfaction of tourists. The basic elements of a tourism destination area or zone are:

- one or more communities to supply the utilities, services and facilities;
- one or more attraction complexes;
- transportation linkages between the communities and the attractions; and
- an entrance or gateway at the destination.

An important principle in the planning and design of tourism destinations is that they be distinctive places with unique internal relationships between the various parts (other places and the various facilities and services). The destination is what attracts the tourist. To be successful, the tourism destination should be planned to maximize:

- the locational advantage;
- the product advantage (in comparison with competitor destinations);
- the advantage of proximate cultural resources and natural resources;
- transport linkages; and
- hospitable host attitudes.

There is no single formula for successful destination tourism, but there are planning and design principles appropriate to the destination scale.

These Include:

- the destination should be integrated into a region-wide strategy;
- the destination should attract (or create) a distinctive image;
- successful destination planning will involve:
- public-private partnership;
- integration; and progressive accumulation of the critical mass of attractions, services, facilities, amenities, and transport linkages-all within carrying capacity limits.

Site scale: The scale of this tourism planning is a particular challenge, because at this scale a single, functional or aesthetic problem can seriously disrupt the image of a tourism destination. If the tourism business on any site fails, it becomes a monument to bad decision-making that may affect an entire destination by association.

At this level, "place" takes on a particular important meaning. It is not only the contribution each place makes to the entire destination, but also a geographical reference point and landmark. It is at the site scale that regional and destination tourism planning yield concrete outcomes, and at this level the projections and predictions of demand for facilities, services and experiences materialize. Therefore, a special understanding of the site characteristics, their potential and constraints, and the contribution of the site to the wider destination area become crucial. It is also critical that the planning, management and monitoring processes be efficient at this scale. In order to avoid the repetition of inappropriate design and development, post-development evaluation should become an integral part of the planning process, especially to determine the validity of the predevelopment design decisions.

Physical Development Strategy

In order to implement the tourism development proposals examined at the various levels (national, regional, destination and site), it is necessary to provide a suitable physical development planning strategy. An important element of any physical development strategy is land use planning. It is important to recognize that many countries may have land use strategies but they are unevenly enforced and lack support at local levels. In some cases, there may not yet be a policy.

There are Four Different Approaches to Land use Planning

Blueprint planning, which is based on the expectation that the full plan as prepared will be implemented exactly and in its entirety. Such an expectation is unrealistic, because no plan ever starts with complete information and functions within a completely controlled operational environment. Such a plan type is too inflexible. Regulatory planning, which relies upon the application of development provenance standards with the possibility of all development eventually conforming to previously set model codes and standards. While easy to implement, the built environment may become monotonous and repetitive. Even so, some fond of regulatory planning is inevitable.

Market-driven planning, which is best suited to individual projects, rather than to planning strategies for entire communities or regions. A systems-driven approach to planning which is becoming more common, especially as planning functions are needed to address increasingly complex situations involving threats to the environment and as development is increasingly scrutinized according to ecologically-sustainable principles. This approach provides for review, monitoring and adjustment as circumstances change in the plan.

The land use planning system most likely will combine the compatible elements of the systems-driven methodology and the regulatory approach to planning.

In many cases, the system of land use planning control is derived from standard European or North American codes of planning practice and then modified to meet the needs of national governments and administrative systems. Usually, a land use planning control system in force for the planning system is backed by appropriate legislation which provides for control over land use and development, specified administrative procedures, and necessary infrastructure development.

For tourism development, the most important issues in land use planning and development will include:

- location of tourism uses;
- accessibility to and travel within tourism districts/zones;
- development standards;
- design standards;
- traffic problems;
- quality of the built environment;
- landscaping of tourism developments;

- free-standing major developments;
- tourism attractions in rural environments;
- location of the major transport interchanges such as airports, and bus/coach terminals; and
- impact of tourism development on local architectural styles and
- important areas of heritage.

To achieve a good standard of land use development, the planning system should:

- coordinate development-relegating frastructurer equipements;
- implement appropriate concepts and ideas in order to achieve acceptable, conventionals tandards of aesthetics, health, convenience and diversity (of interest, experience, and culture);
- promote development where and when appropriate;
- provide the developer with prior knowledge of the development requirements (in the form of performance standards);
- prevent prejudicial development (by type, location, timing, or quality);
- reflect acceptable changes in standards and fashions; and facilitate innovation.

It may be claimed that the best plans and developments have been the outcome of deliberate planning using a systematic planning and decision-making process, but there are examples of successful plans and developments which have not emerged from the application of a systematic process. Such development may be considered to have been fortuitous, fragile, or both. In any case, the pursuit of a systematic process should offer the best chance of successful and harmonious tourism development.

Implementation of a Tourism Plan

It is preferable to consider the planning process as a continuum that integrates the steps of plan creation with its implementation.

Stages of implementation can include the following:

- preparing and putting into practice guidelines, regulations and
- policies necessary to bring the plan to fruition;
- undertaking development in accordance with the plan;
- supervising that development
- preparing the community for the impact of tourism development;
- preparing and providing training facilities for those intending to work in the tourism/travel/hospitality industry;
- collecting information to monitor the progress of the plan as it is put into practice;
- undertaking marketing and promotion to ensure that the tourism destination is known and appreciated for what it has to offer.

A tourism plan is a tool to guide development. Little, if anything, will happen without:

- a suitable legislative and administrative structure;
- suitable sources of finance;
- suitable entrepreneurial interest;
- evidence of demand for the tourism product at the destination; and
- certainty of access by visitors.

In addition, a tourism plan At any level, especially at national and regional levels, will need desegregation so that the various resource needs-land/water, labour and capital-are seen in their spatial, temporal, financial, infrastructure, and social inter-relationships.

An additional consideration is the likely impact of forces external to the destination area, especially the impact of decisions, international airlines that service the region, and the international tour operators who facilitate the arrival of tourists.

Institutional Framework

There is considerable evidence of the need for an effective institutional framework if tourism developments to be coordinated, efficiently supervised, monitored and integrated into the overall scope of national economic, environmental and social planning. It is important that the institutional framework encompasses organizations from both the public and the private sector. A coordinated framework is necessary because of the fragmented nature of the tourism industry.

The tourism palling process provides the catalyst for inputs from the various stakeholders with the outcome of decisions affecting tourism development. Even after the preparation of a tourism development plan, the final outcome is dependent upon the integrated realization of a series of independent development decisions based upon the pursuit of individual opportunities.

The public sector, the private sector, non-profit organizations, the community, and tourists play important roles in tourism planning and development.

In each case, there will be particular perspectives on tourism development, the need for tourism planning, and the shape of that planning. The principal perspective of the public sector is to manage development to achieve community goals in the public interest. For the private sector, the principal function is to provide facilities and services to tourists while maximizing returns on investment. The private sector has also come to accept that it has social and environmental responsibilities. It is recognized that entrepreneurial flair may create tourism development opportunities beyond those identified in the prepared tourism plan.

The formal plan should be composed with sufficient flexibility to accommodate such initiatives, especially if it is responding to shifts in tourist preferences. Some changes in preferences may be identified through the constant monitoring and evaluation of tourism activity by consultants, market research investigators, design professionals and project managers. Financial institutions and corporate lending agencies will have a particular interest in the changes of fashion and the dicates of the tourism market. The World Tourism Organization (WTO) has described the distinct roles of the public and private sector by the principle that governments should not seek to do what the private sector is able and willing to do. However, in many cases of large-scale development, the private sector and government may work in a partnership. Other partnerships may develop where governments assist indigenous landowners to start an enterprise that will be managed eventually by indigenous communities. The perspective of the tourist on tourism planning is different from the other stakeholders.

The interests of every tourist cut across the various independent decisions made by governments and the private sector, and the tourist is concerned with the experience that can be gained. One of the main purposes of tourism planning is to create a harmonious balance between the different interests of the various stakeholders. This balance may be achieved through the establishment of an appropriate multifaceted institutional framework. In some tourism development lands, an effective institutional framework is considered to be one of the principal determinants of successful tourism development.

Sustainable Tourism

Sustainable tourism is an industry committed to making a low impact on the environment and local culture, while helping to generate income and employment for local people. The aim of sustainable tourism is to ensure that development is a positive experience for local people; tourism companies; and tourists themselves. But sustainable tourism is not the same as ecotourism.

Global economists forecast continuing international tourism growth, ranging between three and six percent annually, depending on the location. As one of the world's largest and fastest growing industries, this continuous growth will place great stress on remaining biologically diverse habitats and indigenous cultures, which are often used to support mass tourism. Tourists who promote sustainable tourism are sensitive to these dangers and seek to protect tourist destinations, and to protect tourism as an industry. Sustainable tourists can reduce the impact of tourism in many ways, including:

- informing themselves of the culture, politics, and economy of the communities visited
- anticipating and respecting local cultures' expectations and assumptions
- contributing to intercultural understanding and tolerance
- supporting the integrity of local cultures by favouring businesses which conserve cultural heritage and traditional values
- supporting local economies by purchasing local goods and participating with small, local businesses
- conserving resources by seeking out businesses that are environmentally conscious, and by using the least possible amount of non-renewable resources.

Increasingly, destinations and tourism operations are endorsing and following "responsible tourism" as a pathway towards sustainable tourism. Responsible tourism and sustainable tourism have an identical goal, that of sustainable development. The pillars of responsible tourism are therefore the same as those of sustainable tourism – environmental integrity, social justice and economic development. The major difference between the two is that, in responsible tourism, individuals, organisations and businesses are asked to take responsibility for their actions and the impacts of their actions. This shift in emphasis has taken place because some stakeholders feel that insufficient progress towards realising sustainable tourism has been made since the Earth Summit in Rio. This is partly because everyone has been expecting others to behave in a sustainable manner. The emphasis on responsibility in responsible tourism means that everyone involved in tourism – government, product owners and operators, transport operators, community services, NGO's and CBO's, tourists, local communities, industry associations – are responsible for achieving the goals of responsible tourism.

Responsible Tourism

Responsible Tourism can be regarded as a behaviour. It is more than a form of tourism as it represents an approach to engaging with tourism, be that as a tourist, a business, locals at a destination or any other tourism stakeholder. It emphasises that all stakeholders are responsible for the kind of tourism they develop or engage in. Whilst different groups will see responsibility in different ways, the shared understanding is that responsible tourism should entail an improvement in tourism. Tourism should become 'better' as a result of the responsible tourism approach. Within the notion of betterment resides the acknowledgement that conflicting interests need to be balanced. However, the objective is to create better places for people to live in and to visit. Importantly, there is no blueprint for responsible tourism: what is deemed responsible may differ depending on places and cultures. Responsible Tourism is an aspiration that can be realised in different ways in different originating markets and in the diverse destinations of the world (Goodwin, 2002).

Focusing in particular on businesses, according to the Cape Town Declaration on Responsible Tourism, it will have the following characteristics:

- minimises negative economic, environmental, and social impacts
- generates greater economic benefits for local people and enhances the well-being of host communities, improves working conditions and access to the industry
- involves local people in decisions that affect their lives and life chances
- makes positive contributions to the conservation of natural and cultural heritage, to the maintenance of the world's diversity
- provides more enjoyable experiences for tourists through more meaningful connections with local people, and a greater understanding of local cultural, social and environmental issues
- provides access for physically challenged people and
- is culturally sensitive, engenders respect between tourists and hosts, and builds local pride and confidence.

Sustainable tourism is where tourists can enjoy their holiday and at the same time respect the culture of people and also respect the environment. It also means that local people (such as the Masaai) get a fair say about tourism and also receive some money from the profit which the game reserve make. The environment is being damaged quite a lot by tourists and part of Sustainable tourism is to make sure that the damaging does not carry on.

There are many private companies who are working into embracing the principles and aspects of Responsible Tourism, some for the purpose of Corporate Social Responsibility activities, and others such World Hotel-Link, which was originally a project of the International Finance Corporation, have built their entire business model around responsible tourism, local capacity building and increasing market access for small and medium tourism enterprises.

Responsible Hospitality

As with the view of Responsible Tourism, Responsible Hospitality is essentially about creating better places for people to live in, and better places for people to visit. This does not mean all forms of hospitality are also forms of tourism although hospitality is the largest sector of the tourism industry. As such we should not be surprised at overlaps between Responsible Hospitality and Responsible Tourism.

In the instance where place of permanent residence is also the place where the hospitality service is consumed, if for example a meal is consumed in a local restaurant, this does not obviate the requirement to improve the place of residence. As such, the essence of Responsible Hospitality is not contingent upon touristic forms of hospitality.

While Frideman (1962) famously argued that, admittedly within legal parameters, the sole responsibility of business was to generate profit for shareholders the idea that businesses' responsibility extends beyond this has existed for decades and is most frequently encountered in the concept of corporate social responsibility (Carroll, 1999).

There are numerous ways businesses can and do engage in activities that are not intended to benefit shareholders and management, at least not in the short term. However, often acts of corporate social responsibility are undertaken because of the perceived benefit to business. Usually in hospitality this relates to the cost reductions associated with improved energy efficiency (Pizam, 2009) but may also relate to, for example, the rise in ethical consumerism and the view that being seen to be a responsible business is beneficial to revenue growth. As per the Cape Town Declaration on Responsible Tourism, Responsible Hospitality is culturally sensitive. Instead of then calling for the unachievable, Responsible Hospitality simply makes the case for more responsible forms of hospitality, hospitality that benefits locals first, and visitors second. Certainly, all forms of hospitality can be improved and managed so that negative impacts are minimised whilst striving for a maximisation of positive impacts.

Coastal Tourism

Many coastal areas are experiencing particular pressure from growth in lifestyles and growing numbers of tourists. Coastal environments are limited in extent consisting of only a narrow strip along the edge of the ocean. Coastal areas are often the first environments to experience the detrimental impacts of tourism. A detailed study of the impact on coastal areas, with reference to western India can be an example. The inevitable change is on the horizon as holiday destinations put more effort into sustainable tourism. Planning and management controls can reduce the impact on coastal environments and ensure that investment into tourism products supports sustainable coastal tourism.

Some Conceptual Models in Coastal Tourism

Some of the recent studies have led to some interesting conceptual models applicable for coastal tourism. The 'inverted funnel model' and the 'embedded model' can be good metaphors for understanding the interplay of different stake-holders like government, local community, tourists and business community in developing tourist destinations.

Community-based Management

There has been the promotion of sustainable tourism practices surrounding the management of tourist locations by locals or more concisely, the community. This form of tourism is based on the premise that the people living next to a resource are the ones best suited to protecting it. This means that the tourism activities and businesses are developed and operated by local community members, and certainly with their consent and support. Sustainable tourism typically involves the conservation of resources that are capitalized upon for tourism purposes, such as coral reefs and pristine forests. Locals run the businesses and are responsible for promoting the conservation messages to protect their environment. Community-based sustainable tourism (CBST) associates the success of the sustainability of the ecotourism location to the management practices of the communities who are directly or indirectly dependent on the location for their livelihoods.

A salient feature of CBST is that local knowledge is usually utilised alongside wide general frameworks of ecotourism business models. This allows the participation of locals at the management level and typically allows a more intimate understanding of the environment. The use of local knowledge also means an easier entry level into a tourism industry for locals whose jobs or livelihoods are affected by the use of their environment as tourism locations. The involvement of locals restores the ownership of the environment to the local community and allows an alternative sustainable form of development for communities and their environments that are typically unable to support other forms of development.. However, recent research has found that economic linkages generated by CBST may only be sporadic, and that the linkages with agriculture are negatively affected by seasonality and by the small scale of the cultivated areas. This means that CBST may only have small-scale positive effects for these communities.

Stakeholders

Stakeholders of sustainable tourism play a role in continuing this form of tourism. This can include organizations as well as individuals.

Non-Governmental Organizations

Non-governmental organizations are one of the stakeholders in advocating sustainable tourism. Their roles can range from spearheading sustainable tourism practices to simply doing research. University research teams and scientists can be tapped to aid in the process of planning. Such solicitation of research can be observed in the planning of Cat Ba National Park in Vietnam. Dive resort operators in Bunaken National Park, Indonesia, play a crucial role but developing exclusive zones for diving and fishing respectively, such that both tourists and locals can benefit from the venture

Large conventions, meetings and other major organized events drive the travel, tourism and hospitality industry. Cities and convention centres compete to attract such commerce, commerce which has heavy impacts on resource use and the environment. Major sporting events, such as the Olympic Games, present special problems regarding environmental burdens and degradation. But burdens imposed by the regular convention industry can be vastly more significant.

Green conventions and events are a new but growing sector and marketing point within the convention and hospitality industry. More environmentally aware organizations, corporations and government agencies are now seeking more sustainable event practices, greener hotels, restaurants and convention venues, and more energy efficient or climate neutral travel and ground transportation. Additionally, some convention centres have begun to take direct action in reducing the impact of the conventions they host. One example is the Moscone Centre in San Francisco, California, which has a very aggressive recycling program, a large solar power system, and other programs aimed at reducing impact and increasing efficiency.

Tourists

With the advent of the internet, some traditional conventions are being replaced with virtual conventions, where the attendees remain in their home physical location and "attend" the convention by use of a web-based interface programmed for the task. This sort of "virtual" meeting eliminates all of the impacts associated with travel, accommodation, food wastage, and other necessary impacts of traditional, physical conventions. Travel over long distances requires a large amount of time and/or energy. Generally this involves burning fossil fuels, a largely unsustainable practice and one that contributes to climate change, via CO_2 emissions.

Air travel is perhaps the worst offender in this regard, contributing to between 2 and 3% of global carbon emissions. Given a business-as-usual approach, this could be expected to rise to 5% by 2015 and 10% by 2050. Car travel is the next worst offender.

Mass transport is the most climate friendly method of travel, and generally the rule is "the bigger the better"-compared to cars, buses are relatively more sustainable, and trains and ships are even more so. Human energy and renewable energy are the most efficient, and hence, sustainable. Travel by bicycle, solar powered car, or sailing boat produces no carbon emissions (although the embodied energy in these vehicles generally comes at the expense of carbon emission).

Sustainable Tourism CRC

Sustainable Tourism Cooperative Research Centre (STCRC), headquartered in Gold Coast, Queensland, Australia is an Australian Cooperative Research Centre established by the Australian Government's Cooperative Research Centres Program to establish a competitive and dynamic sustainable tourism industry in Australia. STCRC is a not-for-profit company owned by its industry, government and university partners. STCRC stands as the world's largest travel and tourism research centre.

Organisational Aims

STCRC's aims are the development and management of intellectual property (IP) to deliver innovation to business, community, and government enhancing environmental, economic and social sustainability of tourism – one of the world's largest, fastest growing industries.

In doing so, STCRC aims to develop Australia's long-term tourism research capactities through a vigorous postgraduate research education programme. Presently this programme has produced a number of PhD students and the program is supported by scholarships for students in industry-designed projects, and by developing and distributing education and training products.

Commercialisation Unit

The Commercialisation of STCRC research, sustainability oriented technologies and certification programs is done through EC3 Global which is wholly owned by the STCRC. EC3 Global provides an array of programs and services for companies, communities and other interest groups to set and achieve sustainability targets.

With origins leading back to 1987, EC3's research encompasses 250 tourism and environmental sustainability leaders in 16 universities. EC3's influence has grown to encompass hundreds of projects, creating a strong market presence in over 50 countries. Presently EC3 Global commercialises four main products, Decipher, Earthcheck, IPAT and Green Globe.

History

STCRC was established under the Australian Government's Cooperative Research Centres Program to underpin the development of a dynamic, internationally competitive, and sustainable tourism industry. Since its inception the STCRC has supported over 170 PhD scholars through a suite of scholarships and the provision of a Career Development Program. STCRC currently supports over 90 postgraduate students. All are of exceptional academic standard. Most hold a first class honours degree and many have also received university awards for excellence. All supplementary scholarship holders also hold an APA or university-equivalent scholarship.

University Partners

There are currently 16 Australian universities who are partners with the STCRC, these are listed below.

Charles Darwin University

Charles Darwin University was formed in 2003, with over 50 years history delivering tertiary education to the Northern Territory. Charles Darwin's Main Campus is located in Darwin, Australia and is named after Charles Darwin, the English Naturalist Formed in 2003 through a merger between the Northern Territory University, Alice Springs-based Centralian College, NT Rural

College in Katherine and the Menzies School of Health Research. Charles Darwin University is the largest university in the Northern Territory.

Curtin University of Technology

Curtin University of Technology formed in 1986 is Western Australia's Largest University with over 40,000 students presently. Curtin University has a strong emphasis on innovation and technology, which are the main themes of the university. Curtin University has an important Research & Development history, with an annual income from research of around $12 Million Australian Dollars annually.

Edith Cowan University

Edith Cowan University is the second largest university in Western Australia and has approximately 23,000 students of which over 3,000 originate from countries outside Australia. It was established in 1991, and is the only Australian university named after a woman, Edith Dircksey Cowan. The university specialises in the service professions, and the teaching of education remains a key focus. Joint research and study with other universities and international consultancies remains an important area for the university.

Griffith University

Griffith University is an Australian public university with five campuses in Queensland between Brisbane and the Gold Coast. As of 2008, there were more than 37,000 enrolled students and 3,500 staff. As such, Griffith stands as one of Queensland's largest universities and holds Queensland's oldest academy.

Griffith has diverse multidisciplinary teaching and research fields, and comprises of students and academic staff from over 120 countries throughout the world.

James Cook University

James Cook University is a public university based in Townsville, Queensland, Australia and was proclaimed on 20 April 1970 in Townsville. James Cook University is the second oldest university in Queensland. James Cook University is listed as one of the best universities in Queensland and is one of only 17 in Australia that was listed in the ARWU top 500 academic world universities in 2007.

The main fields of research include marine sciences, biodiversity, sustainable management of tropical ecosystems, tropical health care and tourism. James Cook University receives over $23 Million dollars in research funding annually, highlighting the importance of its ongoing research projects.

La Trobe University

La Trobe University is a multi-campus university in Victoria, Australia. La Trobe is generally considered to be ranked amongst the top ten universities in Australia and in 2005 was ranked in the top 100 universities in the world. Presently La Trobe university has over 28,000 enrolled students and has become a well established centre for teaching, training, scholarship and research.

Monash University

Monash University is a public university with campuses located in Australia, Malaysia and South Africa. It is Australia's largest university with about 55,000 students. Monash consistently ranks amongst the top universities in Australia and the world.

The University has a total of eight campuses, and also a centre in Prato, Italy. This makes it by far Australia's most internationalised university. Indeed, it is arguable that Monash has the greatest international presence of any research-intensive university in the world.

It was recently ranked by The Times Higher Education Supplement (THES) at number 43 in its annual ranking of the world's top 200 universities for 2007.

Murdoch University

Murdoch University is located in Perth, Western Australia and has three campuses at Murdoch, Rockingham and Peel. It currently has a student population of over 15,000 studends including 3,000 international students. Murdoch is a modern Australian university with a national reputation for excellence in teaching and research.

Southern Cross University

Southern Cross University (SCU) is a university based on the Mid North and North coast of New South Wales, Australia. It is a regional University with more than 14,000 students. The University is the country's seventh largest provider of distance education. It also has international students from more than 50 countries. More than 700 students are enrolled on-campus and with on-shore partners in Australia, with a further 1300 enrolled in overseas programs.

The University is renowned for its tourism studies, especially in the local Northern Rivers area.

University of New South Wales

University of New South Wales (UNSW) is one of Australia's largest and most prestigious research institutions, the UNSW has over 40,000 students including 8,800 international students from 90 different countries.

It is a member of Australia's "Group of Eight" lobby group, and is also a founding member of Universitas 21, an international network of leading research-intensive universities. UNSW ranks third for both total funds allocated and the number of grants from the Australian Research Council among Australian universities following University of Sydney and Australian National University, by securing more than $26 million in Discovery Project grants. The University also gains the highest number of Linkage Project grants of any university.

University of Canberra

The *University of Canberra* is an Australian university, located in Canberra, the capital of Australia. It is the second largest university in Canberra. The University was one of nine Australian universities recognised by the Australian government in 2006 for high achievement in learning and teaching. In a 2005 ranking of the international standing of Australian universities, University of Canberra received 44% and ranked approximately two-thirds down the list of Australian universities. Presently it has over 10,000 students, from over 80 different countries and more than 1,000 staff.

University of Queensland

The *University of Queensland* is Queensland's first university, being founded in 1909. Presently it has over 37,000 enrolled students. The University of Queensland also prides itself on being one of Australia's foremest research institutions, the University is a founding member of the Group of Eight, an alliance of research-strong "sandstone" universities in Australia.

UQ remains the most successful Australian university in winning and being shortlisted for Australian Awards for University Teaching since they were established in 1997. On a variety of measures it is one of the top three or four research universities in the country.

University of South Australia

The *University of South Australia* is a public university in the Australian state of South Australia. It was formed in 1991 with the merger of the South Australian Institute of Technology and Colleges of Advanced Education.

The university is a leading expert in technical education and applied research, as well being a founding member of the Australian Technology Network.

University of South Australia is ranked as the 291st university in the 2007 Times Higher Education Supplement Top 400 Universities list. The University has nearly 32,000 enrolled students as of 2008.

University of Tasmania

The *University of Tasmania* is an Australian university, with three campuses in Tasmania. A 'sandstone university', it is the fourth-oldest university in Australia, and was established over a century ago. It was founded on 1 January 1890, and is a member of the international Association of Commonwealth Universities.

The university works with overseas universities to offer students an international experience, with exchange arrangements in place with over 40 institutions throughout Europe, Asia and North America. The university has a particularly notable and long-standing reputation in examining the practical and theoretical challenges involved in addressing social and environmental concerns.

University of Technology, Sydney

The *University of Technology, Sydney (UTS)* is a university in Sydney, New South Wales, Australia. It is part of the Australian Technology Network of universities, and is the third largest university in Sydney in terms of enrollment numbers. Founded in its current form in 1988, it is also the only university with its main campuses within the Sydney CBD. UTS has been ranked in the World's Top 100 universities by the Times Higher Education Supplement and was given A1 ratings across all major disciplines in 2007 by the Federal Government Education department.

Victoria University

The *Victoria University* is a University in Melbourne, Victoria. The University offers both Higher Education and Technical and Further Education (TAFE) courses. Presently there are over 45,000 enrolled students, including over 8,500 international students. Founded in 1916, it is one of Australia's older universities, with a rich history and many successful students.

2

Sustainable Hospitality Planning

The Global Mandate for Protected Areas

A protected area is "an area of land and/or sea especially dedicated to the protection and maintenance of biological diversity, and of natural and associated cultural resources, and managed through legal or other effective means" (IUCN, 1994). A protected area may be a wetland, a tropical or deciduous forest, a cultivated landscape of value, an alpine region, a savannah, a marine area or any number of other types of natural or partially modified ecosystems – or indeed any combination of types of ecosystems. In addition to covering an array of ecosystem types, protected areas are defined in a number of different ways relevant to the objectives and values for which they are managed.

Traditionally one of the most widely used and, arguably, most effective tools for achieving conservation goals, protected areas today play a significant role in supporting local, national, and international biodiversity policies. They also serve as places for scientific research, wilderness protection, maintenance of environmental services, education, tourism and recreation, protection of specific natural and cultural features, and sustainable use of biological resources.

The importance of protected areas is emphasised by international conventions and programmes such as the CBD, the World Heritage Convention (WHC), the Ramsar Convention on Wetlands, the UN Law of the Sea Convention, UNESCO's Man and the Biosphere (MAB) Programme of the United Nations Educational, Scientific and Cultural Organisation (UNESCO) and the global programme of WCPA. Together these agreements and programmes are the backbone of international policy on the establishment and management of protected areas for biodiversity conservation and the sustainable use of natural and cultural resources. The CBD is a particularly important endorsement of protected areas in that: it is globally accepted, with over 170 signatory nations adopting its objectives of conserving biodiversity, sustainably using biological resources, and equitably sharing benefits arising from this use

Category I

An area of land and/or sea possessing some outstanding or representative ecosystems, geological or physiological features and/or species available primarily for research and/or environmental monitoring. A wilderness area is a large area of unmodified or slightly modified land and/or sea retaining its natural character and influence without permanent or significant habitation which is protected and managed so as to preserve its natural condition.

Category II

A natural area of land and/or sea designated to (a) protect the ecological integrity of one or more ecosystems for present and future generations; (b) exclude exploitation or occupation inimical to the purposes of the area; and (c) provide foundation for spiritual, scientific, educational, recreational, and visitor opportunities all of which must be environmentally and culturally compatible.

Category III

An area containing one or more specific natural or natural/ cultural feature which is of outstanding or unique value because of its inherent rarity, representative or aesthetic qualities or cultural significance.

Category IV

An area of land and/or sea subject to active intervention for management purposes so as to ensure the maintenance of habitats and/or to meet the requirements of specific species.

Category V

An area with coast and sea, as appropriate, where the interaction of people and nature over time has produced an area with significant aesthetic, ecological and/or cultural value and often with high biological diversity. Safeguarding the integrity of this traditional interaction is vital to the protection, maintenance and evolution of such an area.

Category VI

An area containing predominantly unmodified natural systems managed to ensure long term protection and maintenance of biological diversity while providing at the same time a sustainable flow of natural products and services to meet community needs.

- it defines biodiversity broadly as the variability among living organisms at the genetic, species and ecosystems levels; and
- it presents a powerful array of actions and tools for implementing a global biodiversity agenda. The CBD envisions a major role for protected areas in national plans for biodiversity. Article 8 calls for the establishment and maintenance of systems of protected areas. As experts, IUCN has given advice on the focus and design of national systems of protected areas – see Davey, A. G. (1998). Article 8 establishes global priorities and policies for the *in-situ* conservation of biodiversity and obliges Parties:
- to establish systems of protected areas or areas where special measures need to be taken to conserve biodiversity;
- to develop guidelines for the selection, establishment and management of protected areas or areas where special measures need to be taken to conserve biodiversity;
- ò regulate or manage biological resources important for the conservation of biodiversity whether within or outside protected areas, with a view to assuring their conservation and sustainable use;
- to promote environmentally sound and sustainable development in areas adjacent to protected areas with a view to furthering protection of these areas; and

- to provide financial and other support for *in-situ* conservation.

The central role of protected areas in Article 8 is reflected in the decisions of the Conference of the Parties (COP). These emphasise the importance of protected areas in achieving biodiversity goals for forest, marine, coastal, and other ecosystems. For example, the third COP (November 1996) recommended that strategies for sustainable forest management be based on an ecosystem approach, which integrates conservation measures such as protected areas and the sustainable use of biological resources. The WHC also provides a global foundation for protected areas by encouraging the identification, protection and preservation of the cultural and natural heritage around the world. The WHC is a mechanism for ensuring that globally important sites are protected and properly managed. Under the WHC, countries submit sites for inclusion on the World Heritage List of sites which are then eligible for funding from the World Heritage Fund. Thus this Convention provides countries with an incentive to create and maintain protected areas of global significance.

Further agreements and action in the international arena also support protected areas. The UN Law of the Sea provides the framework for establishing marine protected areas by allocating rights to territorial seas. The Ramsar Convention encourages mutual commitment from signatories in the designation of wetland protected areas important to waterfowl and which can also promote the "wise use" of wetland ecosystems.

UNESCO's MAB Programme recognises protected areas as key components in the design and management of biosphere reserves and important tools for meeting sustainable use objectives. Through the implementation of the biosphere reserve concept, the programme provides an international framework to: (a) conserve natural and cultural diversity; (b) promote models of land management and of approaches to sustainable development; and (c) improve knowledge on the interaction between humanity and nature through research, monitoring, education and training. IUCN's WCPA is the major global network of protected area specialists. The mission of WCPA is "to promote the establishment and effective management of a representative worldwide network of terrestrial and marine protected areas", as an integral contribution to the IUCN mission. The mission of IUCN is "to influence, encourage and assist societies throughout the world to conserve the integrity and diversity of nature and to ensure that any use of natural resources is equitable and ecologically sustainable". The main purposes of protected area management, as outlined by the WCPA, are: scientific research, wilderness protection, preservation of species and genetic diversity, maintenance of environmental services, protection of specific natural and cultural features, tourism and recreation, education, sustainable use of resources from natural ecosystems, and maintenance of cultural traditions and attitudes.

The need for Innovative Approaches

Strong as this international mandate may be, global conventions and programmes alone are not enough to ensure the continued existence of, and sufficient funding for, protected areas. In times of fiscal austerity and tightening government budgets – especially in developing countries which are home to much of the world's biodiversity – traditional funding sources for protected areas are increasingly under threat. Innovative alternatives to these traditional sources are needed in order to secure the long term viability of protected areas. In addition to strengthening traditional funding, finding additional funding sources has the added benefit of diversifying a protected area's income sources. This makes the protected area more viable and helps it to withstand times of economic hardship.

Where does a protected area manager look for alternative funding sources? What do these potential supporters want from the protected area? And what does the protected area manager communicate to these supporters? Valuation can help the protected area manager find the answers to these questions, and more.

The process of valuation provides protected area managers with information about the protected area's goods and services, the values which people (potential supporters or customers) place on those, which values are being captured and which are not, and which groups could derive more benefits through alternative uses of the protected area and are therefore inclined to be a 'threat' to the protected area. In this way, valuation provides useful information for management and financing decisions regarding protected areas.

A thorough scoping stage of a valuation study identifies the array of benefits flowing from the protected area and the people who value those benefits. This information is likely to expose those who are not contributing to the protected area but derive benefits from it (and are therefore potential sources of funding), as well as those who are excluded from deriving benefits from the protected area but are being asked to 'pay' for the protected area, e.g. through taxes, property loss or foregone opportunities. For instance, a protected area manager searching for additional financing may realise, in the preliminary stages of a valuation study, that the protected area is not capturing any of the value held by bird watchers using the area. To capture this, the manager might decide to start renting out binoculars and bird-books or to start a fund directed at donations from bird-watchers earmarked for bird conservation efforts. On the other hand, if the bird-watchers are a low-income group and unlikely to be able to pay for the benefits they receive, the protected area manager may approach a potential donor, such as the Royal Society for the Protection of Birds or the Ramsar small projects fund, which may be willing to be a benefactor for the bird-watching group. By knowing the benefits and the groups receiving these benefits, alternative avenues for funding protected areas are indicated.

In another instance, a protected area manager might find that neighbouring people are not deriving any benefits from the protected area and, in fact, have been forced to forego opportunities of using the land for agriculture, forestry or other uses due to the establishment of the protected area. This manager needs to look for alternative management practices that enable the protected area's neighbours to derive some benefit from the presence of the area without compromising its overall conservation objectives, thereby reducing the pressure to convert the land to other uses. Alternatives may be to open the protected area to sustainable harvesting of forest products or to develop local capacity to service tourists visiting the protected area. In this case, identifying marginalised groups and the benefits that they have foregone helps the manager solve conflicts and thus reduce threats. The possibility of looking for alternative management practices depends on different factors that should be considered as part of the valuation process:

- What is the management category for the area? A Category V or VI protected area has the potential to accommodate a wide range of uses by zoning the resources within the area. A Category I area offers a much more limited array of use options such as research.
- Is the protected area well managed? Capturing the values attributed to a protected area in turn requires the capacity to manage that area to maintain these values.
- Is the protected area attractive enough? As this paper explains there are a number of different kinds of values attributable to protected areas. Tourism and recreation values are particularly attractive to managers because they are relatively easy to capture and because they can be a source of significant funds.

A New Vision for Protected Areas

But some areas may not have the ability to draw tourists. An economic valuation study conducted at a national level can indicate which areas are most able to obtain funding from tourists and which are not. A system of cross-subsidisation, or a separate funding strategy, can then be used to support wildlife which may be biologically important, but with little appeal to tourists. Such management and finance decisions are not limited to the local protected area manager. Often decisions, such as increasing access fees and the opening up of areas for new tourist concessions, are considered under national or provincial laws and regulations on protected areas. The valuation process, however, can inform decisions taken at national and international levels and should provide recommendations on how to enhance the national legal framework for protected areas management. All governments have limited resources to spend on services for their citizens and must make decisions about how and where to spend these resources. Sectors within government compete for a share of the fiscal budget. Thus protected areas compete with development programmes, health and welfare services, education, and the military, and so forth. Valuing protected areas can provide the economic reasons, to complement the biodiversity ones, why governments – and others – should invest in them.

The 'Client' Approach

Governments, donors, tourists and local people decide what goods and services to buy with their money. In economic terms, such groups are the real or potential 'customers' of the goods and services of protected areas: they are the 'clients' of the protected area. Since protected areas supply goods and services in a generally competitive marketplace they are, in an economic sense, businesses facing a complex array of customers who may wish to spend their limited funds elsewhere. A business is in business to make profits. It makes profits by selling goods and services to customers at a price marginally higher than the cost of producing these goods and services. Though a protected area is in the business of providing biodiversity services, it can use a business approach – profit-centred and entrepreneurial so as to maximise its financial capacity to achieve conservation aims.

To illustrate this client approach, consider some examples of protected areas – a wildlife sanctuary in South Asia, a savannah park in southern Africa, a forest reserve in South America, a protected landscape in Europe or a marine protected area in the South Pacific. All such areas provide a stream of goods and services (benefits) to a host of customers (those who hold a value for the benefits).

What benefits do such protected areas generate and to whom? Are these benefits and their distribution sufficient to ensure that the protected area will be conserved? In particular, do these benefits result in adequate financial flows to maintain the protected area? If not, what measures are needed to generate revenues for managing this protected area and achieve the conservation and development objectives of the protected area?

Think of the customers of the protected area. Think of its neighbours and those living within it as customers. What goods and services do they want from the protected area? Timber to convert into charcoal for fuel? Non-timber products such as fruits and honey? Medicinal plants? Thatching grasses? Do they want access to lands for grazing their livestock or to watering holes during the dry season? Do they want to have access to coral reefs for seafood? What measures are necessary to ensure that the uses they make of protected area resources are sustainable and that they pay for the goods and services provided by the protected area?

Economic Values of Protected Areas

Should the neighbouring or resident community be involved in a collaborative management scheme? Can a system of tradable harvesting permits for timber, honey, fish or grasses be developed? What about access rights for grazing, hunting, or watering? How can support be maintained for traditional land use practices which conserve biodiversity?

Alternatively, think of neighbours or residents as a direct threat to the protected area. Their interest in protected area land for intensive farming or ranching may outweigh their interest in conserving the protected area. Is it in their immediate economic interest to convert the protected area to other uses that threaten biodiversity? If so, why? Are there existing measures, such as agricultural or prospecting subsidies or poorly-defined access rights to wild resources, which threaten biodiversity? Are such "perverse incentives" actually encouraging neighbours to destroy the protected area? Are there positive incentives which can be put in place instead?

Now think of commercial customers of the protected area. What goods and services can be harvested sustainably from the protected area and sold on the open market? Tourism, of course, is often an important non-consumptive service. What about the commercial sales of timber and non-timber products, including medicinal and ornamental plants, honey, bush meat, and so on? Does the protected area offer opportunities for hunting or fishing? Is it a prime site for bio-prospecting? Are there potential genetic resources to be harvested? How can such commercial operations be structured to generate revenues for the protected area so as to support the overall goal of biodiversity conservation? Additionally, there are probably downstream or indirect customers of the protected area. What benefits accrue to downstream communities and enterprises or more generally to the entire country or region? If the protected area serves as a watershed, it provides benefits to downstream water users including farmers, ranchers, miners, manufacturers and villagers.

If it is an area visited by people from cities nearby, then it offers a range of benefits (recreational, educational etc.) to urban dwellers. These groups have a stake in conserving the protected area, but do they have any means to express that interest? What measures will encourage and enable them to support the protected area? Can fiscal measures be used to collect revenues from these downstream customers?

Also, consider the global customers of this protected area. Within the mandates of global environmental agreements, the protected area may provide several global benefits. These could include biodiversity conservation, carbon sequestration, habitat for endangered species and migratory species, replenishing fish stock for traditional and commercial fisheries, mitigation of natural disasters and impacts related to climate change, and so on., What measures will enable the global community to support the protected area? Can the Global Environmental Facility (GEF) be used as a means of finance in such cases?

In short, a protected area can provide a diverse array of biological goods and services to a diverse array of customers. Bringing an entrepreneurial, private sector perspective to protected area management – in the first instance, by thinking of customers for protected area products – can help the protected area to seli goods and services in a way

A New Vision for Protected Areas

That will strengthen the ability of the protected area to support the conservation of biodiversity and sustainable use of natural resources. Valuation is a tool which can help protected area managers to start thinking like a business manager by providing a structured approach for identifying real and potential customers, estimating appropriate prices for goods and services, and signalling ways of capturing those prices.

Economic Values of Protected Areas

Identifying a protected area's goods and services, determining who values those goods and services, and measuring these values is not always a straightforward process. The goods and services include recreation and tourism, plant and wildlife habitat, genetic resources, water supply, protection against natural disasters, and so on. Many of these goods and services are not traded on commercial markets and therefore have no evident market value. The values of non-market goods and services need to be measured and expressed in monetary terms, where possible, so that they can be weighed on the same scale as commercially traded components.

The concept of total economic value (TEV) is now a well-established and useful framework for identifying the various values associated with protected areas. The total economic value of a protected area consists of its use values and non-use values. A protected area's use values are in turn made up of its direct use values, indirect use values, and option values. Non-use values include bequest values and existence values.

The difference between economic valuation and financial analysis should be made clear at this stage. Economic valuation, based on economic value, measures market and non-market values that people hold for a protected area. Financial analysis is a subset of economic valuation and measures the flow only of money through a protected area. Though financial analysis is a very useful tool, it may not be the most appropriate for all situations. This guide uses economic valuation as a framework because it captures a broader array of values.

The direct use values of a protected area are values derived from the direct use of the protected area for activities such as recreation, tourism, natural resource harvesting, hunting, gene pool services, education and research. These activities can be commercial, meaning they are traded on a market (resource harvesting, tourism and research), or non-commercial, meaning there is no formal or regular market on which they are traded (fuelwood collection and informal grazing). The value of commercial uses will generally be a straight-forward process of directly obtaining market-priced values. However, if these prices are administratively set, they may not reflect the true value for the product. Valuing non-commercial uses is more complex and entails a range of techniques which solicit values for goods and services of a roughly comparable nature from other markets.

The indirect use values of a protected area are values derived from the indirect uses of the protected area. Indirect uses are largely comprised of the protected area's ecological functions such as watershed protection, breeding habitat for migratory species, climatic stabilisation and carbon sequestration. Protected areas also provide natural services, such as habitat for insects which pollinate local crops or for raptors which control rodent populations. Indirect use values are often widely dispersed and thus go unmeasured by markets. Alternative valuation techniques discussed later are necessary for measuring them.

The option values of a protected area are values derived from the option of using the protected area sometime in the future. These future uses may be either direct or indirect and may include the future value of information derived from the protected area. Future information is often cited as particularly important for biodiversity as untested genes may provide future inputs into agricultural, pharmaceutical or cosmetic products. Non-use values are values which humans hold for a protected area which are in no way linked to the use of the protected area. Two common examples of non-use values are bequest values and existence values. Bequest values relate to the benefit of knowing that others benefit or will benefit from the protected area. Existence values reflect the benefit of knowing that the protected area exists even though one is unlikely to visit it or use it in any other way. Non-use values are particularly difficult to measure.

A Framework for Valuing Protected Areas

Identifying the values which people hold for a protected area may be an interesting intellectual exercise, but without a framework which embeds the values in a broader context, the process is just that – an exercise. A structured assessment process gives purpose and direction to a valuation study and saves time and money in the end. Such a process identifies what the values will be used for, which values are important to measure, and which techniques of valuation are most appropriate. The assessment process proposed in this section involves three basic steps:

1. Define the audience.
2. Determine the scope of the study.
3. Choose the appropriate analytical techniques.

The decisions taken in these steps are interrelated in that the interests of the audience will help to define the scope of the study and the scope will dictate, to some extent, the relevant techniques.

Define the Audience

Before starting a valuation study, the end use and audience for that study need to be determined. Defining the eventual use of the valuation study gives the study a *raison deter*, enables it to be carried out efficiently and effectively, and ensures that the information arrived at is relevant and clear to those who must use it.

Valuations can be used to procure support for the continued existence of protected areas. But a valuation study can also inform decisions about the management or financing of the protected area. There are many types of decisions which are made by many different groups. Decisions are made about:

- designing and carrying out projects in or adjacent to protected areas;
- designing and carrying out projects which use protected area goods or services;
- designing and carrying out projects upstream to, or downstream from, protected areas which may impact them;
- establishing and implementing sectoral programmes relating to protected areas;
- establishing and implementing policies for protected area management;
- establishing and implementing policies for protected area financing; and
- designing strategic plans at local, regional, national and international levels.

These decisions are made by protected area managers, community members, government officials, sectoral ministries, private enterprise, donor agencies, NGO's, the international community, and more. A brainstorming session with the economist and relevant stakeholders may help the protected area manager to identify the type of decision to be made and the groups that need to be involved.

The type of decision and the nature of the stakeholder groups help determine which values need to be measured and how those measurements should be expressed. For instance, a decision about carrying out a construction project adjacent to a protected area requires information about a set of values different from those needed for a decision about how much global funding to seek in support of maintaining biodiversity in a protected area. Additionally, a group involved in the public enquiry of the construction project will need the information presented in a manner different from a ministry of finance or the GEF.

The perspectives of the relevant stakeholder groups will also influence what is considered a benefit and what is a cost. Assigning the title of benefit or cost is ultimately a subjective process. One person's costs may be another person's benefits. In some cases it may be necessary for a protected area manager to represent what is a 'cost' to taxpayers (civil service jobs) as a 'benefit' to a particular constituency (local communities). Valuation studies can be expensive and time consuming. But not only is it unlikely to be necessary to measure all the values for a protected area, the values arrived at will not be valid for long. Values which people ascribe to a protected area are like preferences and prices, and thus are likely to change over time. Tailoring the valuation study to suit the particular needs of the decision at hand and the targeted stakeholder groups will make for a more efficient and effective study.

Determine the Scope in Terms of the Time, Data, Resources and Institutional Structure

Having determined what the valuation information will be used for and who will use it, the next step is to determine the appropriate scope for the study. The scope of the study must be defined in geographical, temporal and subject terms. It is necessary to know what geographical area the valuation study should cover. Protected areas can cover a vast area of land or water, not all of which may be relevant to the decision-making process. For instance, if a local planner needs to know the impact of an infrastructure project proposed for a site on the northeast corner of the protected area then it is probably unnecessary to measure values of unimpacted goods from the southwest corner. On the other hand, an international donor agency which needs information about the protected area's contribution to the global climate change mitigation is likely to need values relating to the carbon sequestration services of the entire protected area, but not the values of viewing its predators by tourists.

Also, for a valuation study to be relevant, there needs to be a clear idea of the timeline involved in the decision-making process. A valuation study that arrives two years after decisions have been taken is irrelevant – no matter how valid the data. Likewise, the decision-makers using the valuation study need to be realistic about time limitations they impose on the study. The time required to conduct a valuation study depends on the types of benefits being measured, the state and relevance of existing data, the level of measurement required, the amount of certainty desired, the capacity to conduct the study, and so forth. Protected area managers must be realistic about their demands – it is unlikely, for example, that a full contingent valuation study can be done in three weeks – and if time is short, then expectations should be realistic.

Finally, it is important to define the scope of the study in subject terms. That is to say, the scoping stage of the study must identify exactly which values are relevant and should be (and can be) measured. As pointed out in Section 2, people ascribe many types of values to protected areas. The first step to determining which values are relevant is to get a broad idea of the benefits attributed to the protected area and the people who value those benefits – or in other words, the people who are stakeholders in the protected area.

The process of conducting this broad scoping exercise is itself a useful tool for internal management and finance decisions. This is because identifying the various values people hold for the protected area and the groups that derive benefits from the protected area highlights opportunities for obtaining revenues, improving services and minimising exposure to threats. Often the actual measurement of all or some of the values is unnecessary.

Of course, not all values identified through this broad scoping process are relevant to every decision. The next task in the scoping process is determining which values are relevant to the end decision. The type of decision will influence the ranking of the values. For instance, a decision about the impact of a development project on the protected area needs information about the values of goods or services affected by the project – therefore measuring these values should be a priority. On the other hand, a decision regarding alternative uses for the protected area needs information about the most important goods and services that would be foregone if an alternative use were chosen.

It is also important to consider the likelihood of being able to measure the values, and the costs of measuring them. As mentioned before, time and money are likely to be constraints on the study and may limit the types of values which can be measured. This is linked to the next stage in the framework – identifying methods of data collection – because the methodologies used will influence the time required and costs involved.

Choose the Analytical Technique

Measuring the direct use values which are traded on commercial markets is likely to be a more straightforward process than measuring the other values attributed to protected areas. This is because the markets have already done the work of eliciting values from the 'customers' of the protected area. The task of measuring these values involves identifying the markets for them, gathering data about prices paid in these markets, and determining the amount of the good or service traded on the market. For instance, the direct use values of tourism could be measured through the direct sales to tourists which may include expenditures on lodging and meals, entrance fees, concessions, rentals, guides and so on. Where prices such as entrance fees are administratively set and not market driven, however, it may also be necessary to estimate the likely market prices. Indicative methods available to protected area managers for capturing these values are given in the right column. These include collecting rents from those regularly using the land, applying user fees through systems such as hunting or camping permits, charging for access to the land or resources and so on.

A study which arrives at a value by tracing the flow of money through the official market is termed a financial analysis. A protected area's contributions to the financial transactions of the economy are its financial values. Values which fall outside of these financial transactions – such as many non-use and indirect use values –would not be included in a financial analysis. As is revealed in the case studies in Part II, these are the very values which often contribute significantly to the overall economic value of protected areas.

As emphasised before, the type of decision which the valuation information will be used for, and the people making the decision, have a significant influence over the nature of the valuation study. In fact, the group making the decision may hold a set of priorities far different from the protected area manager and the study may take on an entirely different perspective because of this. For instance, the Money Generation Model – used by the US National Parks Service to inform local communities of the value of nearby parks – counts jobs and local tax revenues generated by the park among the benefits attributed to it. Treating jobs as benefits can be rational from the perspective of the local community which may indeed see local jobs created by the park and local tax revenues derived from expenditures in the park as direct and indirect benefits attributable to the park. But from the perspective of the park manager who is running the park like a business, jobs and taxes are costs, not benefits. Taxes are, of course, also a cost to the taxpayers.

It is important to know the priorities of the group which will be using the valuation information as this will further affect which values are chosen and how they are presented. For instance, a local community is likely to be more interested in the number of local jobs created by the protected area, rather than the total number of jobs created. On the other hand a national government will be interested in considering employment prospects overall.

Employment may also take on a different significance when the ratio of foreign specialists to local workers is considered. In comparing protected area employment to other uses for which the area could be considered, a preference for work offered to local people may provide added support for the protected area. Alternatively, as is common in many developing economies, emphasis may be placed on the hard currency earnings and this becomes a determining factor.

As this model is specifically addressing a local community decision of whether or not to support the protected area, it may not provide much useful or appropriate information for a Ministry of Finance deciding how much national funding to allocate to the protected area.

Indeed, national government expenditure on the protected area is measured as a benefit in the Money Generation Model rather than as a cost. Nevertheless, such a model offers a simple approach to capturing some of the values of a protected area, for site-specific, local audience situations.

Where markets do not exist, values held by 'customers' must be elicited. An array of methods for eliciting both market and non-market values from people for environmental goods and services have been developed over the last few decades.

Though still a developing field, some of the more common and widely used methods include:

- contingent valuation,
- hedonic pricing,
- travel cost method,
- change in productivity,
- loss (or gain) of earnings,
- opportunity cost, and
- replacement cost.

The Money Generation Model

The Money Generation Model uses protected area-related expenditures from non-local tourists and Governments to determine the neighbouring communities' benefits in terms of jobs and tax revenues. An example from a study of Federal Interest Lands in South Florida done by FAU/FIU Joint Centre for Environmental and Urban Problems is used here to demonstrate the model.

Tourism

A. Sales benefits;

1. Estimated non-local % of protected area use 90%
2. Annual recreation visitor day................................ 398,120
3. Average daily expenditure.. $119
4. Direct sales (1) x (2) x (3).. $42,638,652
5. Indirect and induced sales multiplier 1.95
6. Sales benefits from tourism (4) x (5)............. $83,145,371

B. Tax revenue benefits from tourism sales;

1. Sales benefits (A.6)... $83,145,371
2. Retail sales tax rate (state and local)........................ 6.5%
3. Sales tax revenue benefits from tourism......... $5,404,449

C. Job benefits from tourism sales;

1. Sales benefits from tourism (A.6) in millions............83.1
2. Multiplier for jobs created per million...................41.4
3. New jobs from tourism sales.................................... 3,440

Federal Government Expenditures 4

A. Sales benefits;

1. Direct sales.. $18,021,448
2. Indirect and induced sales multiplier1...................... 1.8
3. Total sales benefits (1) x (2)............................ $32,438,606

B. Tax revenue benefits from government related sales;

1. Sales benefits (A.3).. $32,438,606
2. Retail sales tax (state and local)................................. 6.5%
3. Sales tax revenue benefits (1) x (2).............. $2,108,509

C. Job benefits from government related sales;

1. Sales benefits (A.3).. $32.4m
2. Multiplier for jobs per million dollars..................... 41.4

3. New jobs from government expenditures.............. 1,341

1. direct and induced sales multipliers (usually 1.2–2.8 for the US) vary with the complexity of the local community. More isolated areas are likely to have lower multipliers because a larger portion of spending will be conducted outside the area. If this multiplier is small, one option for the community is to devise ways of providing more services and goods for tourists in the area.
2. The US retail tax system is comprised of state and local taxes. This is unlikely to be the case inmany countries and the level of government collecting retail taxes will affect whether or not they can be considered 'local' benefits.
3. The jobs multiplier will vary from industry to industry and range from 10 to 50 per million dollars in total sales in the US tourism industry. Additionally, rural areas tend to have larger jobs multipliers than towns and cities.
4. The procedures for calculating the job and tax revenue benefits 'non-local' (State) government expenditures in the protected area follow these Federal Government expenditure procedures.

Managers in developing countries may consider including Donor and International Government expenditures in this model. The contingent valuation method (CVM) uses a direct approach to valuing an environmental good or service in that it asks people through surveys or experiments what they are willing to pay for the good or willing to accept for the loss of the good. Contingent valuation is particularly attractive because it can estimate values where markets do not exist or where market substitutes cannot be found. For these reasons, CVM is widely used to measure existence values, option values, indirect use values and non-use values.

Hedonic pricing uses existing markets – such as the housing or labour markets – to determine the value of an environmental good. The assumption is that property values or wages reflect a stream of benefits, some of which are attributable to the environmental good. The analyst's task is to isolate that value which is attributable to the good.

Hedonic pricing can be used to establish some of the more aesthetic values of protected areas as residential property adjoining a protected area is likely to hold a higher value because the protected area is viewed as a benefit. On the other hand, hedonic pricing can be used to value environmental damages, and their effects on property values or wages. Hedonic pricing becomes problematic where alternative markets are distorted or where information about environmental products is not widespread and data are scarce.

Travel cost method also uses existing markets, determining a person's value of an environmental good from what they spend on travelling in terms of time, travel expenditures and entry fees. Travel cost methods are particularly useful for assessing

A Framework for Valuing Protected Areas

Willingness to Pay and Willingness to Accept

People reveal their value for the benefits derived from a protected area through their willingness to pay (WTP) for those benefits. A person's WTP can be elicited through surveys or surrogate markets. People also reveal their value for an environmental benefit through their willingness to accept (WTA) compensation for foregoing the benefit. In the case of environmental loss, people reveal their values through a willingness to pay to prevent the loss and their willingness to accept compensation to tolerate the loss.

These two concepts of benefit, WTP and WTA, should reveal the same values for the protected area. But empirical studies suggest this is not the case. It is generally believed that this is because people value the things they have more than those things they do not have. Therefore WTP is usually smaller than WTA. An additional problem arising from the concept of WTP in practice is that people with high incomes can afford to pay more than those with low incomes. This is particularly problematic when valuing a protected area in a developing country which is used by developed country tourists because the tourists will be able to place a higher value on their use and non-use benefits than the local people. In order to compare two such sets of value it may be necessary to measure the two sets of values as a percentage of income. Such a split may also support segmented pricing for local and foreign tourists as is increasingly common in developing countries. the non-commercial tourism, recreation and leisure values of a protected area. Travel cost methods, however, can be problematic in that they are data intensive, they rely on restrictive assumptions about consumer behaviour (e.g. multifunctional trips), and they are highly sensitive to the statistical methods used.

Change in productivity methods value the goods and services of a protected area by estimating the change in the value of production of a good or service that occurs as a result of the change in land of the protected area. Measuring the change in productivity is particularly useful when trying to discover the ecological values of a protected area. To take an example, a forested protected area is being considered for a clear-cutting operation. As it stands, the forest provides a service to farmers downstream by keeping the river from silting up. The change in productivity method would measure the current level of productivity and estimate its level after the clear-cutting, and calculate the difference between these levels to derive the loss in productivity. This loss is then a value of the protected area as it correctly stands.

Loss (or gain) of earnings methods evaluate the change in productivity of humans resulting from environmental deterioration (or improvement). Such methods may be useful in determining some of the more concrete effects of a change in the regulatory functions of protected areas. These regulatory functions include watershed protection, storage and recycling of organic matter, nutrients, and human waste, and climate regulation. For example, if water quality improvements reduce the levels of disease resulting from poor water quality, then the loss-of-earnings approach can be used to estimate benefits of clean water.

The opportunity cost approach provides an estimate of the value of a protected area based on the foregone income of the best alternative use of the area. Measuring the opportunity cost of the protected area can give the manager an idea of the competitive threats to the area. In the case of potential threats from people living adjacent to a protected area, the relevant opportunity costs will be the value of alternative land uses they may prefer, such as farming or ranching. Other interest in the area may come from pressures for industrial or urban development, mining or intensely modified recreation uses.

The replacement cost approach can be used to measure the cost of damage done to the protected area by looking at how much it would cost to replace the assets that are damaged. For example, the cost of restoring a protected area could be used as an estimate of the cost of environmental damage to the protected area. These costs are then compared to the costs of preventing the damage in the first place. If the replacement costs exceed the prevention costs then the damage should be avoided.

Case studies in Part II use these and other related methods to determine protected area value. As is evident from the cases, the methods used for a valuation study largely depend on the specific situation of that study and will likely be adapted for the study's specific needs. The methodology for valuing environmental goods and services is continually developing. New methods are devised and old ones amended with every study that is conducted. Deciding on the methods which suit the needs of the study requires imagination and ingenuity. Those described in this section should not be seen as all inclusive, but as an introduction to the possible approaches to valuing protected areas.

Monitoring Tourism in Protected Areas

Sustainable Nature Tourism in Protected Areas

Many of Finland's protected areas are significant tourist attractions. Although the main purpose of protected areas is to protect natural features, they are also beneficially used for scientific research, amateur nature studies and outdoor recreation. The recreational use of protected areas can usually also be described as nature tourism.

Metsahallitus manages almost all of Finland's national parks and other protected areas in areas owned by the state. To help improve nature tourism and the related facilities, Metsahallitus has drafted a special set of principles for sustainable nature tourism in protected areas, wilderness areas and sites in special conservation programmes. Sustainable nature tourism is promoted in cooperation with local residents, the local authorities, firms offering tourist services, and other organisations. These principles for sustainable nature tourism are not simply a list of "dos and don'ts", but rather represent jointly agreed practical guidelines that will help to promote sustainability. These guidelines may be followed in different ways by different organisations, according to local conditions.

Principles for Sustainable Nature Tourism

The following nine principles are intended to guide the operations in protected areas. Explanations and examples are given to illustrate how these principles are put into practice. In protected areas, wilderness areas, and sites in special conservation programmes that are managed by Metsahallitus, sustainable nature tourism is practised according to the following principles:

1. Natural values are preserved and all activities promote nature conservation.
    - Nature is an important reason for visits.
    - Visitors can learn about nature and conservation.
    - Tourism does not disturb nature; not all areas are suited to tourism.
    - Groups are small, and use marked trails wherever possible.
    - Tourism is channelled into areas with suitable facilities.
    - Facilities are designed to fit in with the surroundings; the most beautiful natural areas are left undeveloped.
    - Erosion and other impacts are monitored, with corrective measures taken as needed.
2. The environment is subjected to as little pressure as possible.
    - Nature comes first; every effort is taken to avoid damage or disturbance.
    - Visitors leave no trace behind them.
    - Firewood is used sparingly.
    - Emissions of all kinds are minimised, and renewable energy sources preferred.

- Metsahallitus and other organisations set good examples on environmental protection.

3. Local traditions and cultures are respected.
    - Visitors are encouraged to learn about local cultures.
    - Local cultures are suitably considered in the provision of information and activities.
    - Guides are familiar with local conditions.
4. Visitors increase their understanding and appreciation of nature and cultures.
    - Information is available for visitors before they come.
    - Information is easily available and attractively presented.
    - Visitors can contribute to the management of the area.
    - Guides are well trained.
5. Improved recreational facilities are provided for visitors.
    - The needs of all visitors are considered.
    - Facilities suit local demand and conditions.
    - Visitors can enjoy peace and quiet, as well as guided activities.
    - Facilities and services are developed in cooperation with local firms.
6. Visitors are encouraged to enjoy both mental and physical recreation.
    - Visitors are encouraged to move under their own steam.
    - Facilities are provided for hikers and other visitors.
    - Easy and demanding routes are available.
    - Opportunities exist for a variety of activities in natural surroundings.
    - All trails and other facilities are safe.
7. Local economies and employment are promoted.
    - Local firms' products and services are used where possible.
    - Employment is given to local people where possible,

although outsiders may also contribute valuable ideas to help promote local development.

8. Publicity materials are produced responsibly and carefully.
    - Information is reliable and up-to-date.
    - Publicity work is conducted openly and interactively.
    - Publicity does not work against nature conservation.
9. Activities are planned and organised co-operatively.
    - Visitors' opinions are very important.
    - Training is organised together with local firms.
    - All interested parties may participate in planning.
    - In cooperation work, preference is given to organisations committed to these principles of sustainable nature tourism.

What is Sustainable Nature Tourism?

The goal of sustainable nature tourism is to provide visitors with valuable experiences in natural surroundings in fully sustainable ways. The above principles for sustainable nature tourism in protected areas relate to the various ecological, social, cultural and economic aspects of sustainability. Ecological sustainability involves respecting natural values. Not all areas are suited to nature tourism.

Social, economic and cultural sustainability depend on the impacts of nature tourism on local residents and communities, and also the experiences of visitors. Nature tourism has the potential to improve both economic and spiritual well-being, but poorly planned or badly organised tourism can endanger natural features and local cultures, and also disturb other people using natural areas.

Measuring Sustainability

Metsahallitus is currently developing indicators to evaluate the sustainability of nature tourism. These indicators will be used to monitor the ecological, social and economic impacts of nature tourism in specific areas. Such indicators will also be used in the planning of the use and management of protected areas.

Sustainability through Cooperation

The increasing use of protected areas for nature tourism means that clear rules must be jointly agreed by everyone concerned. Written agreements are made between Metsahallitus Natural Heritage Services and local firms, to define acceptable and sustainable practices. In addition to the contracts entitling firms to organise activities in protected areas, even more detailed cooperation may be established through cooperation and partnership agreements. Sustainability can only be achieved through cooperation.

Visitor Management, A Tool for Sustainable Tourism Development in Protected Areas

Tourism is one of the world's fastest growing industries and its global impacts are immense and highly complex. Given that a high percentage of tourism involves visits to naturally and culturally distinguished sites, there are clearly major opportunities for investing in the maintenance of biological resources.

Tourism can help the sustainable management of protected areas, as a market-based alternative catering to the growing number of discriminating travellers trying to find, understand and enjoy a natural environment.

Tourism can help the sustainable management of protected areas, as a market-based alternative catering to the growing number of discriminating travellers trying to find, understand and enjoy a natural environment. Tourism can support the protection of natural resources, as local residents realize the value of their asset and want to preserve it.

At the same time, our global heritage of living species is threatened as never before, as the protected areas that harbor so much of our biodiversity are exposed to the pressures of unsustainable development. The precautionary approach urges us to be especially concerned about tourism in protected areas, given the risk of damage and destruction to this unique natural resource.

Tourism is a major management issue for many protected areas as the presence and actions of visitors can present serious problems for biodiversity conservation.

Therefore tourism has to be managed with care and site managers must assess and balance the costs and benefits of tourism in protected areas. It is also important to find ways for local people and communities to benefit from tourism linked to conservation, as this helps to demonstrate the economic value of the natural resources being conserved.

Sustainable Tourism Development in Protected Areas

According to the World Tourism Organization sustainable tourism should:

1) Make optimal use of environmental resources that constitute a key element in tourism development, maintaining essential ecological processes and helping to conserve natural heritage and biodiversity.
2) Respect the socio-cultural authenticity of host communities, conserve their built and living cultural heritage and traditional values, and contribute to inter-cultural understanding and tolerance.
3) Ensure viable, long-term economic operations, providing socioeconomic benefits to all stakeholders that are fairly distributed, including stable employment and income-earning opportunities and social services to host communities, and contributing to poverty alleviation.

Sustainable tourism development guidelines and management practices are applicable to all forms of tourism in all types of destinations, including mass tourism and the various niche tourism segments. Sustainability principles refer to the environmental, economic and sociocultural aspects of tourism development, and a suitable balance must be established between these three dimensions to guarantee its long-term sustainability.

Sustainable tourism development requires the informed participation of all relevant stakeholders, as well as strong political leadership to ensure wide participation and consensus building.

Achieving sustainable tourism is a continuous process and it requires constant monitoring of impacts, introducing the necessary preventive and/or corrective measures whenever necessary. Sustainable tourism should also maintain a high level of tourist satisfaction and ensure a meaningful experience to the tourists, raising their awareness about sustainability issues and promoting sustainable tourism practices amongst them. Although the relationship between tourism and protected areas is complex and sometimes adversarial, tourism is always a critical component to consider in the establishment and management of protected areas.

The definition of a protected area adopted by The International Union for the Conservation of Nature (IUCN) is: "An area of land and/or sea especially dedicated to the protection and maintenance of biological diversity, and of natural and associated cultural resources, and managed through legal or other effective means".

Tourism can degrade natural areas, but can also be a reason to protect nature and culture. It can fund nature management and give nature a direct economic value, providing an incentive for local inhabitants and governments to protect nature.

Planning guidelines applicable to government and managers of protected areas include:

- Develop and implement effective land use planning measures that maximize the potential environmental and economic benefits of travel and tourism while minimizing potential environmental or cultural damage.
- Tourism activities should be planned at the appropriate level with a view to integrate socioeconomic, cultural and environmental considerations at all levels.
- Planning for tourism development must be integrated with other planning efforts at the site, regional and national levels, applying tools such as strategic environmental assessment and integrated resource management.

Poor planning and management of tourism development in and around protected areas can have devastating, longlasting and sometimes irreversible effects. Non-sustainable tourism is negative for conservation goals, for local communities and for societies in general.

Visitor Management in Protected Areas

Managing tourism in a sustainable way however requires both a long-term perspective and careful consideration of the many ways in which tourist activities and environment interrelate. What is needed is a systematic approach and a tool kit for planning in order to provide the necessary resources for visitor management. Therefore it is important to provide standardized data and collect them as early as possible.

Increasing recreational use of national parks and protected areas can impact natural and cultural resources and the quality of the visitor experience. Determining how much recreational use can ultimately be accommodated in a park or protected area is often addressed through the concept of carrying capacity.

From a management perspective, visitor impacts are significant because they directly reflect management success in meeting two primary mandates: resource protection and recreation provision. In this respect visitor impacts need to be managed since:

1. Visitor use can negatively affect vegetation, soil, water and wildlife resources as well as the quality of visitor experiences.
2. Visitor crowing and conflict can reduce the quality of visitor experiences.
3. Environmental attributes such as vegetation and soil resistance and resiliency, influence the type and severity of visitor resource impacts.
4. The use/impact relationship limits the effectiveness of visitor use reduction and dispersal strategies.
5. Decision-making frameworks can provide an explicit and flexible means of managing visitor impacts.
6. Indirect management strategies are often less costly to implement and are preferred by visitors.

Visitor management is an administrative action oriented towards maintaining the quality of park resources and visitor experiences. In many but not all situations management tends to focus on the negative impacts resulting from unrestrained visitor activity.

In other situations management acts assertively to create and maintain opportunities for visitors to view, experience, learn about and appreciate their natural and cultural heritage.

Broadly speaking there are four strategic approaches which can be used to reduce the negative impacts of visitors on protected areas:

1. *Managing the supply* of tourism or visitor opportunities, e.g. by increasing the space available or the time available to accommodate more use;
2. *Managing the demand* for visitation, e.g. through restrictions of length of stay, the total numbers, or type of use;
3. *Managing the resource* capabilities to handle use, e.g. through hardening the site or specific locations, or developing facilities; and
4. *Managing the impact* of use, e.g. reducing the negative impact of use by modifying the type of use, or dispersing or concentrating use.

The visitor management techniques available to managers of natural resources include:

- Regulating access by area (zoning);
- Regulating visitation by visitor type (through pricing)
- Implementing entry or user fees;
- Providing interpretation programmes and facilities;
- Regulating visitor behavior (codes of conduct);
- Concentrating on allowing accredited organizations to bring visitors to the site.

Sustainable tourism practice within protected areas is a long-term commitment. But while it is important to think longterm, it is also necessary to set realistic short and midterm goals. Individuals, businesses and organizations must be aware that benefits are long-term, and should not expect to experience them immediately after sustainable practices are implemented. In practice, only a small portion of benefits will arise quickly; most will depend upon many years of continued effort.

Sustainable Tourism in the New Century

The nineteenth and twentieth centuries appear at first glance to have been a golden age when technology began to conquer all. Again Fukuyama says it clearly: "technology makes possible the limitless accumulation of wealth, and thus the satisfaction of an ever expanding human set of desires". That science backed scenario was backed by the philosophers Hegel and Marx in the past, and lives on at the UN, at the World Bank, and in the minds of most people in the developed world. But it is interpreted too simplistically by too many.

Since then progress through technology has been made but in a fashion that has brought new problems of pollution, resource pressures, global terror and war, and fast changing industrial and societal uncertainties. Sail gave way to steam, and then to electricity and now to electronics. Empires have grown and collapsed. Linear change, especially inevitable linear change, has been challenged by chaos and other change theories. The issue of limits to growth – a simple concept – perhaps too simplistic-has become an intense pre-occupation. The success of technology, in raising living standards, in raising expectations and in bringing more people into the developed world, has probably exceeded the earth's carrying capacity. And so-put simply – the ways that we manage the world may have to be changed, moving from unsustainable development to new forms of sustainable development. That change will involve new technologies. It will also involve new management techniques, and *above all* it will involve a very difficult process called behavioural change.

Sustainable Development

Sustainable Development is an old concept. In the agricultural terminology of the past it was called good husbandry or stewardship. It re-emerged in the 1960s, as global economic growth gathered speed after World War 2. A major milestone was reached by the founding of the international Club of Rome in 1968.

In 1980 the International Union for the Conservation of Nature (IUCN) based in Geneva, issued the *World Conservation Strategy*: it brought the cautious and sometimes negative thinking of the conservationist together with the positive but sometimes heedless world of the developer. It set the stage for the publication of the *Brundtland Report* of 1987, a work created by the World Commission on Environment and Development, and the work from which most of the current thinking on Sustainable Development stems.

According to Bruntland, sustainable development is:

> *"development that meets the needs of the present without compromising the ability of future generations to meet their own needs".*

In 1992, at the Earth Summit in Rio de Janeiro, sustainable development became a goal agreed upon by the nations of the world.

Sustainable Development Principles

Four basic principles are crucial to the concept of sustainability:

(1) The idea of holistic planning, cross-sectoral planning and strategy making

(2) The importance of preserving essential ecological processes

(3) The need to protect both human heritage and biodiversity

(4) The requirement that development should be carried out so that productivity does not deplete resources for the long term and future generations

Business watchers will recognise in the above points the making of the case for a new Triple Bottom Line – replacing company and national bottom lines that were concerned with cash alone. The triple bottom line accounting concept requires accounting for financial, social and environmental outcomes. As we shall discuss later, that triple bottom line accounting may be about to give way to Quadruple Bottom Line accounting – with the need to assess climate change responsiveness.

The key words throughout Brundtland are balance and thought-thought about consequences before precipitate action. In addition to all the above Brundtland introduced to the debate the issues of fairness-of intergenerational equity, and also of international equity-requiring a greater convergence between rich and poor nations if the global system was to remain stable. And linked closely to the whole sustainable development discussion are two teasingly difficult areas-the Precautionary Principle and the need for a holistic approach.

Reaction in the USA

Early interest in the concepts of sustainable development was centred on Europe, although there were many thinkers and writers on sustainable development in the USA. Key US developments included the publication by the American Planning Association's Planning Advisory Service of the *Planners Guide to Sustainable Development* (PAS 467), and the work of the Presidents Council on Sustainable Development which worked between 1996 and 1999. Its final report, *Towards a Sustainable America: Advancing Prosperity, Opportunity and a Healthy Environment for the 21st Century,* put forward 140 ways forward to achieve a more sustainable agenda.

Shades of Green

Within the discussion of sustainable development there are two contrasting approaches, the so-called Deep Greens, and the so-called Shallow Greens (these groups are also sometimes called Deep Ecologists and Shallow Ecologists). Deep Greens evolved from the work of the Norwegian philosopher Arne Næss, basing his work on the idea that man is but a part of nature and that the whole environment has a right to live and flourish: all forms of life have intrinsic value. Deep Greens support traditional land use systems and technologies. They have close links to the Gaia movement. Shallow Greens, while supporting sustainable development, are more pragmatic, and at the far end of the shallow green spectrum they are linked to the Wise Use movement in the US. Shallow Greens support and believe in the use of new technologies as a key way to create more sustainable development.

Within the world of sustainable development, there have been changes in polarisation as the threats to the environment created by the acceptance of the existence of climate change have been popularly recognised. But polarity of thinking lives on in many forms: a classic case is the European debate over the sustainability, and even the morality, of short haul air travel.

Overall, however, after 40 years of debate and discussion, the need for more sustainable forms of development is now established and accepted. The problems lie in understanding its *implications*, and in *implementing the ideas* within the paradigm.

Sustainable Tourism

Sustainable tourism was being discussed long before Mrs.

Brundtland's commission delivered its verdict on the general economic development process. It emerged as a theoretical concept in the European Alps and around the Mediterranean Sea in the late 1970s. But theory was long in discussion before it became practice-that had to wait until the late 1980s, and until recently the concept was slow to find widespread implementation.

Tourism has had a long history. Some commentators place its origins in mediaeval pilgrimages, some in the Grand Tours of the eighteenth and nineteenth century, and others in the railway age world of the spa, mountain and seaside resort. But the real rise of tourism as a major pursuit and as a major industry begins in the post war period. UN World Tourism Organization statistics begin in 1950, when 25 million international travellers were recorded. Then the meteoric rise of the tourism industry began, with average year on year growth rates of 6.5% over the period 1950-2007. The year 2007 saw 903 million international arrivals world wide. UNWTO looks forward to 1.6 billion international arrivals by 2020. And far greater numbers holiday in their own countries: it is much easier however to count international arrivals. After 50 plus years of growth, no one working in the industry today can personally recall the pre-growth era. Growth – in numbers – in geographical impacts – in product terms – is regarded as an ongoing and given norm.

But tourism growth can have serious impacts on the environment and the world's peoples:

- It can have powerful physical impacts on places visited-farm and forest land swept away for airport and road construction, hotels and golf courses-often in scenic regions. Physical impacts can be complex and far-reaching-ski run development clearing trees can open the way to soil erosion, leading to landslides and potential major disasters. Heavily used areas can suffer erosion from sheer numbers of visitors-mountain erosion in the Alps, and Himalayas are classic examples. Whole ecosystems can be damaged.
- It can have serious cultural impacts. Tourists are wealthy and demanding guests. They can dismiss local customs,

turn land values and labour markets upside down, make local languages redundant, and shift the balance of political power in favour of distant multi-nationals. In some scenarios tourism can bring vice and crime.

- More subtly, tourism can destroy the future it promises by rendering the destination dependent on its dollars, then declaring a spoilt destination unfashionable and redundant. This, the operation of the tourism cycle, can effect both large resorts and rural retreats, rich and poor countries alike. Tourism is a volatile, fashion industry: it needs to be understood and well managed.
- In recent years, the impacts of the transport systems that are fundamental to modern tourism growth have been increasingly recognised. They burn large quantities of fuel in a fuel hungry world; they produce large quantities of emissions in a world beset by climate change issues. Climate Change and Transport Issues are major issues that loom over the world of tourism and sustainable tourism.

Sustainable tourism was designed not to stop tourism but to manage it in the interests of all three parties involved-the host habitats and communities, the tourists and the industry itself. It seeks a balance between development and conservation. It seeks to find the best form of tourism for an area taking into account its ecology and its culture. It may mean limits to growth, or in some cases no growth at all. The precautionary principle is important here.

Sustainable tourism seeks not just to plan for tourism, but to integrate tourism into a balanced relationship with broader economic development. That is the way in which sustainable tourism fulfils its requirement to think holistically, and one of its approaches to responsibility in business, the triple bottom line. In many rural areas the watchword is that tourism should be a tool for rural conservation, service retention and diverse development-not just a business for its own sake. In many urban areas, tourism can also work with heritage conservation by using redundant historic buildings for tourism purposes, by injecting tourism expenditures into areas needing urban regeneration, and by bringing jobs and re-training to areas with unemployment/social problems. But there is a key caveat. Sustainable development cannot be created by planning alone: it needs to work with the market and it needs to work with businesses great and small.

Progress and Problems

Sustainable tourism began as a purely reactive concept to the above issues, trying to stop negative change. Early outlines simply listed the negative impacts down the left side of the page and then had a wish list of their opposites, presumed to be positive outcomes, down the right side of the page. To be fair to their authors, there were no research findings or exemplars of successful sustainable tourism to draw on.

Only gradually did sustainable tourism become pro-active, trying to create positive change. Many commentators – professional as well as amateur – enjoy criticising tourism. The key to achieving sustainable tourism is, however, to carry out analytical review and criticism, then implement effective management techniques, and then carry on a rolling review, criticism and management process.

What has been Achieved so Far?

Progress in sustainable tourism to date has concentrated on:

- Discussions and definitions, and devising basic assessment/evaluation programmes for small scale sites.
- Testing a range of individual management techniques, notably a range of visitor management programmes, especially those for protected areas, more sustainable accommodation provision, transport centred research and the creation of partnership programmes.
- Local and individual projects, often innovative, many very short term.
- Local Sustainable Tourism Strategies, usually written by or for local governments.
- A number of certification programmes of varying types and varying quality, largely voluntary membership programmes with all the inherent problems that

membership programmes bring with them: such programmes are essentially prisoners of their members, succeeding with the success of their members, failing if their members either dilute their aims or leave the programmes.

- Discussion and trialling of a range of indicators designed to show progress (or lack of progress) in implementing sustainable tourism.
- The thinking through of the ethics and key concepts of the "subject" – one of the most important examples of this has been work by authors such as Bob McKercher, Bryan Farrell, Louise Twining Ward, and John Shultis, which introduced uncertainty, risk, chaos and organic change into the previously linear, inevitable progression development scenario.
- Research and case study work: a wealth of knowledge now exists on some issues. We understand, for example, much more about the role of information provision and interpretation in implementing sustainable tourism. Much research remains to be done, even more remains to be implemented.
- The emergence of a "first generation" of academics who have worked on sustainable tourism. Many members of that first generation are now beginning to reach retirement or to take senior posts that make active research and authorship difficult.
- The peer reviewed international *Journal of Sustainable Tourism* was founded, publishing its first issue in 1993. It is now into Volume 16, with 768 pages each year. It is ranked 4th out of nearly 100 peer reviewed tourism journals in the world. It is one of the few tourism journals on the Thomson Social Science Citation Index. Over 1,000 papers have been submitted to it over the last 16 years: not all have been accepted.

Despite the list above, real progress in sustainable tourism – especially in implementation-has been remarkably slow until recently. Why?

- The tourism industry has not been driven, either by government or market forces, to achieve a more sustainable form of tourism. The industry has successfully opposed attempts to regulate its impacts, often by invoking the idea of self regulation as being the best way forward. The market for tourism remains strongly driven by price and fashion factors, and both the market and the industry remain conservative. Until recently there has been no powerful political, market based, moral or financial case for the industry to change. Denial has been a common approach
- Ecotourism became a development trap for some sustainable tourism advocates. Ecotourism is a subset of sustainable tourism, dealing with rural nature based activities. It was relatively easy to develop and assess small scale sustainable tourism projects in rural areas. These projects appealed to the "small is beautiful" beliefs common amongst many and avoided the problems of contact with the mainstream tourist industry. Many people even assumed, wrongly, that it would be impossible to make "mass" tourism sustainable. It is not impossible: it is a must.
- Governments have been shy to encourage or require change in the tourism sector beyond basic safety regulations. Governments have traditionally practised boosterism towards tourism. In the new privatism that dominates governance, regulation is not welcome. The obvious places to try out regulatory systems, the urban and rural protected areas, are typically weak in tourism management skills, funds, political support and the new ethos required by the sustainable tourism approach.
- Society generally, the wider community, has not understood the need for sustainable development of most kinds. Sustainable development requires thought, change and investment: all are difficult to achieve. Sustainable living needs behavioural change by all stakeholders. Behavioural change is very hard to bring about. It is seen by many as unnecessary and painful.

- The Nature of Holiday Making. Many years ago (1990), the author was asked to address the main board of Thomson Travel about Sustainable Tourism. Thompson was, at that time, the largest tour operator in the UK, with a market share of the outbound holiday market in excess of 40%. The request was one that could not be refused – a major challenge. The address was made. The Board's reply can be summarised as: "nice idea, but the future is bright, the future is Euro-Disney, and we do not need a more sustainable product". A discussion ensued, followed by lunch. I was taken aside by a wise and experienced member of the board, who said, very gently but firmly, that I had to understand that holidays were the 2 weeks of the year when selfishness and thoughtless consumption were possible for everyone, when caution could be relaxed. She was the Director of Marketing. She was, in the real world of that time, correct.
- The academic research community also has to shoulder blame. Very few academic researchers have worked inside the tourism industry, and they remain outsiders, not understanding the pressures and the drivers within the industry, nor how to work with the industry. Equally, the industry has not been keen to work with academics because of the industry's essentially utilitarian, typically short term approach. There is an ongoing tension here.

Why has Sustainable Tourism Moved up the Public Agenda Now?

The fundamental reason is the recognition that climate change is happening, that its consequences could be seriously damaging, and that a series of changes are required in our existing life styles. Those changes could affect us all. And they could impact very strongly upon tourism and its growth. For the first time since 1950 tourism's growth rates are being threatened; for some regions the very existence of the tourism industry is threatened. The media is displaying new interest in green issues, and new anti-travel, anti-tourism pressure groups have developed. Air travel is being scapegoated. It must also be recognised that wider pro-nature, pro-heritage interests are growing in many (but not all) societies and parts of society, with strong implications for non-sustainable tourism. And it must also be said that long distance travel is becoming much more expensive.

New life has been breathed into the concept of sustainable tourism. Suddenly governments, regulators, the media, the industry and even a few travellers are questioning the survival of the status quo. They are less scornful of sustainable development. A powerful driver has emerged. Greed has, to a small extent, been replaced by fear. Sustainable Tourism is reacting to the new challenges by developing new approaches, including Slow Travel and the idea of Carbon-Free Destinations (Gosling 2009).

The concept of the triple bottom line is moving towards the concept of the Quadruple Bottom Line. The Fourth Line, is that of climate responsiveness. This idea was floated by the UN World Tourism Organization at Davos in 2007. (Becken, 2008) North Carolina could be the first state in the US to work on that idea: it has a special interest in railways and a remarkably intact rail net, if only for freight.

Whole new fields of research are developing within sustainable tourism– including behaviour change, market linked interpretation, eco-museum landscapes, social marketing, rail tourism, pluri-activity and life-style entrepreneurialism and new forms of food, beverage and hospitality linkages. They are especially remarkable within the University sector, because so many are multi and cross disciplinary in character.

And coupled with the fear created by climate change is the fear and uncertainty of now, of recession and financial issues. That could, paradoxically, be a powerful if unpleasant tool for behavioural change.

The Planning Process at International & National Scales

Sustainable tourism attracted interest at international level long ago. The United Nation's Environmental Programme (UNEP) published a review of voluntary codes of conduct for tourism in 1993 (Genot, 1995). The World Travel and Tourism Council (WTTC) launched its voluntary Green Globe triple bottom line certification programme in 1994. UN's World Tourism Organization produced a number of advisory publications from 1998 onwards. But few long lasting implementation examples can be directly linked to these activities. At national level the position was also weak, until recently. The UK's English Tourist Board published its plan, *The Green Light: A Guide to Sustainable Tourism*, in 1992, but it was little more than a short wish list. Other nations, such as Spain, have produced similar slight volumes. But in recent years national level progress has gathered speed. Australia has developed its powerful national Sustainable Tourism Cooperative Research Centre (STCRC), the industry backed Australian government initiative to carry out research using University research skills. Work on national sustainable tourism strategies has recently produced useful documents in, for example, Scotland and Norway. In Norway a totally new sustainable tourism strategy, aiming to make Norway into a carbon neutral destination, is being produced at this moment (2008) for implantation in 2010 – aiming to have carbon neutral status by 2025 (Gosling, 2009).

Regional and Local Implementation

It is at the regional and local level that much more tangible progress has been made, and where strongest links have been made with the business and community sectors.

Accommodation Provision

Accommodation is central to tourism. It is also central to sustainable tourism, setting the tone of provision for the visitor, and providing, if successful, employment directly and indirectly for the local area. It is also claimed that aspects of sustainable life styles seen and used on holiday are likely to be taken up by visitors in everyday life.

The Hotel Ucliva, Waltensburg, Graubunden, Switzerland

This is an innovative hotel development in a village far from the main tourism areas in Switzerland. The venture began in 1983, following the decision of a group of villagers to build a new hotel to help retain and expand employment and services in their declining rural area. It is a classic example of the holistic approach that sustainable tourism can develop: it uses tourism as an environmentally/community friendly development tool.

The hotel now has 72 beds and concentrates on family holidays and conference/course work. It uses traditional construction, with components made locally to ensure local jobs and income. Chemically based finishes and plastic were avoided: natural materials were used. It has high levels of energy efficiency and uses local wood and solar energy. Full kitchen and restaurant facilities serve locally sourced and locally processed foods. Farmers in the area were trained to supply the hotel's organic and semi-organic requirements. Ownership and control are local, a status obtained by innovative capital structures.

The hotel was planned and developed with input from University architecture and hospitality department staff as a demonstration project. From the outset the strong ecological design of the hotel and its many special features gave it a unique selling point, which was exploited by skilled PR and marketing, leading to it winning a series of prizes and awards. While collectively owned it has been operated on strict business principles but employing a triple bottom line accounting approach. When, in 1995, the hotel suffered falling customer numbers and revenue, rapid action was taken to replace the manager and introduce new marketing techniques and other improvements.

There have been 18 full time and 18 part time jobs created directly in the hotel, together with more jobs in the area as a result of the multiplier effect, especially in agriculture. Total cash flow to the area is calculated to be well over $4 million per year. Waltensburg's population has risen from 311 in 1984 to 400 in 2002.

The Talbot Inn at Knightwick, Worcestershire, England

In contrast to the Hotel Ucliva, the Talbot Inn is old and is privately owned. The inn has existed since the 14th Century, although it must be stressed that it is very largely a much later building. It is located in a rural area, and like many rural Inns, suffered from falling revenue, conservative management, and little innovation.

It was saved by the arrival home, in 1999, of the two daughters of the owners. While working in other areas of the UK they had begun to understand the principles of sustainable tourism, and notably the importance of *innovation to reintroduce tradition*, the ability to attract market share by offering a sustainable product, and the use of the triple bottom line as an asset rather than a burden. Under their guidance the hotel has been transformed from decline to award winning success, created local employment and income, and helped save the local farming economy.

Key innovations have included:

- Improvements to bedrooms to cut energy consumption, improve comfort, stress heritage links, and raise prices.
- Dramatic changes to restaurant provision to use local produce, grow some produce on site, use free range/ organic produce where necessary, update menus and work on heritage as well as modern dishes. The local farm economy has been boosted. Links have been made to the Slow Food movement.
- The building of a micro brewery on site to attract niche markets, use local barely and hops, save the local hop growers from low cost eastern European competition and create jobs.
- Development and hosting of regular farmers markets, to both boost Saturday daytime trade, market the Inn as a place to visit and help local producers.
- Development of a web site that links to other businesses and communities in the area.
- An effective marketing policy developed, and used to market the area as well as the business itself.

Transport Development

The role of public transport in sustainable tourism is an especially important one in Europe, where a dense bus and rail public transport network is slowly dying because of competition from airlines over long distances and cars over short distances, and because of unimaginative management, unaware of customer needs. Public transport is important to retain for older people, those without cars, or access to cars, to maintain employment, cut emissions and fuel use, and to engender long term behavioural change.

The examples below focus on the work of two UK Universities, Bristol and Plymouth, to encourage private railway companies to develop their slow local train services in rural areas for visitor use, boosting user numbers by over 25% within 4 years, and thus retaining the services for local people

The key to success in both cases lay in unlocking access to additional funding, developing partnership working to aid marketing, understanding market needs, and creating new products that built on the natural advantages of the local train and often indirectly developed additional more sustainable forms of tourism. The role of the Universities lay in their access to innovatory ideas, their market research skills, their knowledge of partnership management, their honest broker role and their ability to understand the ways to access public sector project funds.

Key developments included:

- The creation of short self guided walks from stations along the lines, carefully routed to pass interpreted points of interest, inns and cafes. Similar provision has been introduced for cycling.
- The introduction of line by line web site provision
- Linkages of rail travel to local food and drink providers – a classic on both lines has been the creation of Rail Ale Trails.
- Researching community and visitor needs to help develop better timetabling and ticketing.
- Motivating customer care amongst front line rail staff.
- Drawing into a meaningful partnership local councils, and/or the community to promote rail services.
- Obtaining funding from national and EU sources by stressing the triple bottom line approach, tapping into environmental and community support funds.
- Making rail services easy to use, by producing understandable and informative timetables.
- Making a rail trip an experience rather than a way of travelling from A to B.

Non-motorised Transport Provision

The development of cycle holiday companies is in some ways the ultimate form of transport for sustainable tourism. CountryLanes is a good example of this sort of private venture which has achieved triple bottom line success, making money, conserving the environment and helping local communities and other local business.. This company offers cycle hire and cycle holidays at several destinations across rural England, using skilled web site marketing, working closely with the media, local councils, communities and businesses and injecting large amounts of revenue into often remote areas. The business has been revamped several times over the last 15 years as markets and competition has changed.

Heritage Conservation

Heritage sites: Sustainable Tourism management techniques have been applied to a range of heritage sites in the UK to re-invigorate markets and product offer, cut emissions and work with and maintain local communities and businesses. Two good examples include:

- Hadrian's Wall, (a major Roman legacy) An important factor here has been the creation by a partnership of agencies of a private sector company, Hadrian's Wall Ltd. to deliver a sustainable tourism plan against a set of economic and environmental targets.
- The Blaenavon World Heritage Site in Wales, where a new Visitor Experience Plan and related Interpretation Plan will boost off peak visitor numbers, steer visitors into underused areas, avoid fragile environments, introduce new bus services and help regenerate the community and its businesses while increasing visitor satisfaction.

Landscape and Farm Conservation: Unmanaged tourism into heritage landscapes and farming areas can be a problem. The application of sustainable tourism marketing, management and monitoring techniques can give valuable triple bottom line benefits to such areas. Food trails have been especially valuable in remote mountainous parts of northern England, in helping farms recover from the disaster of the 2001 Foot and Mouth disease. The success of this trail has allowed traditional high cost farming to survive and the landscape patterns and associated ecologies to be conserved by targeted marketing and diversification in managed tourism. Some protected areas in the UK now use the vehicle of sustainable tourism to come to terms with visitor management and the private sector businesses. And others have used the concept of Food Heroes to market traditional food and farming.

Sustainable Tourism Strategy Planning

Over much of the developed world, the creation of regional, district and local sustainable tourism strategy plans has enabled business, community and environmental interests to come together to learn, discuss and develop viable sustainable tourism strategy plans, to guide and inform investment by the private sector, non-profits and public sector interests. The creation of the West Oxfordshire Sustainable Tourism Strategy in the UK was an example of the success of this technique. It used carefully mediated stakeholder involvement to understand the needs of business, environmental and community interests. It assessed by market survey and asset review the optimum way forward for each part of the district, a total area of 276 square miles. It used visitor management techniques to channel visitors into key areas. And it helped create partnerships between businesses to market and manage the strategy.

Similar techniques have been very successful in other areas. They require an effective knowledge of sustainable tourism management techniques, of partnership creation and business advice services.

But what could be done in North or East Carolina?

The success of the schemes described above can be related to a number of factors, many of which could be replicated in North or East Carolina. These include:

1) The ability of University staff to provide a lead into this new and complex area, by providing technical assistance, information, awareness raising, training and leadership.
2) The willingness of public sector and non-profits to work with business interests and to understand the economic realities of business.

3) A knowledge of, and the ability to implement, partnership working.
4) Accurate and targeted market knowledge and the skills to access those markets.
5) Knowledge and understanding of success stories in sustainable tourism, and the ability to adapt – not copy – those stories to the North/East Carolina situation.
6) Finding and supporting informed risk takers from, and risk taking by, all sectors.
7) Leadership – coming from all sectors.
8) Determination and Flexibility – in business there is little time for conflicts between deep and shallow ecology.

Taking that background into account, what tangible measures could be taken on the ground to make North/East Carolina a leader in sustainable tourism within the USA?

Political support is essential – to provide a platform for persuasion, to convince local officials and elected members, to supply start up funding for new infrastructure and marketing projects. The University has an important advice and lobbying role here.

Jealousy and example are also key, if surprising, factors. Potential stakeholders are best convinced by example; successful example engenders jealousy amongst others to achieve or exceed the outcome of those examples. In practice the use of the jealousy factor requires pilot projects to be created to demonstrate good and bad practice. The choice of pilot projects is central to success – they must be areas or businesses likely to succeed – through both the drive and skills of the individuals involved or the suitability of the assets that areas and people have.

Media support is also essential – to obtain broader support for initiatives across the region, and maintain political support.

Marketing skill – to sell the concept to communities, to business and to tourists. And here recent research has confirmed something many have long suspected. Marketing appeals to save the earth are ineffective. The adoption of behavioural change requires people to believe that they personally will gain, often in a tangible way, from change. They will gain financially, or increase their comfort, prestige or choices. Going green is just not enough for the great majority.

Financial support will also be important to provide incentives and advice – that support could come from agencies, from environmental or community support funds, from state tourism marketing agencies, from large companies with non tourism related triple bottom lines, from foundations or from the regions private investors. Technical expertise and technical contacts worldwide are also important – and the University of East Carolina is well placed to supply that role.

A start list might be:

1) Create a university/private sector/public sector/non profit group to steer Project East Carolina Sustainable Tourism 2020. The choice of its members is critical – no passengers can be taken.
2) Work out a practical manifesto and action plan for that Project. That Manifesto must be plausible, inspiring, link all sectors, and aim high enough to gain potential national recognition. It must however be achievable. It must contain sure fire winners. Nothing succeeds like success.
3) Hold one or more stakeholder meetings to get public support for the Manifesto.
4) Start a series of local projects of various kinds including farm related, community regenerating related, heritage related and others. Pay special attention to media coverage, and ensure that the products and marketing work. Try the Food Heroes concept; Find a Trial Area where a sustainable tourism strategy can be tested; Work with the North Carolina Train Host Association, with its over 100 volunteers serving as North Carolina's goodwill ambassadors on board the *Piedmont* and *Carolinian; set up the Heritage Region concept in one or more key areas, following Canada's experience; try to create your own group of "Sustainable Hotels" following the example of the Talbot Inn, and the Hotel Ucliva. It may even be possible to test Austria's Soft Mobility project at a selected location.*

5) The Austrian Ambassador would be happy to personally declare that project open !
6) Produce an East Carolina Sustainable Tourism Strategy – and remember that your aim is as much the adaptation of existing businesses and assets as it is the creation of new businesses and assets. Take heed of market requirements. Understand the key measures for changing visitor behaviour with particular reference to social marketing, targeted information provision, targeted heritage interpretation, and the value of personalities. Above all – remember that tourism is a fashion business, visitor experiences must be enjoyable and rewarding – but greenwash is soon exposed.

Remember, sustainable tourism is not just a planning technique, or a marketing device, or an unreachable aim, it is an adventure with rewards. Those rewards could be especially strong here. North Carolina is a train trip away for millions of people, no airline is necessary; even a car trip – with 2 or more people – is more sustainable, given an eco-friendly car. It is a remarkable opportunity for business and Universities and non-profits and the public sector to work together, first in learning networks, leading to effective action partnerships.

Problems of Sustainable Tourism

While authorities want to stop the access to forest lands and natural resources of village people, another group of people-namely tourism developers and tourists with lots of money to spend-are set to gain access to the area. While authorities believe that local people, who have often lived in the area for generations, are not capable of managing and conserving their land and natural resources-under a community forestry scheme for example-they believe they themselves in cooperation with the tourist industry can properly manage and conserve 'nature' under a national ecotourism plan. Taking the above quote seriously, cynics may be tempted to say there is obviously a gap between 'human rights' and 'animal rights'.

How is this story linked to globalization? First of all, that humans cannot live in the forest is-of course-not a Thai concept.

It is a notion of Western conservation ideology-an outcome of the globalization of ideas and perceptions. Likewise, that ecotourism under a 'good management' system is beneficial to local people and nature is also a Western concept that is being globalised. In fact, Thailand's forestry chief thinks globally and acts locally. A lesson that can be learned from this is that the slogan 'Think Globally, Act Locally' that the environmental movements have promoted all the years, has not necessarily served to preserve the environment and safeguard local communities' rights, but has been co-opted and distorted by official agencies and private industries for profit-making purposes. The tourism industry is demonstrating this all too well.

Many developing countries, facing debt burdens and worsening trade terms, have turned to tourism promotion in the hope that it brings foreign exchange and investment. Simultaneously, leading international agencies such as the World Bank, United Nations agencies and business organisations like the World Travel & Tourism Council (WTTC) have been substantially involved to make tourism a truly global industry.

However, tourism in developing countries is often viewed by critics as an extension of former colonial conditions because from the very beginning, it has benefited from international economic relationships that structurally favour the advanced capitalist countries in the North. Unequal trading relationships, dependence on foreign interests, and the division of labour have relegated poor countries in the South to becoming tourism recipients and affluent countries in the North to the position of tourism generators, with the latter enjoying the freedom from having to pay the price for the meanwhile well-known negative impacts in destinations.

Transnational Corporations

Travel and tourism has emerged as one of the world's most centralised and competitive industries, and hardly any other economic sector illustrates so clearly the global reach of transnational corporations (TNCs). Over recent years, the industry has increasingly pressured governments around the world to liberalise trade and investment in services and is likely to benefit tremendously from the General Agreement on Trade in Services-a multilateral agreement under the World Trade Organisation (WTO).

GATS aims to abolish restrictions on foreign ownership and other measures which have so far protected the services sector in individual countries. For the hotel sector, for example, GATS facilitates franchising, management contracts and licensing. Moreover, foreign tourism companies will be entitled to the same benefits as local companies in addition to being allowed to move staff across borders as they wish, open branch offices in foreign countries, and make international payments without restrictive regulations.

Foreign investment will also be increasingly deregulated under the GATT/WTO system. According to the Agreement on Trade-Related Investment Measures (TRIMs), foreign companies will no longer be obliged to use local input. The Multilateral Agreement on Investment (MAI) proposed by Organisation for Economic Cooperation and Development (OECD) countries goes even further, calling for unrestricted entry and establishment of foreign firms, national treatment, repatriation of profits, technology transfer, etc.

Accordingly, the WTTC has recently presented its 'Millennium Vision' on travel and tourism, including the following key areas:

- Get governments to accept travel and tourism as a strategic economic development and employment priority;
- Move towards open and competitive markets by supporting the implementation of GATS, liberalise air transport and deregulate telecommunications in international markets;
- Eliminate barriers to tourism growth, which involves the expansion and improvement of infrastructure-e.g. the increase of airport capacity, construction and modernisation of airports, roads and tourist facilities.

On a tour through South-East Asian countries in February 1998, WTTC president Geoffrey Lipman also strongly supported the privatisation of state enterprises, particularly airlines and airports. His visit in Thailand, for example, coincided with the announcement of British Airways-a prominent member of the WTTC-that it was interested in taking over 25% of Thai Airways

International. And the British Airport Authority promptly followed up by proposing to buy a major equity share in the provincial airports of Chiang Mai, Phuket and Hat Yai, which are all located at popular tourist spots. However, the selling out of state companies to foreigners has been facing growing public opposition in Thailand so that privatisation is not progressing as planned.

Meanwhile, even the voices of the tourism industry in Asia are urging a cautious approach towards globalization. Imtiaz Muqbil, a renowned tourism analyst based in Bangkok, warned: 'The independence of thousands of small and medium size enterprises, including hotels and tour operators, is at risk.' This is because most local enterprises will hardly be able to compete with foreign companies. Moreover, Muqbil suggested that as an outcome of globalization, Asian countries may face 'the prospects of huge growth in leakage of foreign exchange earnings.' In conclusion, he said, 'The radical restructuring of travel and tourism... could strike at the heart of national economies.'

It is already a well-established fact that in some developing countries, more than two-thirds of the revenue from international tourism never reaches the local economy because of the high foreign exchange leakages. Now, as the new free trade and investment policies are being implemented, their balance sheets may even worsen because the profits and other income repatriated by foreign companies is likely to grow larger than the inflow of capital. That means, the claims that globalization and liberalisation of tourism will bring wealth, progress, social achievements and improved environmental standards to developing countries need to be seriously questioned.

A recently published document by the UN Conference on Trade and Development (UNCTAD) states that Asia-Pacific countries urgently need to bolster their bargaining positions in the field of tourism services and negotiate better terms in exchange for opening their markets. However, governments have barely had time to examine the potential impacts of globalization, and many local tourism-related companies are already in financial trouble due to the economic crisis. So it is very unlikely that they can strengthen their negotiating power. Even major Asian airlines can hardly survive in this crisis-hit business environment; the recent temporary closure of Philippine Airlines is an illustrative example.

Economic globalization has also generated considerable criticism because it comes along with the erosion of power of governments. Opponents argue that local and national institutions will no longer be able to properly fulfil their responsibilities such as providing social services, preserving the environment, and implementing sustainable development programmes.

Indeed, the multilateral agreements facilitating globalization have shown little, if any, concern for social and ecological issues. On the environment front, the WTO has discussed proposals to introduce 'environmental standards' and 'eco-labels' developed by international setting bodies.

Critics say this move is likely to be dominated by TNC interests, which attempt to appropriate the environmental agenda and push for self-regulation. Meanwhile, existing national environmental policies and laws adopted by democratically elected governments will be undermined.

The WTTC, for example, vows to 'promote sustainability in travel and tourism' through its Green Globe programme, but-as its 'Millennium Vision' document states-'strongly believes that the environmental policy agenda should focus on (the industry's) self-improvement, incentives, and light-handed regulation as the preferred approach'.

Concerns

The increasing influence of private sector interests on international forums negotiating the environmental agenda has reinforced concerns that genuine efforts to set up a more stringent framework for the tourism industry may be jeopardised. In this context it is important to note that the seventh session of the UN Commission on Sustainable Development (CSD) this year will include important discussions on the issues of sustainable tourism.

So far, the UN General Assembly has adopted a resolution on 'Sustainable Tourism' as part of its 'Programme for the further implementation of Agenda 21', the action programme adopted at the Rio Earth Summit. This resolution acknowledges the need to consider further the importance of tourism in the context of Agenda 21. Among other things, it states: 'For sustainable patterns of consumption and production in the tourism sector, it is essential to strengthen national policy development and enhance capacity in the areas of physical planning, impact assessment, and the use of economic and regulatory instruments, as well as in the areas of information, education and marketing.'

Furthermore, the resolution calls for participation of all concerned parties in policy development and implementation of sustainable tourism programmes.

What is important to keep in mind is that this UN resolution stresses the need for a democratic regulation of tourism development, which is in stark contradiction to the lobbying efforts by the agents of tourism globalization towards deregulation and an industry-led and self-regulated scenario.

This conflict featured prominently at the fourth Conference of Parties to the UN Convention on Biological Diversity (COP4) in Bratislava, Slovakia, last May, which included discussions on the integration of biodiversity into sectoral activities such as tourism.

Many government delegates there resisted attempts by the German government to get approval from the Ministerial Roundtable at COP4 for a programme to develop global guidelines on biodiversity and sustainable tourism. Observers noted that the increased promotion of interests of the powerful German tourism industry at the UN level by the German government has been conspicuous over recent years.

Official and NGO representatives were surprised by the insistence of the Germans to work on global guidelines and to seek endorsement for this programme from the CSD. The delegate from Samoa, for example, reiterated that sustainable tourism is a complicated issue that will be dealt with by the CSD next year and complained: 'We are not in favour of some of the top-down approaches we have seen here (at COP4).' Other delegates expressed concern over the relevance, objectives and funding of the proposed programme.

Significantly, critical observers warned that an ill-advised proposal on global guidelines under the Convention could have devastating consequences for local and indigenous communities-socially, culturally and ecologically. 'The tourism industry's propensity towards unrestricted growth and its commoditisation of indigenous cultures must be recognised as clearly unsustainable,' commented an NGO representative during the Bratislava Conference.

Meanwhile, there are justifiable fears that under the new economic globalization schemes, sustainable and ecotourism activities will even further enable TNCs to gain commercial access to ecologically sensitive areas and biological resources and accelerate the privatisation of biodiversity, all to the detriment of local communities' land and resource rights and the natural environment. As the Austrian environment minister told delegates at COP4, 'Sustainable tourism offers new market opportunities.'

Vague, with Buzzwords

Indeed, the debate on tourism principles and guidelines is a tricky one-not only because it is heavily overshadowed by politics of global players. Another point of concern is that guidelines and programmes, as discussed and adopted by advocates of sustainable tourism at the international level, naturally remain very vague. Usually, they are also overly euphemistic, with buzzwords abounding: e.g. empowerment of local communities; local participation and control; equitable income distribution; benefits to nature conservation and biodiversity protection; etc.

A tourism researcher from the University of British Columbia, Nick Kontogeorgopoulos, suggested that attempts to implement tourism projects based on such guidelines are bound to fail altogether because it is simply impossible to apply them to highly disparate and heterogeneous destinations. He says, 'While these altruistic principles are laudable in theory, the absence of place-specific context strips them of empirical evidence.' In conclusion: Not the global game, but local circumstances and conditions represent the essential determinant of success for sustainable development. In Asia, social and environmental activists argue that the inflationary tourism policies in the context of globalization have greatly contributed to the present economic crisis. During the era of the so-called bubble economy, indiscriminate and unsustainable investments led to the rapid conversion of lands into massive tourism complexes, including luxury hotels, golf courses and casinos, and related infrastructure such as airports, highways, and dams to generate electricity. With economic liberalisation, the tourism, real estate and construction industries boomed, backed by local banks and global speculative capital. An essay written by renowned tourism critic and media activist Ing. K. reflects the anger of many Thais about the developments that have led to the country's bankruptcy. She presents the hard facts as follows:

'Land speculation became a national pastime, permeating every beautiful village, however remote. Land prices skyrocketed. Villagers sold agriculturally productive land to speculators. Practically overnight, fertile land became construction sites. The plague kept spreading; corruption got out of control. National parks and forest reserves were encroached upon by golf courses and resorts...

'Many instant millionaires were made, but much of this new rich money was not wisely invested in productive ventures. Instead, most of it was spent on luxury "dream" products and services, in pursuit of the consumer lifestyle.

'Many of these people were merely imitating tourists and were influenced by the prevailing free-spending frenzy. Greed and consumerism devastated whole communities all over Thailand, raising the temperature even higher, on every level of society...

'In the end, we have nothing to show for it but whole graveyards of unsold high-rise condominiums, shophouses, golf course and resort developments and housing estates.'

Now, all discussions and work programmes relating to the implementation of global and local Agendas 21 and sustainable development appear-more than ever-removed from reality in view of the unfolding Asian crisis-a human disaster with millions of unemployed and landless people falling below the poverty line. According to the latest figures from UN agencies, more than 100 million people in the region are newly impoverished. And there are growing fears that the machinations of unregulated global speculative capital now threaten to ruin not only Asian economies but the rest of the world as well.

A major question that needs to be addressed in this context: Where will all the money come from for sustainable development and tourism projects? In Thailand, for example, the World Bank and the Japanese OECF have agreed to provide loans to improve and expand tourism as part of a social investment programme (SIP) aimed at tackling the problems of unemployment and loss of income arising from the economic crisis. It has been stressed that tourism development is crucial for the country's economic recovery, and 'community participation' and 'sustainability' are mentioned as major components in projects. But critics have warned that firstly, tourism is not a quick commodity that can pull the country out of its economic pains. And secondly, much of the borrowed money will be used for new developments in national parks and biodiversity-rich areas in the drive to promote 'ecotourism'.

Let me confront you with a provocative idea now. It is not the longstanding efforts by the many experts promoting and working on the implementation of global and local Agendas that bring us closer to sustainable tourism. Ironically, it is rather the current all-embracing crisis which may eventually make tourism more sustainable-at least in environmental terms. Why?

First of all, a basic problem of sustainable tourism has been the rapidly expanding numbers of travellers. But as a result of the crisis, tourism growth has come to a standstill. Due to currency devaluation, increasing unemployment, declining income and deflation, Asian markets are collapsing. Even the numbers of Japanese going abroad for holidays are now declining for the first time in 18 years. European and American holidaymakers have also shunned South-East Asian countries because of 1997's smog disaster, caused by forest fires in Indonesia, and political turmoil in the region-e.g. in Burma, Cambodia and-more recently-Indonesia.

As the economic contagion is spreading, the travel fever that had gripped Russia and other East European countries after the fall of the Soviet Union is also on the wane, as the Russian currency, the rouble, has plummeted dramatically and the economy slumps. Moreover, amid the decline of business activities in Asia, stockmarket slumps and fears of a global recession, nervous companies around the world are limiting corporate travel spending. The WTTC, which had earlier in 1998 forecast growth averaging 7% a year throughout 2008, now expects the global tourism market to remain flat in the next years. This may be bad in terms of economics but, unquestionably, the environment will benefit from stagnating or even decreasing tourist numbers.

For instance, the air travel industry has been identified as one of the biggest environmental villains in tourism. With fewer people travelling, however, the Asia-Pacific aviation industry is now flying into a deep recession. Airlines are fighting for survival by closing or cutting unprofitable routes, selling aircraft and cancelling orders for new aircraft. Governments are forced to cut budgets for airport expansion and construction. Ultimately, that means less pollution and less environmentally damaging developments.

The real estate and construction industries, which are both inextricably linked to the tourism industry, were the first industries that crash-landed when the Asian bubble economy burst. As a result, many speculative and unsustainable hotel and resort development projects have been abandoned, and new construction is down to a trickle. An excellent example is golf, which became a symbol of globalised leisure and tourist lifestyle in Asian tiger societies. But as the frenzy to build luxurious golf course complexes-including hotels, housing estates and shopping centres-has almost stopped completely, and middle-class people affected by the crisis are turning away from the expensive sport of golf, environmentalists can be relieved: The malaise of rampant land grabs, national park encroachments, deforestation, etc. related to golf courses is no longer as threatening as it was a few years ago.

On the other hand, while many tourism-related companies may have scrapped or postponed potentially harmful projects, one needs to acknowledge that because of the financial crunch, public and private investments in environmental protection are also being cut. Moreover, there have been warnings that the crisis has resulted in an upsurge of crime, prostitution, drug abuse and other social vices related to tourism.

Failed

But most importantly, Asian societies are beginning to realise that the current global economic capitalist system has utterly failed to bring achievements in all terms. Now burdened with having to pay for the activities of unscrupulous speculators and additionally suffering from free-market-oriented structural adjustment programmes imposed by the International Monetary Fund (IMF), people are losing faith in a globalised economy. Some experts even go so far as to say that free trade and investment liberalisation is 'yesterday's story'. Malaysia in particular has recently taken decisive steps to shut itself off from global markets by strictly controlling foreign capital flows.

Asian governments are now likely to move towards greater self-reliance as they are pressured by people of all walks of life to look into economic strategies that are chiefly based on domestic financial resources and the domestic market. This involves the strengthening of the agricultural sector and local industries to protect people's livelihoods in the first place. Forces still seeking to further prop up economically risky service industries such as tourism are likely to be weakened. Moreover, the crisis has also created considerable public debate about the impacts of global culture and lifestyle, including the issues of consumerism and the wasteful and unproductive use of resources. In several Asian countries-such as Korea, Thailand and Malaysia-outbound tourism is now being discouraged as it is seen as conspicuous consumption that has contributed to the negative balance of payments.

The issues of democracy and human rights are also gaining momentum in the region. As never before, people are making use of their civil rights and call for transparency and democratic procedures to phase out corruption and harmful government policies and development plans. The growing opposition of Thai environmentalists and villagers to the move of the government to open up protected areas for 'mass ecotourism' is just one example.

All in all, I believe, the current Asian crisis, which is likely to become a global crisis, poses a fundamental challenge-and an important opportunity-to re-evaluate the issues of globalization, sustainable development and tourism. As Asian societies begin to acknowledge that rapid economic growth under global regimes has devastating effects on people's lives and the environment, we may find that a stringent regulation of tourism, which involves a stricter limitation of tourist numbers and a halt to the unlimited spatial expansion of tourism, is better than further promoting tourism growth and hoping that this growth can be handled with 'good management', education of tourists, etc. What the current crisis really appears to confirm is-what many tourism critics have been saying all along-the global tourism industry just cannot be propelled towards sustainability under the conventional economic and political structures. That means, efforts to implement social and environmental agendas and sustainable tourism are unlikely to progress unless profound structural changes take place in the global system.

Understanding the Market for Tourism

Understanding tourism marketing has become essential in professional scenario of today. As the market is consolidating, the role of marketing as a driving force in a business endeavor is also being recognized. With growing competition, organisations in tourism business have no option but to engage in organised marketing. A professional approach to marketing always helps, whether it is on the tour operators' end or at destinations. Guides, escorts, restaurants, hotels, transporters, shops etc. closely compete and have to out-market one another to stay ahead. A proper tourism marketing strategy at national level needs close cooperation between the government, tourism industry and the local population.

Evolution of Marketing

Marketing as a concept has evolved in the last 30 years. Development of marketing and modern business practices has three stages: Production Era, Sales Era and Marketing Era. Marketing era arrived when organisations began to produce what they could sell rather than trying to sell what they produced. While planning and designing a product, consumers' needs, tastes and satisfaction are considered. Growth of competition prompted organisations to frame new marketing techniques. Changing tourism trends also demanded a new approach. The emergence of long haul tourist created the need for marketing research which took into account market trends, consumer behavior and ascertained procedure to make products which satisfied the users of tourism products. Gradual social and economic development culminated in segmentation of mass market into specialized target markets. Tackling these markets needed new approach and understanding of tourism marketing.

Selling and Marketing

Selling and Marketing are two different concepts. Selling concentrates on the needs of the seller while marketing concentrates on the requirements of the buyer. A marketing oriented organisation focuses on customer needs and earns profits through customer satisfaction. Many organizations in tourism sector are product oriented. They stress on the available services of products but ignore consumers' needs or attitudes. A marketing oriented tourist organisation takes totally different approach.

Business Philosophy

A marketing oriented business philosophy keeps consumer needs at centre-stage of all activities. An organisation could offer quality tourism products but if it lacks supporting infrastructure, it would have no takers. A tourist organisation needs to look after the needs like accessibility, accommodation, leisure and entertainment facilities. Tourists have their own needs, preferences and tastes, and these have to be taken into account while developing a product for them.

Marketing and Research-know Your Markets

To succeed in a competitive environment, it is important to tailor your business to the wants and needs of your customer.

Marketing is about matching every part of your business with your customers so that:

- You meet their needs.
- They are aware that you meet their needs.
- They are motivated to buy from you.

- They are motivated to keep buying from you.

Market research is an essential tool in assisting you to do this.

Undertaking market research will allow you to:

- define the essence of your business so you know what you are offering visitors;
- determine who your potential visitor markets are; and
- Establish their needs and how you will go about meeting those needs.

Define Your Business

- Your product or service;
- Your geographic marketing area—neighbourhood, regional or national;
- Your competition;
- How you differ from the competition—what makes you special;
- Your price;
- The competition's promotion methods;
- Your promotion methods;
- Your distribution methods or business location

Define Your Customers

- Your current customer base: age, sex, income, neighborhood;
- How your customers learn about your product or service-advertising; direct mail, word of mouth, Yellow Pages;
- Patterns or habits your customers and potential customers share e.g. what they read, watch, listen to;
- Qualities your customers value most about your product or service-selection, convenience, service, reliability, availability, affordability;
- Qualities your customers like least about your product or service-can they be adjusted to serve your customers better?
- Prospective customers like least about your product or service but whom you aren't currently reaching.

Tourism Queensland provides research on a number of areas of the tourism industry and access to regionally specific research and information. This includes:

- International market research
- Domestic and International aviation research
- Destinations-including a regional update, regional snapshot, visitor surveys, aviation information and fact sheets.

Owners of the Heritage Tea Rooms, Allan and Michelle Sharpe discuss the importance of market research in being able to foresee changes in the market, and adapting to those changes.

Create a Marketing Plan

With knowledge backed by research about your customers, a marketing plan brings together the planned activities and opportunities to promote your product or service. The key sections in developing a marketing plan are outlined below.

Background

- Overview of your business, your industry and the current state of the market place.
- Mission.
- Goals.
- Competitive advantage-what is special about your business.

Situation analysis:

- External and internal factors affecting your business success.
- Strengths Weaknesses Opportunities Threats (SWOT) analysis.
- Competition analysis.

Market identification:

- Target markets-who are they, how do they behave?
- Segmentation-how can you split your market up for the purposes of targeting them?

Marketing mix:

- Product (or services)-e.g. tours, accommodation, camping, souvenirs, restaurant, bush tucker etc.
- Packaging-how do you 'wrap up' your tourism product to market it? e.g. 2 night camping package with a bush tucker tour and breakfast included.
- Place-where will you promote yourself, and how will you achieve this e.g. in Europe through inbound travel agents, in my nearest town through tour desks etc.
- Price.
- Promotion.

Action Plan:

- Who is going to do what, and by when?

Budget:

- How much have you got to spend or how much will you need to spend to be effective?

Monitoring and Evaluation:

- How will you track which strategies have converted into bookings?
- What is the yield of the visitors you are attracting?

Packaging

Visitors are seeking experiences more so than specific products and services when they visit destinations. This requires the seamless provision of a coordinated range of products and services that collectively offer particular experiences desired by visitors.

The definition of packaging is the combining of two or more facilities/services/attractions as a single unit for sale to visitors to an area. The overall aim of any packaging is to produce an integrated, interesting product to encourage visitors to increase their stay within the region.

Working together with other tourism operators to provide packages also helps you to achieve economies of scale in relation to marketing costs and provides further opportunities to raise the profile of your tourism business. Not only does each individual operator benefit by such arrangements, but the region in general benefits by greater visitor numbers and increased expenditure.

In turn visitors benefit from new, innovative and interesting experiences reflecting a particular region's attributes.

Distribution

Distribution is making sure that your product or service information reaches the visitor. There are three distinct groups that you can work with to distribute your product or service:

- consumers
- trade including travel agents, wholesalers
- other industry and sector associations or professionals including RTOs, VICs, media, industry suppliers

From these three groups there are many different types of distribution channels available:

- Cooperative marketing initiatives
- Regional tourism brochures or travel planners
- Visitor Information Centres
- Australian Tourism Data Warehouse
- Online-regional websites, online booking systems
- Direct to the consumer-via brochure or website
- Retailers, travel agents or booking agents
- Wholesalers.

Visitor Information Centres

There has been increased recognition of the role of visitor information centres and their importance in providing high quality tourist information. In Queensland, accredited visitor information centres provide, local, regional and state wide information to visitors. They are recognisable by the italicised yellow on blue *'i'* sign. Visitor Information Centres that are accredited in Queensland provide a high quality level of service and facilities.

Online distribution

Traditional and emerging online distribution channels are converging. Technology is rapidly evolving and is one of the most significant factors affecting the tourism sector. Emerging online technologies can effectively facilitate information flows and transactions, and improve efficiencies within the tourism distribution chain. Travellers look for information before going on a trip to help them plan and choose between options. They also need more information during their trip as the trend towards more independent travel increases.

The use of employing Internet distribution channels is one way to meet these needs. Some of these include:

- Online booking systems
- Online travel planners
- State and regional websites
- Search engines such as Yahoo, ninemsn travel services.

Online Presence

The Internet has become one of the most significant communication tools for businesses and individuals all over the world. Users turn to the Internet to search for information and interact with other users such as friends, peers and communities.

It comes as no surprise that travellers use the "net" extensively to plan and organise their trip, more than 80% of travellers do so according to international research.

The increased accessibility of markets and speed of communication facilitated by the Internet is a double-edged sword. Tourism industry suppliers and operators need to be increasingly flexible and responsible to changing consumer needs, trends and preferences.

Why Should I be Online?

The Internet is the quickest and cheapest way of reaching potential travellers anywhere in the world. It will allow you to be connected with your customers, suppliers, partners and competitors to access an enormous amount of information.

The Internet provides new ways for you to deliver the information and services to customers and suppliers, with the benefits including:

- more effective marketing and the identification and development of new markets;
- improved customer service and relations;
- cost savings in communications, accounting, banking, financial
- management and purchasing; and
- efficiencies in linking 'back office' systems with external requirements etc.

Owners of Hidden Valley Cabins express the positive affect the Internet has had on increasing the number and frequency of visitors to their business.

By creating a mechanism by which visitors can book online, Hidden Valley Cabins were able to increase the number of both and domestic and international visitors.

Starting your online presence

As a tourism operator it is essential that you consider what the Internet can do for you and your business, as well as the possible consequences to your business development if you do not take advantage of the Internet and its services.

The following issues need to be taken into account:

- Your future communication needs
- Your business' growth expectations
- How you will conduct business in the future and with whom
- How much value Internet connection will add to your competitiveness
- Staff training and motivation to embrace the changes required.

It is important to consider when you're thinking about going online, the commitment of management and staff to dealing positively with the change. Success on the Internet requires rethinking how business is done, communicating with customers to staff training and motivation, and to how different sections of the organisation work together.

Improving Your Online Presence

Get smarter about e-marketing knowledge through step-by-step lessons. The Tourism E-kit is a complete suite of tutorials that covers everything from the basics of developing a good web site to the more complex issues of Google ad words, search engine marketing and online product distribution.

Trade Distribution

Wholesalers are the vital link between the originating manufacturers and businesses at the point of sale. Wholesalers package tour programs including travel, accommodation, and tours that are sold to the public via retail travel agents. Wholesalers do not sell directly to customers. Wholesalers link individual tourism operators with retailers. They consider what type of tour program would appeal to a particular market and package the program accordingly. They offer goods in large quantities at a trade price to those who are seeking to resell the products for retail purposes rather than personal use. Wholesalers-what is their commitment to your product?

- Product development
  - sourcing
  - negotiating special rates from participating products and services
  - creating packages
- Producing a brochure which is the major sales tool for travel agents to use and recommend your business
- Distribution of brochure to consumers through travel agents
- Advertising to visitors and travel agents
- Travel agents training on products and services offered
- At point of sale (e.g. travel agency), in-store merchandising, and window displays.

Retail travel agents sell travel services direct to customers and act on their behalf to book and purchase holiday packages, travel, accommodation, tours and so on. Wholesalers package tour programs including travel, accommodation, and tours that are sold to the public via retail travel agents. Wholesalers do not sell directly to customers.

Inbound tour operators act on behalf of national and international tour wholesalers to organise the 'land/ground' content of a tour program. Inbound tour operators act as intermediaries between wholesalers and tourism operators. They are usually able to negotiate better rates due to the volume and regular use of the tourism products they book.

International Marketing

Have you considered whether your product is suitable for the international market? A number of issues need to be considered when promoting your product internationally.

Ask yourself the following questions:

Accessibility-is your product close to a regular air/bus/train service?

Usually overseas visitors are limited in the amount of time they can spend in any particular location; therefore access to your product is vital. In certain circumstances investment in a transfer facility should be a major consideration.

Service-does your establishment or product reflect high levels of service expected by international visitors? High service standards have become synonymous with the tourist industry in Australia and constant reviewing and training is essential to maintain these levels.

Distinctive-does your product reflect an Australian experience to the customer?

Visitors to Australia want to experience our way of life. Ensure that there is as much "Australiana" as possible in your product. However, you must differentiate between "Australiana" and "Ocker"

Credibility-is your product already established in the Australian domestic market? It is important that you already have a customer base, which illustrates your product's credibility.

Remember, not all tourism products are suitable for marketing overseas on an individual basis. It is important to arrange your product as part of a package of attractions, then contact Inbound Tour Operators and sell them your product or package.

Have you selected a specific target market?

Don't try to enter every market at once, for it is far more important to select your market carefully. An overview of the international markets is included in this publication.

Are you a member of the local Regional Tourist Organisation?

Your local Regional Tourist Organisation can assist you in promoting your product and keep you abreast of invaluable opportunities as they occur. They are also an excellent source of information and advice.

Is your current domestic brochure adaptable to the overseas marketplace?

Make sure that when producing a brochure you are aware of the experiences or key selling points of your product for both your domestic and international markets and produce a brochure accordingly. Experiences in the domestic market may not be appropriate for the International market and while it is important to retain the Australian flavour in your prose.

Ensure that your property, attraction or service is well presented. The overseas traveller is accustomed to seeing informative, well-conceived and attractively produced material whereby decisions are often made. If you are planning to distribute your brochure to both the trade and consumer, the following information is essential in brochure design:

- A concise description of the product
- Where it is located (include a map with Australia, Queensland and the Region)
- When it operates (use months, as seasons are reversed)
- How to get there (use both miles and kilometres)
- How to book (your full address, telephone, fax numbers (with area codes), email address and web address)
- How much it costs (use Australian dollars and approximate local currency equivalent or exchange rate at time of printing).

- Allow space for the travel agent's stamp and sticker-usually on the back of the brochure.
- Ensure your brochure conforms to appropriate envelope sizes (this can bring down your costs considerably).

If you plan to distribute your product through wholesalers, it is not compulsory to have your prices in local currency. Your product may be featured as a component in the wholesalers' brochures.

Is your product readily available?

You must ensure that your product can be booked quickly and efficiently in the overseas market, as travel agents and consumers will usually not contact. Australia for bookings or information.

Have you considered a sales visit to meet the major wholesalers and agents in the relevant markets?

Maintaining regular contact with your distribution system and providing them with updated information on your product is very important. There are several do's and don'ts when conducting business with international wholesalers:

Dos:

- Source information about the market you wish to target and the type of product that is saleable in your target market
- Do your research and have your prices fully prepared for negotiation
- Expect to negotiate-buyers invariably have a choice of product
- Take advantage of the opportunity to meet buyers at the annual trade shows held in Australia, such as the Australian Tourism Exchange (Adelaide, 2006)
- Pre-schedule all appointments (well in advance) and reconfirm the visit a day or two beforehand
- Make your presentation brief and to the point

Don'ts

- Don't visit during the public holiday periods, including Christmas and New Year

- Also avoid visiting when large major travel shows are being held elsewhere in the world
- Don't arrive unannounced
- Don't play one operator off against another
- Don't commit to rates or services without keeping written records
- Do not pay brochure support. Your inclusion in a wholesale operator's brochure will not necessarily guarantee that an operator will sell your product.

You will have to allow for levels of between 20-30% to cover an Inbound Tour Operator, an overseas Wholesaler and Retailer to deliver and sell your product internationally. You must also be prepared to quote firm prices well in advance-up to 18 months ahead and ensure it is fully understood that your rate is gross or net. Be careful that your international pricing is not higher than your domestic rate and be flexible but realistic when setting your price levels.

3

Sustainable Development of Tourism

The New Realities of Tourism in an Era of Global Climate Change

Compelling evidence indicates that global climate has changed compared to the preindustrial era and is anticipated to continue to change over the 21st century and beyond. The Intergovernmental Panel on Climate Change (IPCC) declared that "[...] *warming of the climate system is unequivocal.*" The global mean temperature has increased approximately 0.76°C between 1850–1899 and 2001–2005 and the IPCC concluded that most of the observed increase in global average temperatures since the mid-20th century is very likely (> 90% probability) the result of human activities that are increasing greenhouse gas concentrations in the atmosphere. Discernible human influences now also extend to other aspects of climate, including ocean warming, continental-average temperatures, temperature extremes and wind patterns. Widespread decreases in glaciers and ice caps and warming ocean surface temperature have contributed to sea level rise of 1.8 mm per year from 1961 to 2003, and approximately 3.1 mm per year from 1993 to 2003. The biological response of ecosystems and individual species has been recorded on every continent.

The IPCC has projected that the pace of climate change is very likely (> 90% probability) to accelerate with continued greenhouse gas (GHG) emissions at or above current rates, with the best estimate that globally averaged surface temperatures will rise by

1.8°C to 4.0°C by the end of the 21st century. Even if atmospheric concentrations of GHGs were stabilized at current levels, the Earth would continue to warm as a result of past GHG emissions and the thermal inertia of the oceans. The biological response to this continued warming and sea level rise would continue for several centuries.

Future changes in temperatures and other important features of climate will manifest themselves differently across the regions of the world. According to the IPCC, it is very likely that hot extremes, heat waves and heavy precipitation events will continue to become more frequent. It is likely that future tropical cyclones (typhoons and hurricanes) will become more intense, with larger peak wind speeds and more heavy precipitation associated with ongoing increases of tropical sea surface temperatures. There is less confidence in projections of a global decrease in numbers of tropical cyclones. The extension of the regions that will be primary affected by these extreme events with major tourism destinations highlights the need for awareness and preparedness for natural hazards at the local level through systematic capacity building and strategies for disaster risk management. Extratropical storm tracks are projected to shift poleward, with consequent changes in wind, precipitation and temperature patterns, continuing the broad pattern of observed trends over the last half-century. Observed decreases in snow cover are also projected to continue.

The environmental and economic risks of the magnitude of climate change projected for the 21st century are considerable and have featured prominently in recent international policy debates. The IPCC concluded with very high confidence that climate change would impede the ability of many nations to achieve sustainable development by mid-century. The Stern Review on the Economics of Climate Change found that the costs of taking action to reduce GHG emissions now, are much smaller than the costs of economic and social disruption from unmitigated climate change.

Our lifestyles, economies, health and social well-being are all affected by climate change, and although the consequences of climate change will vary on a regional basis, all nations and economic sectors will have to contend with the challenges of climate change through adaptation and mitigation. Tourism is no exception and in the decades ahead, climate change will become an increasingly pivotal issue affecting tourism development and management. With its close connections to the environment and climate itself, tourism is considered to be a highly climate-sensitive economic sector similar to agriculture, insurance, energy, and transportation. The regional manifestations of climate change will be highly relevant for tourism destinations and tourists alike, requiring adaptation by all major tourism stakeholders. Indeed, climate change is not a remote future event for tourism, as the varied impacts of a changing climate are becoming evident at destinations around the world and climate change is already influencing decision-making in the tourism sector.

At the same time, the tourism sector is a non-negligible contributor to climate change through GHG emissions derived especially from the transport and accommodation of tourists. Tourism must seek to significantly reduce its GHG emissions in accordance with the international community, which at the "Vienna Climate Change Talks 2007" recognized that global emissions of GHG need to peak in the next 10– 15 years and then be reduced to very low levels, well below half of levels in 2000 by mid-century. * The tourism sector can not address the challenge of climate change in isolation, but must do so within the context of the broader international sustainable development agenda. The critical challenge before the global tourism sector is to develop a coherent policy strategy that decouples the projected massive growth in tourism in the decades ahead from increased energy use and GHG emissions, so as to allow tourism growth to simultaneously contribute to poverty alleviation and play a major role in achieving the United Nations Millennium Development Goals (MDG). "*Climate change as well as poverty alleviation will remain central* issues for the world community. Tourism is an important element in both. Governments and the private sector must place increased importance on these factors in tourism development strategies and in climate and poverty strategies. They are interdependent and must be dealt with in a holistic fashion."

Francesco Frangialli, UNWTO Secretary-General (2007) Tourism can play a significant role in addressing climate change if the innovativeness and resources of this vital global economic sector are fully mobilized and oriented towards this goal. The concern of the tourism community regarding the challenge of climate change has visibly increased over the last five years. The World Tourism Organization (UNWTO) and several partner organizations, including UNEP, convened the First International Conference on Climate Change and Tourism in Djerba, Tunisia in 2003. This event was a watershed in terms of raising awareness about the implications of climate change within the international tourism community.

The Djerba Declaration recognized the complex inter-linkages between the tourism sector and climate change and established a framework for future research and policy making on adaptation and mitigation.

A number of individual tourism industry associations and businesses have also shown leadership on climate change, voluntarily adopting GHG emission reduction targets, engaging in public education campaigns on climate change and supporting government climate change legislation.

"Far sighted action by the US$ 880 billion international tourism industry will send important signals to governments, industries and the public that mitigation and adaptation to the climate change challenge make economic and environmental sense. It is the kind of leadership that can encourage others to look not only to their exposure and to the risks posed by climate change, but also to the abundant opportunities and benefits of cost effective action." Achim Steiner, UN Under-Secretary General and UNEP Executive Director (2007) The scientific community has also responded, doubling the number of scientific publications that examine the interactions of tourism and climate change between 1996–2000 and 2001–2005 and significantly advancing the place of tourism in the IPCC 4th Assessment Report (AR4) relative to previous assessments.

In 2006, the World Meteorological Organization (WMO) established an Expert Team on Climate and Tourism in collaboration with the UNWTO, with the broad mandate to advance the application of weather and climate information in the tourism sector and understanding of the implications of climate change.

Impacts and Adaptation at Tourism Destinations

The tourism industry and destinations are clearly sensitive to climate variability and change. Climate defines the length and quality of tourism seasons and plays a major role in destination choice and tourist spending. In many destinations tourism is closely linked with the natural environment. Climate affects a wide range of the environmental resources that are critical attractions for tourism, such as snow conditions, wildlife productivity and biodiversity, water levels and quality. Climate also has an important influence on environmental conditions that can deter tourists, including infectious disease, wildfires, insect or water-borne pests (e.g., jellyfish, algae blooms), and extreme events such as tropical cyclones.

There are four broad categories of climate change impacts that will affect tourism destinations, their competitiveness and sustainability.

Direct climatic impacts: Climate is a principal resource for tourism, as it codetermines the suitability of locations for a wide range of tourist activities, is a principal driver of global seasonality in tourism demand, and has an important influence on operating costs, such as heating-cooling, snow-making, irrigation, food and water supply, and insurance costs. Thus, changes in the length and quality of climate-dependent tourism seasons (i.e., sun-and-sea or winter sports holidays) could have considerable implications for competitive relationships between destinations and therefore the profitability of tourism enterprises. Studies indicate that a shift of attractive climatic conditions for tourism towards higher latitudes and altitudes is very likely. As a result, the competitive position of some popular holiday areas are anticipated to decline (e.g., the Mediterranean in summer), whereas other areas (e.g., southern England or southern Canada) are expected to improve. Uncertainties related to tourist climate preference and destination loyalty require attention if the implications for the geographic and seasonal redistribution of visitor flows are to be projected. There are well established vulnerabilities among winter sports destinations to projected declines in natural snowfall. Even with increased snow-making, contractions in the ski industry are very likely in the European Alps, Eastern and Western North America,

Australia, and Japan, although projected impacts on destinations in these nations vary in magnitude and over different time horizons.

The IPCC has concluded that changes in a number of weather extremes are probable as a result of projected climate change, including: higher maximum temperature and more hot days over nearly all land areas (very likely), greater tropical storm intensity and peak winds (likely), more intense precipitation events over many land areas (very likely), and longer and more severe droughts in many mid-latitude continental interiors (likely). Such changes will affect the tourism industry through increased infrastructure damage, additional emergency preparedness requirements, higher operating expenses (e.g., insurance, backup water and power systems, and evacuations), and business interruptions.

Indirect environmental change impacts: Because environmental conditions are such a critical resource for tourism, a wide-range of climate-induced environmental changes will have profound effects on tourism at the destination and regional level. Changes in water availability, biodiversity loss, reduced landscape aesthetic, altered agricultural production (e.g., wine tourism), increased natural hazards, coastal erosion and inundation, damage to infrastructure and the increasing incidence of vector-borne diseases will all impact tourism to varying degrees. In contrast to the varied impacts of a changed climate on tourism, the indirect effects of climate induced environmental change are likely to be largely negative. Mountain, island, and coastal destinations are considered particularly sensitive to climate-induced environmental change, as are nature-based tourism market segments. UNESCO has also identified several World Heritage Sites that are critical tourist destinations, to be vulnerable to climate-induced environmental change (e.g., Venice, Italy – sea level rise, Great Barrier Reef, Australia – coral bleaching and mortality, Glacier-Waterton International Peace Park, USA and Canada – glacier retreat, Chan Chan Archaeological Zone, Peru – El Nino-Southern Oscillation (ENSO) caused flooding and eroding). While our understanding of the impacts of climate change for various destination types has improved since the Djerba Conference, it is important to emphasize that there remain major regional gaps in our knowledge of how climate change will affect the natural and cultural resources critical for tourism in Africa, the Caribbean, South America, the Middle East and large parts of East Asia.

Impacts of mitigation policies on tourist mobility: National or international mitigation policies – that are policies that seek to reduce GHG emissions – are likely to have an impact on tourist flows. They will lead to an increase in transport costs and may foster environmental attitudes that lead tourists to change their travel patterns (e.g., shift transport mode or destination choices). There has been substantial recent media coverage on this topic, specifically as it relates to air travel. Long-haul destinations can be particularly affected and officials in Southeast Asia, Australia-New Zealand, and the Caribbean have expressed concern that mitigation policies could adversely impact their national tourism economy. On the other hand, emission scenario projections developed for this report indicate that opportunities may arise for low carbon emission transport modes like coach and rail. This may also help to revitalize destinations that are nearer to the main markets.

Indirect societal change impacts: Climate change is thought to pose a risk to future economic growth and to the political stability of some nations. The Stern Report on the Economics of Climate Change concluded that although a global warming of only 1°C might benefit global GDP, greater climate change would eventually damage economic growth at the global scale, including the stark conclusion that unmitigated climate change could cause a reduction in consumption per capita of 20% later in the 21st century or early 22nd century. Any such reduction of global GDP due to climate change would reduce the discretionary wealth available to consumers for tourism and have negative implications for anticipated future growth in tourism; however there has been no in-depth interpretation of the Stern Report 54 for the tourism sector.

Our actions over the coming few decades could create risks of major disruption to economic and social activity, later in this century and in the next, on a scale similar to those associated with the great wars and the economic depression of the first half of the 20th century.

Climate change is considered a national and international security risk that will steadily intensify, particularly under greater warming scenarios. Climate change associated security risks have been identified in a number of regions where tourism is highly important to local/national economies.

Destination vulnerability hotspots: The integrated effects of climate change will have far-reaching consequences for tourism businesses and destinations. Importantly, climate change will generate both negative and positive impacts in the tourism sector and these impacts will vary substantially by market segment and geographic region. The implications of climate change for any tourism business or destination will also partially depend on the impacts on its competitors. A negative impact in one part of the tourism system may constitute an opportunity elsewhere. Consequently, there will be 'winners and losers' at the business, destination and nation level. Due to the very limited information available on the potential impacts of climate change in some tourism regions, this qualitative assessment must also be considered with caution.

Until systematic regional level assessments are conducted a definitive statement on the net economic or social impacts in the tourism sector will not be possible. Furthermore, the outcome most likely will depend on the extent of climate change. The impact on the tourism sector may strongly parallel that of the global economy, where a 1°C temperature rise may result in a net benefit for the world economy, but greater increases increasingly show net declines.

Destination level adaptation: It is now recognised that regardless of the emissions reduction efforts, there is an inevitable need for societies around the world to adapt to unavoidable changes in climate. It is essential to emphasize that regardless of the nature and magnitude of climate change impacts, all tourism businesses and destinations will need to adapt to climate change in order to minimize associated risks and capitalize upon new opportunities, in an economically, socially and environmentally sustainable manner.

Tourists have the greatest adaptive capacity (depending on

three key resources: money, knowledge and time) with relative freedom to avoid destinations impacted by climate change or shifting the timing of travel to avoid unfavourable climate conditions. Suppliers of tourism services and tourism operators at specific destinations have less adaptive capacity. Large tour operators, who do not own the infrastructure, are in a better position to adapt to changes at destinations, because they can respond to clients demands and provide information to influence clients' travel choices. Destination communities and tourism operators with large investment in immobile capital assets (e.g., hotel, resort complex, marina or casino) have the least adaptive capacity.

The dynamic nature of the tourism industry and its ability to cope with a range of recent major shocks, including SARS, terrorism attacks in a number of nations, or the Asian tsunami, suggests a relatively high adaptive capacity within the tourism industry overall. The capacity to adapt to climate change is thought to vary substantially between sub-sectors, destinations, and individual businesses within the tourism industry.

> *"It is vital for tourism destinations [...] to anticipate the coming changes and to draw their consequences, starting now. [Adaptation] is a long-term project that must be anticipated and carefully prepared beforehand; it is not easy to see this through successfully, because it entails, all at the same time, modifying economic circuits, introducing new technologies, carrying out intensive training, investing in the creation of new products, [...] changing the minds of public authorities, entrepreneurs, host communities and tourists."*

Francesco Frangialli, UNWTO Secretary-General (2007)

The tourism sector has been adapting its operations to climate zones worldwide, using a diverse range of technological, managerial, educational, policy and behavioural adaptations to deal with climate variability. However, adaptation has figured less prominently in climate change research on tourism than in some other economic sectors (e.g., agriculture). There has been a range of research activities focusing on climate change impacts for destinations or specific tourism sectors (e.g., ski operations), but they generally have not identified properly the range of adaptation options available to tourism stakeholders. Due to a lack of integration of adaptation measures in impact analysis studies, the perspectives on projected impacts may be misleading.

Much more needs to be done to incorporate adaptation into future impact assessments in the tourism sector given its high adaptive capacity. Second, knowledge of the capability of current climate adaptations to cope successfully with future climate change remains rudimentary. An important lesson learned from Hurricane Katrina and the extremely warm winter of 2006–2007 in the European Alps is that adaptations can be overwhelmed by events unexpected and beyond the range of experience of the tourism sector. Such events should be anticipated under climate change, and consequently there is a critical need for the tourism sector to evaluate the effectiveness of current adaptations under projected climate conditions. In an era of global climate change, it will no longer be sufficient to rely on past experience. The information requirements for effective, anticipatory climate change adaptation will be substantial and therefore adaptation is a critical area for future research.

Climate change is slowly entering into decision-making of a range of tourism stakeholders (e.g., investors, insurance companies, tourism enterprises, governments, and tourists); studies that have examined the climate change risk appraisal of local tourism officials and operators have consistently found relatively low levels of concern and little evidence of long-term strategic planning in anticipation of future changes in climate.

There is also some evidence that local tourism operators may be overestimating their adaptive capacity (e.g., capacity to make snow under the warmest scenarios). The incorporation of adaptation to climate change into the collective minds of private and public sector tourism decision-makers ('mainstreaming') remains several steps away. Consequently, there is a real need for effective communication between the climate change science community and tourism operators at the regional and local scale, particularly with respect to the development of climate change scenarios and indicators catered toward local tourism decision-making.

Implications of Climate Change for Tourism Demand Patterns

Climate, the natural environment, and personal safety are three primary factors in destination choice, and global climate change is anticipated to have significant impacts on all three of these factors at the regional level. Tourists also have the greatest capacity to adapt to the impacts of climate change, with relative freedom to avoid destinations impacted by climate change or shifting the timing of travel to avoid unfavourable climate conditions.

As such, the response of tourists to the complexity of destination impacts will reshape demand patterns and play a pivotal role in the eventual impacts of climate change on the tourism industry. Understanding and anticipating the potential geographic and seasonal shifts in tourist demand will remain critical areas of research in the future.

The evidence available from studies that have explored the potential impact of altered climate conditions for tourist demand suggests that the geographic and seasonal redistribution of tourist demand may be very large for individual destinations and countries by mid-to late-century. Anticipated impacts include a gradual shift in preferred destinations to higher latitudes and to higher elevations in mountainous areas. Tourists from temperate nations that currently dominate international travel (e.g., Northern Europe) are expected to spend more holidays in their home country or nearby, adapting their travel patterns to take advantage of new climatic opportunities closer to home.

Tourism seasons will be altered with possibly more tourists travelling in shoulder seasons, or in winter seasons, as climate will be more appealing. This shift in travel patterns may have important implications, including proportionally more tourism spending in temperate nations and proportionally less spending in warmer nations now frequented by tourists from temperate regions. The direct effect of climate change might be significant enough to alter major intra-regional tourism flows where climate is of paramount importance, including Northern Europe to the Mediterranean and the Caribbean, North America to the Caribbean, and to a lesser extent North East Asia to Southeast Asia.

However, the net effect of a change in climate on tourist demand at the global scale is expected to be limited, as there is no evidence to suggest that a change in climate will directly lead to a significant reduction of the global volume of tourism. It is important to emphasize that it is the holistic impact of climate change on tourism environments that tourists will respond to, not just changes in climatic conditions.

Tourism demand at the regional scale will also be affected by the range of indirect environmental and social impacts brought about by global climate change. The indirect impacts of global climate change are anticipated to influence tourist demand for specific destinations and perhaps at the regional level where political destabilization may occur, but not affect tourism demand at the global level, unless, as some economic analyses indicate, global economic growth were to be adversely affected by climatic change.

The perceptions of future impacts of climate change are likely to play the central role in the decision-making of tourists and tourism investors alike, as perceptions of climate conditions or environmental changes are just as important to consumer choices as the actual conditions. Perceptions of climate change impacts in a region are often heavily influenced by the nature of media coverage. Speculation and misinformation about the impacts of climate change on tourism destinations already abounds in the media, particularly with regard to the demise of the ski industry and extreme summer temperatures in the Mediterranean region. The combination of increased awareness of the potential environmental impacts of air travel, as reflected in a number of recent public opinion polls, and national or international mitigation policies that increase the costs of travel, will also have important implications for shaping tourist demand. Current understanding of how price increases for travel may alter tourist mobility remains low.

Past studies that have analysed the price sensitivity of air passengers, for example, show moderate inelasticity (–0.7). Recent market surveys have also identified highly varied willingness to pay to offset the environmental consequences of air travel. The perception of transport, and in particular air travel, in relation to its carbon footprint is also likely to be an important influence on tourists' responses to price changes. Information on tourist climate preferences and key thresholds (i.e., temperature limits for a beach holiday), tourist perceptions of the environmental impacts of global climate change at destinations (i.e., perceptions of coral bleaching, diminished or lost glaciers, degraded coastlines, reduced biodiversity or wildlife prevalence), and tourist perceptions of the environmental impacts of tourism related travel and their willingness to pay to reduce this impact, remain important knowledge gaps that need to be addressed if potential long-range shifts in tourist demand are to be more accurately projected. There is also limited understanding of how climate change impacts will interact with other longer term social and market trends influencing tourism demand (e.g., globalization and economic fluctuations, fuel prices, aging populations in industrialized countries, increasing travel safety and health concerns, increased environmental and cultural awareness, advances in information and transportation technology).

Emissions from Global Tourism: Status and Trends

The contribution of tourism to human-induced climate change has never been comprehensively assessed. This report represents the first attempt to calculate emissions of CO2 from three main tourism sub-sectors – transportation, accommodations, and activities – as well as the contribution to radiative forcing (i.e. including all greenhouse gases) for the year 2005. Tourism in this report refers to "[...] *the activities of persons traveling to and staying in places outside their usual* environment for not more than one consecutive year for leisure, business and other purposes not related to the exercise of an activity remunerated from within the place *visited.*"

Existing databases on tourism are not directly suitable for emission inventories, so the UNWTO prepared a specific database for this project with data provided for the baseline year of 2005. In order to refine calculations of GHG emissions from the tourism sector and effectively monitor progress on GHG emission reductions in the future, a strategic reassessment of the current system of tourism statistics will be required so that appropriate data are collected at the necessary spatial and temporal resolutions.

While CO_2 is the most important greenhouse gas from human activities, other greenhouse gases also make significant contributions to global warming. In the tourism sector, this is particularly relevant for emissions from aviation, which, at flight altitude, has an enhanced impact on global warming. Radiative forcing is thus used to calculate the entire contribution of tourist (air) travel to global warming.

Radiative forcing measures the extent to which emissions of greenhouse gases raise global average temperatures now or at a specified year in the future (estimates of tourism contribution to radiative forcing will be analyzed in the full report). International and domestic tourism emissions from three main sub-sectors are estimated to represent between 3.9% and 6.0% of global emissions in 2005, with a best estimate of 4.9%.

The analysis also showed that emissions can vary greatly per tourist trip, between a few kilograms of CO_2 up to 9 t CO_2 for long-distance, cruise-based journeys. A globally averaged tourist journey is estimated to generate 0.25 t of CO_2 emissions. A small share of tourism trips was found to cause the main share of emissions: while the aviation based trips account for 17% of all tourism trips, they cause about 40% of CO_2 emissions from tourism. Long-haul travel by air between the five UNWTO world tourism regions represents only 2.2% of all tourist trips, but contributes 16% to global tourism-related CO_2 emissions. In contrast, international tourist trips (i.e., overnight tourist trips) by coach and rail, which account for an estimated 16% of international tourist trips, stand only for 1% of CO_2 emissions generated by all international tourist trips (transport emissions only).

These results show that mitigation initiatives in the tourism sector will need to strategically focus on the impact of some particular forms of tourism (i.e., particularly those connected with air travel) if substantial reductions in CO_2 emissions are to be achieved. This also implies that climate change mitigation should primarily focus on a minor proportion of tourist trips.

Mitigation Policies and Measures

Climate change mitigation relates to technological, economic and socio-cultural changes that can lead to reductions in greenhouse gas emissions. Tourism-related emissions are projected to continue to grow rapidly under 'business-as-usual' conditions in contrast to the substantial emission reduction targets the international community agreed was required in the latest round of UNFCCC negotiations ("Vienna Climate Change Talks 2007"), where it was recognized that global emissions of GHG need to be reduced to well below half of the levels in 2000 by mid-century.

Mitigation is thus of particular importance in tourism; however, mitigation policies need to consider a number of dimensions, such as the need to stabilize the global climate, the right of people to rest and recover and leisure, and attaining the United Nations Millennium Development Goals.

As the emission reductions required for tourism to contribute meaningfully to the broader emission reduction targets of the international community are substantial, mitigation should ideally combine various strategies, such as voluntary, economic, and regulatory instruments. These can be targeted at different stakeholder groups, including tourists, tour operators, accommodation managers, airlines, manufacturers of cars and aircraft, as well as destination managers. Instruments could also be applied with different emphasis in different countries, so as not to jeopardize the development and poverty reduction opportunity offered by tourism in developing countries. It is clear that for those actors being pro-active in addressing climate change, mitigation offers a range of business opportunities. Given current societal trends, it seems that there will be new, permanent and growing markets for environmentally oriented tourists and many opportunities to develop new low-carbon tourism products.

Four major mitigation strategies for addressing greenhouse gas emissions from tourism can be distinguished:

- reducing energy use;
- improving energy efficiency;
- increasing the use of renewable energy, and;
- sequestering carbon through sinks.

This report has systematically investigated the various options with regard to technological improvements, environmental management, economic and policy measures, and behavioural change, arriving at a number of conclusions:

Reducing energy use is the most essential aspect of mitigation, which can be achieved by altering destination development and marketing (tour operators), destination choices (tourists) as well as shifts in transport use from car and aircraft to rail and coach. Changing management practices can be of importance for business tourism (videoconferencing). Tour operators play a key role in this process, as they bundle products into packages that are advertised to and purchased by tourists. Tour operators can also increase length of stay, which would very effectively reduce the carbon footprint per tourist day and increase economic opportunities for destinations.

It has to be considered however that current tourism trends show an increase of short stays. Overall, tour operators have a considerable influence on creating demand for less carbon intensive journeys by creating attractive products that meet tourists' needs and desires.

Regarding the most important sector, aviation, the industry favours emission trading over the taxation of fuel or emissions. Aviation is likely to soon enter the European Union Emission Trading Scheme, which will increase the speed at which new technologies are introduced. An even better alternative might be to create an emissions trading scheme entirely for aviation. More efficient technology would be introduced faster, while the profitability of the aviation sector could grow rapidly, as prices for tickets can be increased despite stable costs for operating aircraft.

Improving energy efficiency can be another mechanism to decrease energy demand. New technology will significantly reduce the emissions of aviation in a 'business-as-usual' scenario, simply because it saves fuel-costs and improves aircraft performance. Reductions in emissions per pkm are likely to be in the order of 32% between 2005 and 2035. Additional efforts to bring aviation technology to the theoretical limit (50% reduction of emission factors between 2005 and 2035), would contribute to an overall reduction of total emissions from tourist travel (excluding same-day, including all transport modes) by 14% with respect to the 'business-asusual' scenario.

The same overall emissions reduction (14%) may be achieved with strong reductions in the accommodations sub-sector. New technology within car transport has a potential of reducing 7% of all tourist emissions. Note however, that the introduction of new air transport technology takes decades as the market introduction of new technologies is slow, because fleet renewal stretches overseveral decades due to the long operational life of aircraft. The more rapid introduction of new technologies is thus dependent on environmentally pro-active management decisions that need to be aided by government policy, such as emission trading.

This study found that virtually all sources of renewable energy are relevant for tourism, including wind, photovoltaic, solar thermal, geothermal, biomass and energy regeneration from waste. Several studies have explored the extent to which renewable energy sources can be used for tourism, in particular in island destinations where energy supply based on fossil fuels is expensive and at risk of supply interruptions.

These studies come to the conclusion that the use of renewable energy sources is generally economical and technically feasible. For example, in a vast number of destinations in the tropics, investments in solar energy can pay off in as little as two years. Biofuels are another option to contribute to more sustainable transport systems, even though it should be noted that several problems remain unsolved, particularly relating to the sustainability and efficiency of biofuel production and increasing competition over land, especially arable land area. Also the maximum share of biofuels for use in (all) transport is estimated at less than 10%.

CO_2 can also be stored in biomass (e.g., through afforestation and avoided deforestation), in aquifers or oceans, and in geological sinks (e.g., depleted gas fields). Within the tourism industry, this is currently practiced through carbon compensation or carbon offsetting, which means that an amount of greenhouse gas emissions equal to that caused by a certain activity (i.e., a flight), will be reduced elsewhere (i.e., through the planting of additional trees). There is still a lot of confusion among tourists about what carbon offsetting is, and there is also evidence that particularly hyper-mobile travellers, who account for the major share of the distances travelled and emissions caused, are not ready to support voluntary carbon offsets.

There is also a risk that carbon offsetting, which has been initiated as a voluntary form of carbon reductions, is now becoming the means used by the industry to 'reduce' emissions. This effectively means that producer responsibility is turned into customer responsibility, which may be problematic if no action to reduce fuel use is taken.

As such, carbon offsetting can be seen as a controversial solution to climate protection, because it potentially diverts from the real causes of the problems and therefore bypasses the structural and technological changes that need to be made to achieve long-term greenhouse gas reductions in the tourism sector. Nevertheless, carbon offsetting does have a role to play in future mitigation efforts in tourism.

In the framework of this report, the expert team developed several scenarios considering different mitigation options, in order to estimate how emission pathways in the global tourism sector might develop in the future. In case of the 'business-asusual' scenario (which takes into account the UNWTO's *Tourism 2020 Vision* forecast of an average 4% annual growth of international tourist arrivals up to 2020) it was estimated that CO_2 emissions in the global tourism sector may experience a growth of 161% by 2035.

- If maximum assumed technological efficiencies were achieved for all transport modes, accommodations and activities, this may result in 38% lower emissions.

- Reducing energy use by a combination of transport modal shifts, shifts to shorter haul destinations and increasing average length of stay may result in emission reductions by 44%.

Considering the projected dynamic growth of tourism activities, there is a large task ahead if tourism is to reduce its emissions to the same extent as other economic sectors. For an effective reduction of emissions, the tourism sector needs to apply a combination of mitigation measures. Under the most effective mitigation projection, using a combination of both above measures, the 'business-as-usual' scenario emissions in 2035 could be reduced by 68%, thus achieving a 16% reduction of emissions with respect to the emissions in 2005.

The Way Forward to Adaptation and Mitigation in Tourism

Concern about climate change is increasing worldwide and the IPCC has made it clear that global climate change is only just beginning. The impacts of climate change on the tourism sector will steadily intensify, particularly under higher emission scenarios. Climate change would redistribute climate resources for tourism geographically and seasonally and poses a risk to ecosystems worldwide.

The nature and intensity of climate change impacts will differ for tourism destinations around the world. The most vulnerable regions are in developing countries, which generally also have less adaptive capacity, and this will be a particular challenge for their tourist destinations and their host communities. Climate change impacts on the tourism sector could influence other economic sectors, such as agriculture and local business networks supplying tourism. Conversely, the tourism sector must also be cognizant of the implications of climate change adaptation in other economic sectors, which could have significant impacts on tourism. As the financial sector incorporates a company's climate change strategy, or lack of one, into its investment criteria, it will influence credit rating and insurance rates. Climate change mitigation requires the transformation of energy and transportation systems worldwide, with implications for the cost of travel and tourist mobility. Climate change also has the potential to have an adverse effect on the global economy and poses a security risk in some regions. Consequently, climate change is anticipated to have profound implications that could fundamentally transform aspects of the global tourism sector.

> *"Given that climate change is expected to pose an increasing threat to tourism operations in many destinations [...], WMO urges governments and the private sector to increasingly use climate information generated through National Meteorological and Hydrological Services [...], and to take additional steps towards incorporating climate considerations in tourism policies, development and management plans."*

The unmistakable conclusion of this report is that the significance of climate change to tourism is not in some distant and remote future. Climate change is already influencing decision-making within the tourism sector, including tourists, forward looking tourism businesses and investors, and international tourism organizations. The next generation of tourism professionals will need to contend with virtually all of the broad range of impacts outlined in this report.

Tourism can and must play a significant role in addressing climate change as part of its broader commitment to sustainable development and the United Nations Millennium Development Goals. Tourism as a non-negligible contributor to climate change has the responsibility to reverse the growth trajectory of its GHG emissions over the next three decades to a more sustainable emissions pathway consistent with the actions of the international community. The climate change mitigation potential is thought to be relatively high in the tourism sector because efforts to lower energy consumption and GHG emissions in the sector are still largely in their infancy, and thus far have been generally taken without any vision of a coordinated sector-wide strategic response. 106 Also in this study it is shown that several combinations of strong efforts, including decoupling of the growth of tourism from the growth of tourism transport volumes and technological innovation, may significantly reduce emissions in 2035, without jeopardizing the growth of world tourism in number of trips or guest-nights.

Regardless of the success to reduce GHG emissions by the international community, there will undoubtedly also be costs associated with climate change adaptation. These costs cannot be borne solely by those affected, especially as those most affected are likely to be those less able to take action to cope with the changes (e.g., LDCs, SIDS and local tourism SMMEs). The capacity of the tourism sector to adapt to climate change is thought to be relatively high due to its dynamic nature and therefore there will be important opportunities for tourism to reduce the vulnerability of communities to climate change.

The United Nations Secretary General Ban Ki-moon has called for action by the international community on climate change to be taken in close coordination with action on poverty alleviation and the Millennium Development Goals. The IPCC further contends that there are significant synergies that can be exploited in bringing climate change to the development community and critical development issues to the climate change community. There is an important opportunity for the tourism sector to show leadership in the development of a coherent policy agenda that integrates both development and climate change perspectives.

This is the time now for the tourism community to collectively formulate a strategy to address what must be considered the greatest challenge to the sustainability of tourism in the 21st century.

4

Environmental Issues in Sustainable Tourism

Introduction

It has been said many times and by many actors: Tourism is a double-edged activity. It has the potential to contribute in a positive manner to socio-economic achievements. At the same time, its fast and sometimes uncontrolled growth can be the major cause of degradation of the environment, and loss of local identity and traditional cultures. Tourism's relationship with the environment is highly complex. There are obvious economic benefits involved for countries and societies, and obvious options for an increased interest in conservation and concern for nature and the protection of fragile environments. At the same time, there are equally obvious ecological risks of ecosystem and habitat depletion and destruction due to the pressure of growing tourism.

Tourists may, literally speaking, love nature to death. According to a much-quoted Asian saying: "Tourism is like fire-you can cook your dinner on it, or it can burn your house down". UNESCO stresses the following on tourism and the management of protected natural areas, including many biosphere reserves: "Yet tourism is ambivalent, by its very nature. On the one hand, tourism generates well-known advantages. Visitor fees, concessions, and donations provide funds for restoration and protection efforts. Visitors are recruited as 'friends' of a site and can aid in generating international support. Tour operators and hotel chains can play a role in the management of a site either with financial contributions, aiding monitoring efforts, or encouraging their clients to follow guidelines of responsible tourism. Tourists can support artisan activities and help to strengthen threatened cultural values. Tourism also generates well-known problems. Tourism growth is difficult to control. Guiding development is a time-consuming process involving establishing policies, ongoing dialogue with stakeholders, and monitoring to determine if desired conditions are being met. Tourism activities require environmental impact assessments and carrying capacity studies. At sites with limited budgets and staff, increasing tourism can stretch scarce resources taking managers away from protection efforts. While tourism's benefits can contribute to protection and restoration efforts, it can be difficult to strike a balance between economic gain and unacceptable impacts."

Or thus summarized in a SCOPE (International Council for Science/Scientific Committee on Problems of the Environment) research programme and symposium on "Placing tourism in the landscape of diversities", on the tourism–biodiversity interaction, opposition and possible symbiosis:

Interactions: The interactions between tourism and biodiversity can be both negative and positive. They are negative when tourism results in a progressive decrease of biodiversity and cultural diversity, to the point that this diminution adversely affects the potential of tourism itself.

Positive interactions may include an increase or steady maintenance of biodiversity, enhancement of cultural diversity, economic growth, as well as increasing the potential for quality tourism. Most depends on the type of landscape planning and management, and of societal adaptation. When tourism implies positive interactions, one may speak of sustainable tourism. Even if interactions are more often negative in the world's tourism, there are many cases and examples of positive interactions within similar regions and ecosystems. A comparison of case studies of success and of failure of tourism, under similar geographic and ecological initial situations, is therefore a key to understand the dynamics of the process of tourism development.

Opposition: Tourism activities often originate a self-destruction cycle. As tourism becomes more massive, intensive and spread out in a region, and when there is an excessive urban growth, there is a progressive degradation of biodiversity. This negative impact is especially important concerning the diversity of landscapes, and the type of exploitation that takes place on them.

It may eventually lead to a lack of quality and diversification that will no longer attract tourists. The economic profitability of tourism decreases, the return on investments is too low, and there is a progressive trend towards uniformity of both tourists and landscapes. Tourism operators are forced to lower prices to attract tourists, tourism becomes even more massive and low quality, and the self-destructive cycle is increasingly strengthened, up to the moment that tourism may eventually end.

In general, as mentioned by the World Bank, *the features of the natural and socio-cultural environment that are important resources for tourism attract people because of aesthetic, recreational educational/ scientific value. However, many of the same features are particularly sensitive to disturbance by human activities. Negative impacts resulting from inadequately planned and uncontrolled tourism development can easily damage the very environments on which the success of the project depended... This in turn may severely reduce project benefits. In other words, without careful attention to the balance between the volume and type of tourist activity and the sensitivities and carrying capacities of the resources being developed, tourism projects can be not only environmentally harmful but also economically self*

For example, an increased number of hotels sited to attract tourists to a coral reef fail after a. few years, because hotel effluents discharged offshore rapidly impair-or kill-the reef.

More specifically, the negative environmental impacts of tourism development may be the result of the following activities:

- planning tourism development and policy making
- siting tourism facilities
- construction of tourism infrastructure
- maintenance and operation of tourism infrastructure
- tourism related transport and activities
- use by tourists of the territory.

In general, many environmental impacts in the Seychelles are due to a lack of enforcement of existing legislation and lack of obedience of existing guidelines, e.g. those of the Planning Authority.

Planning Tourism Development and Policy Making

Lack of proper integration of environmental concerns into tourism planning may result in:

increasing the gap between visitors' expectations in environmental terms and their actual experience,-increasing the gap between the required infrastructure and the availability of services for proper environmental management and the actual number of tourists to accommodate,-lack of attention to the shift in demands for environmental services by the tourists,-lack of attention given to new promising environmentally conscious tourism customers community.

Over estimating the tourism carrying capacity of the various islands will also result in negative environmental impacts.

Implicitly admitting too many tourists compared with the carrying capacity will increase de facto the environmental problems generated by the tourism industry.

Tourist education is not a significant part of the present tourism policy in Seychelles.

Siting Tourism Facilities

Facilities have been constructed and are being operated at distances too close to the beach and coastline, resulting in increased coastal erosion, flora and fauna destruction and more generally sensitive ecosys disturbance. As most tourism facilities are sited on coastal areas, see Guideline 2 for more on coastal zone management.

The improper siting of tourism facilities may result in:

direct destruction of valuable ecosystems, e.g. during the land clearing operations,

overburden to the natural environment in connection with the carrying capacity of the ecosystems.

can either be due to high tourist concentrations in an average ecosystem, or reasonable tourist concentration in a fragile environment.

Examples of the latter in the Seychelles include most of the small islands.

We have long been proud of the fact that mass-tourism has a greater impact on the world than we do, and rightly so; backpackers generally tend to stay away from the large resorts, and because we try to get off the beaten track our tourist dollars benefit those outside the more well-trodden parts of the world. Unfortunately, our numbers mean we are having a profound effect on the places we visit, and in 2007 the 119,000 British backpackers who flew to Australia created a sobering 480,000 tonnes of CO_2 through their flights.

When tourism and its environmental impact is discussed in the media, an 'industry spokesperson' will appear to reassure us that everything is being done to blah, blah, blah... but the 'tourist industry' is not an IATA or ATOL accredited travel agent in your high-street. The tourist industry is a luxury hotel in Bombay which employs cleaners for bed and board, or an Italian owned resort in Honduras which throws hundreds of empty plastic water bottles into a local landfill everyday. The tourist industry is the tourists themselves-us.

In an age where back packing and gap-year travel have become the norm, sustainable travel is not just about the impact you have personally, it all comes down to numbers. There are an awful lot of backpackers out there and we are just as capable of damaging the areas we visit as package tourists are. Rather than sticking to the illusion that we are the last of the world's explorers, it is vitally important now that we begin to see ourselves as part of the much larger group we represent. The key is to imagine that you are actually quarter of a million customers, not just one. If everyone is carrying the same guidebooks and eventually everyone reaches the same page then you're certainly not the only person buying a piece of that snake skin, and a quarter of a million bits of snake skin is more than just a couple of dead snakes. We need to get back to using our guide books as 'guides', not just the only option.

Marco Polo's been dead for 700 years and if there is anything left to be discovered it won't be done by back packers, so it's time for us to be honest. We are still pioneers, but unfortunately it's for the travel industry and a back packer centre now will be a tourist resort in ten years time. Our responsibility now is not just to be responsible travellers in what we do ourselves, but to show those parts of the world we visit that we value what they can offer us, be it virgin rainforest or a full-moon party, and that we want them to preserve not their lifestyles (a dubious idea anyway) but the environment as it exists now.

Sustainable travel is not expensive, nor is it a barrier to local people making the life for themselves that they wish-but it is a chance for us to influence how the tourist industry, as defined above, treats its local environment. We are not explorers in the Marco Polo sense of the word-the world has been mapped and is waiting for us to arrive-but we can be pioneers for a new kind of environmentally and socially sustainable travel.

Public-sector Planning for Control and Conservation

Tourism is one of the world's fastest growing industries as well as the major source of foreign exchange earning and employment for many developing countries, and it is increasingly focusing on natural environments. However, tourism is a double-edged activity. It has the potential to contribute in a positive manner to socio-economic achievements but, at the same time, its fast and sometimes uncontrolled growth can be the major cause of degradation of the environment and loss of local identity and traditional cultures. Biological and physical resources are in fact the assets that attract tourists. However, the stress imposed by tourism activities on fragile ecosystems accelerates and aggravates their depletion. Paradoxically, the very success of tourism may lead to the degradation of the natural environment: by depleting natural resources tourism reduces the site attractiveness to tourists, the very commodity that tourism has to offer.

As far as economic benefits are concerned, tourism certainly constitutes an opportunity for economic development, economic diversification and the growth of related activities, in developing countries especially, contributing around 1.5 per cent of world gross national product. Tourism is also a major source of income and employment. Tourism based on the natural environment (ecotourism) is a vital growing segment of the tourism industry and, despite the negative impacts, and given the fact that tourism generates a large proportion of income and that a growing percentage of the activities are nature-based, tourism does present a significant potential for realizing benefits in terms of the conservation of biological diversity and the sustainable use of its components.

Among the benefits are direct revenues generated by fees and taxes incurred and voluntary payments for the use of biological resources. These revenues can be used for the maintenance of natural areas and the contribution of tourism to economic development, including linkage effects to other related sectors and job-creation. Sustainable tourism can make positive improvements to biological diversity conservation especially when local communities are directly involved with operators. If such local communities receive income directly from a tourist enterprise they, in turn, increase their evaluation of the resources around them. This is followed by greater protection and conservation of those resources as they are recognized as the source of income. Moreover, sustainable tourism can serve as a major educational opportunity, increasing knowledge of and respect for natural ecosystems and biological resources. Other benefits include the provision of incentives for maintaining traditional arts and crafts, traditional knowledge, and innovations and practices that contribute to the sustainable use of biological diversity.

In considering the role of tourism in the sustainable use of biological resources and their diversity, it is important that the potential adverse impacts of tourism are fully considered. These are roughly divided into environmental impacts and socioeconomic impacts, the latter generally being those imposed on local and indigenous communities. Although such impacts on biological resources may be less easy to quantify and analyze systematically, they may be at least as important as, if not more important than, environmental impacts in the long term.

Direct use of natural resources, both renewable and non-renewable, in the provision of tourist facilities is one of the most significant direct impacts of tourism in a given area. Land use for accommodation and infrastructure provision, the choice of the site, the use of building materials are all essential factors. Deforestation and intensified or unsustainable use of land also cause erosion and loss of biodiversity. Direct impact on the species composition and on wildlife can be caused by incorrect behaviours and unregulated tourism activities (e.g. off-road driving, plant-picking, hunting, shooting, fishing, scuba diving). Moreover, tourists and tourist transportation means can increase the risk of introducing alien species and the manner and frequency of human presence can cause disturbance to the behaviour of animals. Construction activities related to tourism can cause enormous alteration to wildlife habitats and ecosystems.

Tourism has for many years been focused on mountain and coastal areas. Pressures from tourism activities on biological resources and their diversity are enormous and includes: erosion and pollution from the construction of hiking trails, bridges in high mountains, camp sites, chalet and hotels. Tourism activities have a major impact also on the marine and coastal environment, the resources they host and the diversity of those resources. Most often, those impacts are due to inappropriate planning, irresponsible behaviour by tourists and operators and/or lack of education and awareness of the impacts by, for example, tourist resorts along the coastal zones.

Tourism is also a water-intensive activity with a large production of waste. The extraction of ground-water by some tourism activities can cause desiccation, resulting in loss of biological diversity. Moreover, the disposal of untreated effluents into surrounding rivers and seas can cause eutrophication and it can also introduce a large amount of pathogens into the water body. Disposal of waste produced by the tourism industry may cause major environmental problems.

Socioeconomic and cultural impacts of tourism include influx of people and related social degradation, impacts on local communities and on cultural values. Increased tourism activities can cause an influx of people seeking employment or entrepreneurial opportunities, but who may not be able to find suitable employment, thus causing social degradation. Sudden loss of income and jobs can also be experienced in times of downturn, if the economy is not diversified and it heavily relies on tourism. When tourism development occurs, economic benefits are usually unequally distributed among members of local communities. In the case of foreign direct investment, much of the profit may be transferred back to the home country. Therefore, tourism can actually increase inequalities in communities, and thus relative poverty.

Tourism has a highly complex impact on cultural values. Tourism activities may lead to intergenerational conflicts and may affect gender relationships. Traditional practices and events may also be influenced by the tourist preferences. Tourism development can lead to the loss of access by indigenous and local communities to their land and resources as well as sacred sites.

Sustainable tourism is therefore in everybody's interest. Given that a high percentage of tourism involves visits to naturally and culturally distinguished sites, generating large amounts of revenue, there are clearly major opportunities for investing in the maintenance and sustainable use of biological resources. Along with the efforts to maximize benefits, efforts must be made to minimize the adverse impacts of the tourism industry on biological diversity.

In this context, one the challenges for the Convention on Biological Diversity is to develop, promote and disseminate guidelines for the sustainable planning and management of tourism activities in vulnerable terrestrial, marine and coastal ecosystems and habitats of major importance for biological diversity.

The Public-private Sector Interface in Sustainable Tourism Development

The ever-growing threat to environmental support systems and the continuing lack of progress toward sustainability are ringing alarm bells. As a result, environmental issues have surged to the forefront of public consciousness, and are rewriting the rules for business, investors and consumers. Some of the rising pillars of a sustainable future include: environmental economics, environmental markets, new ways of measuring environmental impact, renewable energy technologies, eco-technologies, payments for ecosystem services, biodiversity offset schemes, innovative approaches to applied ecology in industry, and new action networks for sustainability. IUCN believes that private enterprise has a strong interest and an important role to play in securing our natural heritage and using it sustainably for human benefit.

The promise of a vibrant economy that meets human needs depends in large part on society's ability to sustain the biodiversity that underpins all economies. There is a need for stronger action on the part of governments, business and consumers to make environmental protection and poverty reduction integral to the pursuit of individual, corporate or national prosperity..

The Structure of Tourism Industry

The Tourism Chain of Distribution

Distribution (or place) is one of the four elements of marketing mix. An organization or set of organizations (go-betweens) involved in the process of making a product or service available for use or consumption by a consumer or business user. The other three parts of the marketing mix are product, pricing, and promotion.

The Distribution Channel

Chain of intermediaries, each passing the product down the chain to the next organization, before it finally reaches the consumer or end-user. This process is known as the 'distribution chain' or the 'channel.' Each of the elements in these chains will have their own specific needs, which the producer must take into account, along with those of the all-important end-user.

Channels

A number of alternate 'channels' of distribution may be available:

- Distributor, who sells to retailers
- Retailer (also called dealer or reseller), who sells to end customers
- Advertisement typically used for consumption goods

Distribution channels may not be restricted to physical products alone. They may be just as important for moving a service from producer to consumer in certain sectors, since both direct and indirect channels may be used. Hotels, for example, may sell their services (typically rooms) directly or through travel agents, tour operators, airlines, tourist boards, centralized reservation systems, etc.

There have also been some innovations in the distribution of services. For example, there has been an increase in franchising and in rental services-the latter offering anything from televisions through tools. There has also been some evidence of service integration, with services linking together, particularly in the travel and tourism sectors. For example, links now exist between airlines, hotels and car rental services. In addition, there has been a significant increase in retail outlets for the service sector. Outlets such as estate agencies and building society offices are crowding out traditional grocers from major shopping areas.

Channel members

Distribution channels can thus have a number of levels. Kotler defined the simplest level, that of a direct contact with no intermediaries involved, as the 'zero-level' channel. The next level, the 'one-level' channel, features just one intermediary; in consumer goods a retailer, for industrial goods a distributor. In small markets (such as small countries) it is practical to reach the whole market using just one-and zero-level channels.

In large markets (such as larger countries) a second level, a wholesaler for example, is now mainly used to extend distribution to the large number of small, neighbourhood retailers or dealers. In Japan the chain of distribution is often complex and further levels are used, even for the simplest of consumer goods. In Bangladesh Telecom Operators are using different Chains of Distribution, especially 'second level'.

In IT and Telecom industry levels are named "tiers". A one tier channel means that vendors IT product manufacturers (or software publishers) work directly with the dealers. A one tier/ two tier channel means that vendors work directly with dealers and with distributors who sell to dealers. But the most important is the distributor or wholesaler.

The Internal Market

Many of the marketing principles and techniques which are applied to the external customers of an organization can be just as effectively applied to each subsidiary's, or each department's, 'internal' customers.

In some parts of certain organizations this may in fact be formalized, as goods are transferred between separate parts of the organization at a 'transfer price'. To all intents and purposes, with the possible exception of the pricing mechanism itself, this process can and should be viewed as a normal buyer-seller relationship. The fact that this is a captive market, resulting in a 'monopoly price', should not discourage the participants from employing marketing techniques. Less obvious, but just as practical, is the use of 'marketing' by service and administrative departments; to optimize their contribution to their 'customers' (the rest of the organization in general, and those parts of it which deal directly with them in particular). In all of this, the lessons of the non-profit organizations, in dealing with their clients, offer a very useful parallel. But in spite of this many, organizations prefer not to operate at a 'transfer' price because costs gradually increase as they undergo the distribution process.

Channel Decisions

- Channel strategy
    - Gravity
    - Push and Pull strategy
- Product (or service)<>Cost<>Consumer location

Managerial Concerns

The channel decision is very important. In theory at least, there is a form of trade-off: the cost of using intermediaries to achieve wider distribution is supposedly lower. Indeed, most consumer goods manufacturers could never justify the cost of selling direct to their consumers, except by mail order. Many suppliers seem to assume that once their product has been sold into the channel, into the beginning of the distribution chain, their job is finished. Yet that distribution chain is merely assuming a part of the supplier's responsibility; and, if they have any aspirations to be market-oriented, their job should really be extended to managing all the processes involved in that chain, until the product or service arrives with the end-user. This may involve a number of decisions on the part of the supplier:

- Channel membership
- Channel motivation
- Monitoring and managing channels

Channel membership

1. Intensive distribution-Where the majority of resellers stock the 'product' (with convenience products, for example, and particularly the brand leaders in consumer goods markets) price competition may be evident.
2. Selective distribution-This is the normal pattern (in both consumer and industrial markets) where 'suitable' resellers stock the product.
3. Exclusive distribution-Only specially selected resellers or authorized dealers (typically only one per geographical area) are allowed to sell the 'product'.

Channel Motivation

It is difficult enough to motivate direct employees to provide the necessary sales and service support. Motivating the owners and employees of the independent organizations in a distribution chain requires even greater effort. There are many devices for achieving such motivation. Perhaps the most usual is 'incentive': the supplier offers a better margin, to tempt the owners in the channel to push the product rather than its competitors; or a competition is offered to the distributors' sales personnel, so that they are tempted to push the product. Dent defines this incentive as a Channel Value Proposition or business case, with which the supplier sells the channel member on the commercial merits of doing business together. He describes this as selling business models not products.

Monitoring and Managing Channels

In much the same way that the organization's own sales and distribution activities need to be monitored and managed, so will those of the distribution chain. In practice, many organizations use a mix of different channels; in particular, they may complement a direct salesforce, calling on the larger accounts, with agents, covering the smaller customers and prospects.

The supply chain comprises the suppliers of all the goods and services that go into the delivery of tourism products to consumers. It includes all suppliers of goods and services whether or not they are directly contracted by tour operators or by their agents (including ground handlers) or suppliers (including accommodation providers). It should also be considered that some tourism goods and services are supplied direct to tourists and are purchased by consumers themselves and it should not be forgotten that tour operators can influence their customers in this area too. The initiatives reviewed in this report focus on improving benefits to the destination, consumers and the tourism industry. These initiatives are focused around four main points in the tourism supply chain:

- Accommodation
- Transport
- Ground handlers, excursions and activities
- Food and crafts

These include a variety of different activities-from increasing the proportions of local goods and services used in the tourism sector, to working on environmental and socio-cultural issues, such as waste management practices, employment training and combating illegal forms of tourism. Many of these initiatives are being put into practice by one or a few tourism businesses, sometimes working with partners across different points in the supply chain. We have also included some initiatives designed to support more sustainable tourism that are being undertaken at destination level.

Tourism and Supply Chain Management

The impacts of a tour operator come from the impacts of all components of the products they sell, including use of raw materials and their processing and production, as well as impacts from transport and distribution. Understanding the sustainability of each tourism product means going right back to the raw materials from which they are produced, through suppliers, and so on, right back to source, as well as ensuring that a company meets sustainability criteria in its own internal operations.

Tourism, like all other supply chains, operates through business-to-business relationships, and supply chain management can be applied to deliver sustainability performance improvements alongside financial performance, by working to improve the business operations of each supplier in the supply chain. The main differences between tourism supply chains and those of other sectors, are that tourists travel to the product, and the product that they buy has a particularly high service component-in other words, it involves a higher proportion of people in the immediate production of the holiday experience.

A good example of supply chain management from another sector is the DIY retailer, B&Q, which has developed and implemented a major supply chain management programme, first addressing environmental impacts, and now incorporating social impacts as well, for all its 40,000 products. In order to assess its overall sustainability as a retailer, B&Q analyses the sustainability of its products going right back to the raw materials from which they were produced, through suppliers, and so on, right back to source, as well as ensuring that B&Q meets sustainability criteria in its own internal operations. For B&Q, the ethics of a product-including employment and working conditions-are an important part of quality and sustainability. Supply chain management in any sector, including tourism, covers all parts of a product's 'life cycle': raw materials, processing, manufacture, distribution, retailing, customer use and final disposal. Overall, the sustainability of a tourism product, depends on issues including the environment and working conditions in destination countries; safety, including safety of customers and staff in delivering all aspects of a tourism product; and resource use and disposal, including proper handling, reuse and recycling of waste materials, and measures to increase the efficiency of resource use.

Tourism supply chains involve many components-not just accommodation, transport and excursions, but also bars and restaurants, handicrafts, food production, waste disposal, and the infrastructure that supports tourism in destinations. These all form a part of the holiday product that is expected by tourists when they purchase holidays-whether or not the suppliers of those components are directly contracted by a tour operator. Just as no tour operator would provide 1-star transport to take customers to a 5-star holiday hotel, the sustainability of a holiday, like quality, depends on performance at all the links in the tourism supply chain.

A further aspect of the tourism supply chain is the activities of customers while on holiday, particularly in relation to their behaviour, and what they source for themselves in destinations. Tour operators are marketing the whole holiday experience to customers, and this includes opportunities to experience a destination's local products and services. Tour operators can play a significant role in providing appropriate advice to their customers about local products and services, and in ensuring that local producers and service providers have access to tourists on a fair basis. Many tour operators already supply some information on these aspects, but there is scope to do more.

Transport to & from destinations* Tour operating includes advertising, purchasing, package development, marketing and sales, and purchasing* Ground operations include ground transport and excursions Some of the components of tourism products... Tour operators contract suppliers to provide some of these components directly: others are obtained by suppliers and their suppliers. Allsuppliers providing component goods and services that go into delivery of a tourism product are part of the supply chain for that product.

Assessment of Current Practices: Adequacy, Implementation, Motivations & Challenges

We have assessed information on tourism supply initiatives against actions and policies for sustainable tourism that have been outlined by international organisations, tourism industry organisations and NGOs. Socio-economic and cultural issues encompass a number of aspects, including contribution to the economic development and the well-being of local communities; preservation of cultural identity; respect for human rights local communities' and indigenous peoples' rights. Environmental aspects include sustainable transport development and sustainable use of resources; reducing, minimising and preventing pollution and waste (e.g. solid and liquid waste, emissions to air); conserving plants, animals, ecosystems and protected areas (biodiversity); and conserving landscapes, cultural and natural heritage. Examples of practices here include environmental auditing and management in hotels, as well as supply chain management actions. The principles embodied in the various actions and policies advocated for making tourism more sustainable, are well summarised in the definition of fair trade tourism-a "commitment to finding positive and practical solutions for the tourism industry as well as consumers, local communities and destination governments, so as to benefit local communities through trade, in preference to aid". Fair trade principles can be applied to investments, business benefits including wages and working conditions, direct tourist expenditure, and use of natural resources.

Overall, we conclude that proven examples and practical expertise to implement initiatives addressing most aspects of sustainability are already available, and that the main challenges are to apply these more widely, and in some cases to extend their breadth. We also note that widening the opportunity to implement such initiatives in mass tourism from the UK, may require a shift to business models based on destination sustainability and value-for-money, rather than price and asset yield alone, and therefore may raise issues about brand values and consumer marketing which at present often focus heavily on price.

While all the sectors reviewed have some examples of good practice, there is a significant variation between tour operators in their efforts to promote sustainability in their supply chains. The range of actions available is sufficient for all tour operators to engage at some level, although analysis indicates specific challenges in each sector:

Accommodation

Within those actions undertaken to improve the sustainability of accommodation, our research found a range of activities, but not many of these were the result of tour operator demand or support. So far it is the mass tour operators that have been able to set sustainability programmes for their accommodation suppliers, whilst small operators state that they do not have the purchasing power to change behaviour.

The emphasis of sustainable tourism activities, such as those from MyTravel Northern Europe, Kuoni and Hotelplan, is on the environment, mainly focusing on the reduction of costs from energy, water and waste. Fewer activities are evident in relation to employment conditions and staff development. Most small tour operators rely on selecting suppliers that already meet their sustainability requirements, partly because these smaller operators work with niche markets for whom many of the characteristics of sustainability (small properties, local food, host contact) are part of the product. Developments such as the AITO preferred supplier scheme and the Green Travel Market, as well as the increase of sustainability certification standards are expected to help in this respect.

Socio-economic Issues

The accommodation sector requires considerable numbers of staff, and so has the potential to provide employment for nearby communities. However, many jobs in the accommodation sector are low paid and involve long hours and difficult shift patterns. Because of the restricted length of the tourism season in some destinations, many jobs are temporary and insecure. There is also a tendency to employ non-local labour, especially in large hotels. Improving working conditions and pay and encouraging greater employment of local labour, are all part of improving sustainability performance, and hotels and tour operators are starting to address some of these issues. There are examples of good practice on training and employing local people in hotels (such as Serena Hotels, and the Movenpick, Carlson and Taj hotel chains), or providing education for staff families (eg. Tongabezi Lodge in Zambia), and a range of smaller tour operators prefer to use locally-owned hotels with good standards rather than international foreign-owned hotel chains (Trips Worldwide, Explore Worldwide, MAD Adventures Guerba World Travel, Inntravel, Exodus, SNP, Worldhorseriding amongst others). Members of the TOI and other large tour operators support the ECPAT Code of Conduct against Child Sex Tourism, and deliver training modules on the Code and its implementation to all staff, including accommodation suppliers in pilot destinations, as well as including specific clauses on the issue in hotel contracts.

Environmental Issues

Action on some environmental issues, such as energy efficiency is widespread in larger hotels (eg. Maldives, Lanzarote, Kingfisher Bay-Australia, and Mauritius), and more use is being made of renewable energy technologies, especially in remoter areas (eg. Rottnest Island and Couran Cove-Australia, Cousin Island-Seychelles). Some also use water saving devices, and recycle wastewater ('grey water') for irrigation. Large hotel chains (eg. Marriott, Radisson SAS, TUI Hotels and Resorts, and Accor) often include training on environmental issues as part of staff training programmes, and in other cases, tour operators may provide environmental training for hotels-examples are My Travel and Kuoni Switzerland.

In a scheme supported by members of the TOI operating in Side (Turkey), a joint action plan on waste management has been developed through a multi-stakeholder process including local hotels, the Side Tourism Association, and the Side Municipality. As part of this, waste separation bins have been introduced in approximately 100 hotels in Side (representing an overall capacity of around 20,000 beds), training provided for hotels and key workers dealing with waste management, and a waste handling and recycling scheme set up by the municipality.

Many of these actions help to reduce operating costs as well as improving environmental performance. However, little attention has so far been given to the siting and design of hotels to minimise their environmental impacts. Smaller hotels generally take less action on environmental issues, but some accommodation owners, especially in remote areas, use solar and wind energy.

Management Issues

A variety of management tools and standards are available and being applied for improving sustainability performance in the accommodation sector. These include standards and certification (including ecolabelling), auditing and environmental management systems, as well as development of action plans and designation of clear management responsibilities.

Many of these tools were originally developed to manage environmental aspects of business, but can be (and in some cases have been) extended to incorporate social aspects too. Working conditions and employment aspects can be integrated into human resource management.

Some large tour operators have developed environmental standards backed by training materials to assist and encourage improvements in performance by their accommodation suppliers (Kuoni Switzerland, TUI, My Travel Northern Europe, First Choice, Hotelplan); environmental management systems are being implemented in hotel chains (Marriott, Radisson, Hilton, Accor) while a few programmes are integrated with tour operator demands or incentives such as the agreement between the Swiss tour operator Hotelplan and the Spanish hotel chain Iberostar, and some destinations are operating certification schemes to audit and reward good performance by tourism businesses on environmental aspects (Red Sea, Rimini-Italy, Alcudia-Spain, Bolivia, Seychelles, Lloret de Mar-Spain, Phuket Yacht Club-Thailand).

A number of these also provide technical advice and support to help businesses improve standards ranging from the municipality of Rimini in Italy to the nation-wide Costa Rican Certificate for Sustainable Tourism.

Conservation issues

Some hotels are developed within old and historic buildings giving them a new life and preserving a part of a destination's architectural heritage. Smaller buildings, such as former fishermen's cottages and barn conversions, traditional properties and colonial buildings are also preserved by restoring them as holiday accommodation (eg. the Laona Project, supported by Sunvil, Cyprus, Laskarina, Inntravel, Worldhorseriding, Pure Crete, and Gites de France). As well as preserving local heritage, these also offer communities a new source of income from tourism.

Transport

Transport by air, land and sea is a major area of environmental impact for the tourism industry, and one that can only partly be managed through switching to less polluting forms of transport or upgrading to more efficient transport. The emphasis in transport has been on environmental issues, rather than on social ones and this has meant that opportunities to use airlines for instance as a communication medium to captive audiences have often been missed by operators.

Environmental Issues

Tour operators maintain that they do not have the ability to influence the sustainability of air transport and the few examples are mainly focused on offsetting carbon emissions. However, tour operators do have some choice over mode of travel, and over the operation of ground transportation that they use. A few tour operators have schemes to promote a modal change towards use of forms of transport with lower environmental impacts, such as using trains instead of planes as the preferred form of transport for their products where feasible (Studiosus, Forum Anders Reisen). SNP, the largest soft adventure tour operator in the Netherlands, always offers train transport first for all package holiday destinations under 1,000 kilometres away and offers to quote for train transport for all other destinations.

Ground transportation operators can promote greater fuel efficiency by ensuring that their fleets are well maintained, and by requiring drivers to switch off engines when vehicles are stationary (Vasco Travel). And in the Pantanal region of Brazil, World Horse Riding has supported its suppliers to replace environmentally unfriendly two-stroke boat engines with cleaner four-stroke engines and small solar-powered electric motors.

Because of the difficulties in reducing environmental costs, some tour operators use carbon offset schemes (eg. Future Forests, Climate Care, C Level and Coolflying) which calculate carbon dioxide emissions from air transport and promote offsetting of these generally through reforestation projects, or in some cases through investment in renewable energy supplies. Some tour operators provide information on these schemes in their brochures

(Kuoni Switzerland, Guerba, Trips Worldwide, Island Holidays, Naturetrek, The Adventure Company) and websites (Journey Latin America, The Gambia Experience) and encourage contributions by their customers on a voluntary basis. Other operators-usually at the higher end of the market-include contributions to these schemes in the price of the packages they sell (High and Wild, Greentours, The Expedition Company, Discovery Initiatives, Club Robinson-part of TUI, South American Experience Ltd, The Last Resort, Wildlife World, Crystal Holidays). In discussions with industry experts it was stated that these programmes won't make a real difference to the problem of climate change, but can raise awareness and lead to more advanced proposals.

Socio-economic Issues

Some airlines deliver sustainability messages through their in-flight presentations, such as magazines and videos, and the few examples available (such as destination-specific videos produced by Tourism Concern) could be replicated. For example, Air France and Austrian Airlines show ECPAT video spots in their flights highlighting the issue of sexual exploitation of children.

Ground Handlers, Representatives, Excursions, and Activities

Most of the examples found of sustainability requirements from ground handlers come from smaller, nature and ecotourism operators, and even amongst those, there are relatively few examples of ongoing impact assessments of excursions and other products. There are however good examples of destination training, both for the operators' own representatives and those of its suppliers. In particular, it is important that tour guides and local representatives are trained in minimisation of environmental impacts, and maximisation of local economic benefit and educating customers on the social workings of a region so as to maximise positive local impact, so that they can play their part in implementing company policies. These examples however are small compared to the portfolio of excursions, since tour operators are often unwilling to deselect unsustainable and poorly managed products that are otherwise popular with customers.

Like the accommodation sector, ground handling and related activities are staff-intensive, and often provide only low-paid jobs with poor working conditions as well as suffering from the seasonality of tourism. However, there are a number of examples of good practice on sustainability issues. Most of these come from ecotourism and nature tourism companies and excursions, where experienced staff with detailed knowledge of local culture and environments are vital for delivery of quality holidays. But these are also equally relevant and applicable to mass market operators too.

Socio-economic Issues

Our research found that some operators (eg. Rainbow Tours, Inntravel and Guerba) emphasise the importance of selecting suppliers based on community and work force issues before environmental concerns, and/or are working on introducing responsible tourism criteria in their purchasing policies to cover these issues. Some take steps to employ local staff (Guerba, Worldhorseriding, and Andean Trails), and/or promote visits to community projects or tourism enterprises (Sunvill Africa, Dragoman, Abercrombie & Kent, Exodus, and Andean Trails). A number of mainly smaller tour operators have provided financial investment to assist their ground handlers to improve the quality of their services (Guerba, Alternative Travel Group) and, indirectly, the sustainability of their operations, or have provided basic equipment needed for specialist excursions, such as field guides, binoculars and telescopes (Naturetrek). Importantly, nearly 40 tour operators that offer trekking holidays are implementing policies on porters rights and working conditions, based on Tourism Concern's Porters' Rights Campaign. Some operators state they will stop using suppliers if standards are not met, but have never actually had to carry through this approach (Imaginative Traveller, Explore, Audley).

Environmental Issues

A variety of practical measures are available to address environmental quality issues. Some tour operators are working with their customers and local suppliers to reduce the amount of waste generated by their tours (Andante Travel, Thomas Cook,

Laskarina, and Exodus), and most adventure tour operators interviewed take home all waste materials to prevent litter in the sites they visit. Some tour operators set standards for key excursion and activity suppliers operating in protected or sensitive areas such as marine environments. TOI member companies are working with Conservation International and CORAL to establish guidelines for marine recreation standards, to support resorts and tour operators in selecting more sustainable suppliers.

Conservation Issues

Nature and wildlife are key parts of some holiday packages and excursions, yet just the pressure of sheer numbers of visitors can do serious damage to wildlife and sensitive sites. Provision of information combined with simple management controls can help visitors experience the natural environment while protecting it for others to enjoy in the future.

Most tour operators provide an element of customer education on conservation, especially advising customers not to buy products made from endangered species, such as from coral, shells or ivory, which are in any case protected by national and international legislation (Thomas Cook in Cuba, Jamaica and Egypt, TUI UK in Tunisia and Kenya); and in many parts of the world, tourists diving around coral reefs must first take a local induction programme on how to avoid damage to corals (eg. Bonaire Marine Park, Accor hotel group in the Red Sea, Hotel association in Fiji). Some tour operators encourage and develop nature-based tours which can help raise awareness of the environment and conservation issues amongst tourists (eg. TUI UK turtle appreciation excursion in Greece).

Food and Crafts

Food and crafts can generate considerable profits for the local population, when volume production and delivery at set quality standards can be met by local producers. Key issues for local sourcing of food supplies in the tourism sector are quality, reliability and quantity of supply. Promotion of local sourcing therefore requires training and technical support and investment-for example in storage and distribution facilities-to meet quality and reliability standards, as well as the development of production and distribution networks to gather supplies from different local producers into the quantities required by hotels.

Socio-economic Issues

Few tour operators have supply chain initiatives on the production and distribution of local, sustainable food and crafts, but some work with their local suppliers to promote local sourcing of food and other local products. Small hotels are more likely to buy from local suppliers, while some large hotels have developed programmes to encourage local production at the standards they require. This generally requires constant supervision and commitment, and success is often linked to championing of local sourcing by hotel chefs. Most large hotels that have worked with local food producers have found it requires constant supervision and commitment, and success is often linked to championing of local sourcing by hotel chefs-examples include Grecotel's organic vegetable program linked to promoting local products in hotel restaurants, and the Sheraton Lombok's fish programme that has created a number of local jobs. Local sourcing and production will usually improve the contribution of tourism to the local economy, both financially and in terms of employment, and may also help to preserve local skills in craft production, such as the production of local crafts in Malta, provide a source of diversification and reduce seasonality in employment.

In many cases tour operators use local food and crafts as one of the tourist attractions of their packages. There is also scope for tourists to visit local bars and restaurants to experience local produce and cuisine. Local crafts retail outlets and restaurants are often key to the holiday experience, for example the Canadian Economuseum Society opens craftmakers's workshops to visitors, and the 'Eurotext' initiative in Finland, Greece and Portugal uses the production of traditional textiles as a tourist attraction. Tour operators and representatives can play an important role in suggesting visits to appropriate places through the holiday information they provide to customers when they book, and at destination meetings. Tour operators are in a tremendous position to educate their customers about local food and crafts and to encourage their appreciation, which can help to make a real difference to the preservation of local skills and jobs. However there are few examples were available of tour operators considering the potential depletion of local food (for example fish and seafood) or the outcome of rises in prices for locals.

Destinations

In relation to the tourism supply chain and direct inputs to tourism, destinations provide infrastructure and services. Destination initiatives for sustainable tourism seek to improve the quality of infrastructure-for example, through improvements to waste management infrastructure for solid wastes and waste (eg. Cirali and Side (Turkey), Menorca and Calvia (Balearics), Hanauma Bay (Hawaii), Cape Town, Phuket Yacht Club (Thailand), and Rio de la Plata (Uruguay)) and awareness raising programmes on waste management practices (eg. the Maldives, Lanzarote, Lloret de Mar and Mauritius), to transport systems and to reduce vehicle impacts (Hanauma Bay (Hawaii), Tres Islas (Mexico), Alcudia, Lloret de Mar and Sant Feliu de Guíxols (Spain), Cap d'Agde (France), Rottnest Island, and Couran Cove)-and to increase the ability of the destination to gain from tourism. Several destinations have worked to improve the sustainability performance of suppliers (eg. Red Sea Sustainable Tourism Initiative), and marketing and product developments being used by mass tourism destinations to offset seasonality in tourism (eg. Calvia and Sant Feliu de Guixols in Spain, and Bermuda). Other initiatives include the promotion of linkages between tourism sites, and promotion of a wider range of tourism activities to encourage tourists to sample different aspects of the country and thereby diversify and spread the economic benefits of tourism.

A number of initiatives in destinations in many developing countries are designed to enhance local employment in tourism, such as by supporting the substitution of locally-grown and locally-manufactured products in place of imports in the tourism sector (Western Samoa), the establishment of investment and loan funds to assist local tourism businesses to start and expand (Zambia), or the setting up of employment bureaux to match employees with tourism jobs (Macedonia).

Some destinations have set up local quality of life and sustainability programmes using sustainability indicators to monitor environmental quality (Lanzarote and Calvia), and in some cases, biodiversity (St. Lucia Marine Park and Cousin Island), as well as monitoring visitor satisfaction and changes in tourism markets. Marketing, products and operations can then be adapted according to the monitoring information obtained. Associated environmental initiatives often include general environmental education programmes (Rottnest Island, and Calvia), as well as various approaches to protect biodiversity, which may include the protection of a single species or site, such as turtle protection (Belek, and some Brazilian sites), establishment of environmental monitoring and restoration programmes, and environmental impact studies and indicators (Couran Cove, and the Maldives). Measures for protection of cultural heritage are also in place in a number of destinations, ranging from requirements for new developments to be of appropriate architectural designs and built of local materials (eg. Mauritius and Tres Islas) to the development of visitor management infrastructure and encouragement for visitation to historic monuments and archaeological sites (eg. Honduras and Turkey).

Trade Stability as Pre-condition to Sustainability Improvement in Supply Chains

Suppliers are more willing to adopt tour operator requirements when they have long term contracts that guarantee the return on investment. A large part of sustainable supply chains depends on first ensuring the socio-economic sustainability of the suppliers. The move in the early 1990s towards "guaranteed" accommodation contracts, in which operators would guarantee payment regardless of occupancy, was designed to secure accommodation and to mitigate financial risk, but in fact laid the foundations of a more sustainable supply chain partnership.

A secure income stream, with stable contracts and foreseeable contracting conditions including prices is paramount, both to facilitate the necessary investments by the supplier, and to cement the trust in the relationship. Because projects require time for companies to build knowledge and develop relationships, supply chain initiatives are unlikely to produce measurable short term, quick fix results. Tour operators interviewed reported that it is necessary to develop initiatives gradually and that results are based on solid working relationships that have been built up over time and reflect a mutual respect between both parties. Tour operators tend to require a steady and significant volume of operations with a supplier or destination if they are to make a significant contribution and expect changes in local operations, whether this is in terms of contracting local people or influencing decision-making of suppliers. Therefore three necessary conditions must to be met in the tour operator-supplier relationship:

- Long-term partnership;
- Fair pricing;
- Consistent volume of operations.

Many improvements in the supply chain are not the result of projects *per se*, but of advice and support provided to suppliers through long term working relationships and the security of a stable client. Smaller tour operators with long term links to destinations have a greater tendency to fund projects that improve local quality of life, whilst creating new tourist products that their customers can visit on excursions.

Approaches to Implementation of Good Practices

Two main types of approach can be identified. The first involves businesses working though their own internal management procedures and/or through their business networks and relationships with suppliers. The second approach involves actions outside the direct supply chain, through partnerships with stakeholders in the public sector, private and voluntary sectors, including local enterprises, host communities and destination NGOs.

Internal Management, Supplier Networks and Direct Business Relationships

A tour operator may adopt practices to reduce the environmental impacts of their office and sales operations, including addressing issues such as brochure production, energy and waste management at their premises. However, the main opportunities for improving the sustainability of their holiday products are to be found in the hotels, airlines, ground transport and other suppliers that are contracted directly. In this tour operators are in a similar position to any retailers where most of its impact as a business comes not from its internal operation, but from the products it sells.

Tour operators direct and influence the volume of tourism, the tourist destinations and facilities that are used. Through this, tour operators have enormous influence over activities throughout the tourism supply chain and the opportunity to use their influence to help in promoting general improvements in sustainability performance as part of good commercial practice.

A detailed review by the TOI of initiatives in the management of supply chain relationships by companies in partnership with their suppliers, shows that a defined series of steps are applied to supply chain management by tour operators. These steps are set out in the TOI Supply Chain Management Handbook, and comprise the following:

Establish a Sustainable Supply Chain Policy and Management System

1 Create a clear company policy on sustainability and co-ordinate implementation across relevant departments.
2 Conduct a baseline assessment using consultation to assess the performance of a sample of suppliers against criteria defined in the sustainability policy, and identify priority areas for improvement.
3 Prepare and implement an action plan drawing on the baseline assessment, and working with suppliers to improve their sustainability.

Support Suppliers in Reaching Sustainability Goals

1 Raise awareness on sustainability issues amongst suppliers and demonstrate why sustainability performance is important.
2 Provide suppliers with technical support on actions to improve their sustainability performance

3 Offer incentives to sustainable suppliers to recognise and reward them for improvements on key environmental, social and economic issues.

Integrate Sustainability Criteria into Suppliers' Contracts and Preferentially Contract Suppliers that Meet those Criteria

These steps are equally applicable to development of action within individual companies. Within these frameworks we have found a series of tools that are being implemented, with some overlaps in use, including:

- Standard setting and use of certification schemes
- Performance monitoring through special surveys and through customer satisfaction questionnaires
- Provision of a range of incentives, such as long term relationships and preferential marketing
- Partnerships, such as investment assistance
- Provision of technical support and advice
- Preferred contracting
- Avoidance or deselection of suppliers that do not meet basic requirements

The successful implementation of sustainability management systems relies on systematic data gathering. For tour operators that are not already doing this, there are a variety of tools available that offer frameworks that they can use. These include the GRI reporting indicators for tour operators, the socio-economic and environmental indicators that form part of the IHEI's Benchmark tool for accommodation, and the forthcoming supply chain management handbook, and marine purchasing guidelines from the Tour Operators' Initiative for Sustainable Tourism Development (TOI). It would be valuable to encourage use these or similar tools in order to gather baseline information which can then be used by tour operators in setting clear objectives and programmes for implementation of sustainability improvements in their internal operations and in their supply chains, which together make up the mainstream business activities of tour operators.

The basic methodology for information gathering can be developed around existing expertise with sustainability indicators, including the work of the GRI and TOI on sustainability reporting indicators for tour operators, and the TFIU's Integrated Responsible Tourism Programme which includes a section on assessing the impact of products and services. It would be possible for information gathering to be done collectively, for example through the TF or the FTO, or to be done or commissioned by individual tour operators for specific destinations. Whichever approach is adopted, it is essential that tour operators buy into the process, as it is they who will primarily act upon the information gathered.

Financing for supply chain initiatives based on internal management and business-to-business relationships of this type generally comes from the budgets of the businesses concerned, and can be obtained from budgetary reallocations, as well as through cost savings that may be made in some areas of sustainability implementation. The majority of actions taken through this approach are self-financing, although in some cases external funding support may also be provided, for example through programmes funded by governments or by overseas development aid that are aimed at improving various aspects of business performance linked to sustainability.

Partnerships Involving the Public, Private and Voluntary Sectors

When the World Tourism Organization analysed 49 sustainable tourism good practices, they found that, irrespective of whether they were in developed or developing countries, the success of these projects is linked to local community involvement in the planning, development and management of the projects in over 40% of examples. Partnerships such as that in Side supported by the TOI, or Tourism Concern's work to develop its Porters' Rights campaign are critical to ensure that a good understanding is built up between all those who need to take action in a supply chain or in a destination, and that common actions with clear responsibilities are established from the outset of a project aimed at creating sustainability improvements. It should also be noted that NGOs can and do play an important role in drawing attention to some supply chain issues-the Porters' Rights campaign being a good example.

Partnerships involving two or more groups of stakeholders are the second main approach used to promote sustainability in tourism supply chains. The stakeholders involved in these initiatives can include national and local government organisations, business associations (such as the Caribbean Alliance for Sustainable Tourism and the Caribbean Hotels Association), local communities (often through community associations), and NGOs. Some of these projects incorporate components that are directly aimed at assisting the private sector to improve performance in some aspects of sustainability. One example is the programme of environmental auditing for hotels-EAST: Environmental Audits for Sustainable Tourism-that has been set up in Jamaica.

A number of these partnerships deal with infrastructure for environmental and resource management at destination level-particularly solid and liquid waste management, and water quality and supply-through supporting investment and through establishment of improved management systems.

Other partnership projects deal with a range of areas covering:

- Marketing, ecolabelling and certification
- Promotion of economic development and employment, including development of economic linkages between tourism and other local economic activity
- Legislation enforcement and standard raising
- Training and awareness raising
- Protection and restoration of natural and cultural heritage

Financing for initiatives based on partnerships often comes mainly from national governments and overseas development aid, with varying degrees of contributions from the private sector and local government. Some initiatives-generally smaller schemes-can also involve funding from NGOs or are self-financed by tourism enterprises.

The recent work of the Association of Independent Tour Operators (AITO) is a good example of partnership approach to using market mechanisms to promote sustainable suppliers, by developing a system to promote the use of sustainable suppliers for AITO members' new product development. Details of tourism service suppliers that have met sustainability criteria will be stored in a database and directory, which AITO members can search when preparing new packages. Current suppliers of these tour operators will be encouraged to demonstrate that they meet the criteria to be included in the database, while the service will be promoted to other suppliers with good sustainability credentials that aim to work with AITO tour operators.

As a multi-stakeholder organisation, the TF is well placed to encourage partnerships that integrate a number of tour operators working in the same destination, as this reflects specific TF aims, to which TF Forum members have signed up to through the UK Sustainable Tourism Initiative Commitment, in which they have undertaken to:

- "develop a policy and associated strategy to integrate and implement sustainable tourism practices into their mainstream business activities with indicators to track progress and to engage with other stakeholders to achieve the goals of the initiative."
- "work together in a process of continuous improvement in sustainable tourism practice."
- "Implementation of preferred codes of practice supported by practical tools that allow continuous improvement in the environmental and social performance of supply chain partners in destinations."
- "Building multi-stakeholder partnerships in destinations to identify and address priority areas in promoting sustainable tourism practice."
- "Developing a communication process that will engage consumers and other stakeholders in sustainable tourism issues.

Business Issues and Motivations

Good practice covers both what a business aims to achieve, and the processes and approaches by which it seeks to implement such aims. The cases reviewed for this report demonstrate a range of good practices, which have potential to be applied widely across the industry by tour operators and their supply chain partners. However, at present, apart from some basic environmental technologies, such as use of energy efficient lighting, few of the good practices recorded in this report are being applied very widely.

Tour operators make strict health and safety demands in their supplier contracts, but they tend not to set local labour and employment conditions, even though these can also contribute to the quality of their customers' holiday experience, by encouraging the development of high quality local staff. Some of the actions are tokenistic and short term and use philanthropic actions to make up for an inability of internalising sustainability in core business operations.

Most suppliers are chosen on overall quality, but at present the tourism sector only rarely includes sustainability issues as part of the quality equation. Sustainability issues are most evident as a quality issue amongst smaller and specialist tour operators. The mass tourism sector is just at the very early stages of incorporating sustainability as a product quality issue, focusing mainly on environmental issues, but now starting to address a few social issues such as working against child sex tourism through implementation of the ECPAT code. However despite examples such as Serena Hotels, specific action to improve employment and working conditions within mass tourism businesses is still a rarity.

Yet good practices recorded in this report are clearly viable as part of the business practices of those businesses that have adopted them, and indeed provide a range of business benefits that maintain and increase competitiveness. These include gains from brand reputation, to better staff morale and retention, to stronger long term business relationships with key suppliers. This suggests that there is huge scope for good practices to be adopted by tourism businesses throughout the supply chain on both social and environmental aspects of sustainability.

However there are some very good examples that genuinely incorporate sustainability into supply chain management and contractual relationships: these need to be encouraged. Pro-active, forward looking tourism firms have much to gain from selecting, developing and retaining sustainable and responsible suppliers.

The TOI members and the World Travel and Tourism Council have separately reported similar benefits from corporate social leadership and actions to improve sustainability performance. Seven categories of business benefit have been identified by the TOI from a series of case studies of good practices by TOI members:

- Retention of your clients, as there they increasingly expect responsible behaviour even from those not willing to pay for it
- Increased revenue
- Reduced costs and improved operational efficiency, remaining competitive to assess and respond to risks and opportunities in the market
- Management of risks and staying ahead of legislative requirements
- Enhanced staff performance, achievement of better recruitment and staff retention, as satisfied staff are a key asset
- Protection of the core assets of the business (environment and culture)
- Enhanced brand value, reputation and market share, protecting image and status, particularly for companies publicly quoted on stock markets

These business benefits match those highlighted by the WTTC in their 2002 report "Corporate Social Leadership".

Promoting Sustainable Suppliers: Green Travel Market

The Green Travel Market (GTM) is a business to business service launched in 2003 to help European and North American tour operators become more aware of sustainable products, integrate them into the packages they offer, and reach relevant markets. GTM offers a range of services: a network of over 500 tour operators aiming to promote sustainability amongst their suppliers; a match-making service to support new product development for tour operators and for tourist destination firms to seek new markets, promotion at key European travel fairs, consumer marketing, information know-how and training materials.

Central to GTM is a database of tourism suppliers with information and credentials on their sustainability performance. This project benefits from the over 1000 European accommodation providers certified by one of the ecolabels under the VISIT initiative. Information included on the database includes receipt of sustainable or environmental awards, being members of key industry associations with sustainability codes of conduct and a solid track record of implementation, or having undergone a screening process from GTM. The list of suppliers in the GTM database ranges from organic farms in Eastern Europe, to car-free resorts in the Alps, community projects in Costa Rica and incoming tour operators from Latin America.

Providing Benefits and Developing Skills for the Local Community: Klein's Camp

Klein's Camp in Tanzania is one of the Conservation Corporation Africa's (CC Africa) group of small safari lodges and it is committed to CC Africa's core principle "Care of the Land, Care of the Wildlife, Care of the People". Klein's Camp is set against the most breathtaking scenery in Tanzania adjacent to the northern boundary of the Serengeti. Klein's Camp – CC Africa and the Ololosokwan (Maasai) community have reached a land lease agreement under which Klein's Camp can only use 3,000 acres while the remaining 22,000 acres are shared by the camp for safari operations and the locals for their needs. Under this agreement a joint management committee has been established consisting of equal number of members from both the local community and the Klein's Camp lodge, and which is responsible for making all land-related decisions. The agreement gives the Maasai unrestricted access to water and the salt licks.

Following the land agreement Klein's Camp and the CC Africa have launched a number of initiatives that support the Ololosokwan community and its environment. Klein's Camp helped the development of the Ololosokwan Community clinic and employs a medical assistant who treats staff and community members. Apart from medical facilities, Klein's Camp helps the communities to build and fully equip classrooms and provides skills training such as carving, building, weaving and ironmonger that help the locals not only to improve their lives but also to increase their revenue by selling handicrafts to guests. Klein's Camp supported locals to establish vegetable gardens, and this project has proved so successful that the garden keepers now supply not only Klein's camp, but all the Serengeti camps and two local villages.

Other initiatives include AIDS education, scholarship sponsored, employment opportunities in the camp and reintroduction and re-establishment of endangered wildlife populations. A significant portion of the revenue from Klein's Camp is given to the community and to the local conservation authority in order to care for the local people and wildlife.

Environmental Standards for Accommodation Suppliers: Kuoni Switzerland

Kuoni Switzerland developed in 2000 an in-house scheme, the Green Planet Award, to encourage and reward environmental management for its beach accommodation suppliers. In assessing candidates for the award, Kuoni focuses on how hotels deal with energy, waste and water. In order to achieve this Kuoni developed a questionnaire to provide measurable data. The key issues of the questionnaire are the quantity and quality of the information the hotel provides on its energy consumption, its waste and waste-water management and its use of water resources. Great importance is also given to details on aspects such as information provided to guests on each hotel's environmental efforts, and on training provided to the staff on how to operate their duties in more environmentally-friendly ways. Space is also provided for further information about their future environmental development goals.

The initiative was launched in the summer of 2000 in all seaside resort-destinations where Kuoni does business: since then, 641 beach resort hotels have been approached and by May 2002, 43 of these had met the criteria and were presented with the award. Kuoni conducts its survey once a year and publicises the winners in its catalogues and on its webpage, enabling its customers to select their holiday accommodation in line with their environmental principles. Each hotel that receives the award can retain it for one year only and has to prove each year that it still meets the criteria through participating in Kuoni's annual survey.

Through this Kuoni's accommodation partners can demonstrate systematic environmental management, their willingness to innovate and put environmental action into day-to-day practice.

The award enables Kuoni to work with its partners to achieve more sustainable tourism development. Through this, both parties-accommodation suppliers and the tour operator-not only can acquire new clients but also to increase customer loyalty as a result of the strong reputation they built through the award. Through the Green Planet Award Kuoni has achieved to build its suppliers' environmental awareness and motivated them to implement better practices. By receiving this award a hotel can develop a distinctive profile that can be used for promotional purposes and also gains competitive advantage in the market, as well as benefiting from long term cost savings by implementing water and energy conservation strategies.

Tour Operator and Destination Partnership for New Product Development: Pantanal Association of Nature Tour Operators

Pantanal is a protected area in Brazil covers 2.3. million hectares of mainly private land in 197 different Fazendas, as well as some land owned by local and regional authorities. A partnership approach has been used to plan the use of tourism as a tool for sustainable development, with the involvement of seven selected specialist tour operators through a familiarisation trip that involved stays in several pousadas (ranches) starting tourism businesses to complement their traditional sources of income. After the trip a two day workshop brought together pousada-owners and tour operators for feedback on both activities and accommodations offered, including comments and suggestions for improvement. The tour operators were invited by the Pantanal Park as the area considers it needs tourism income to maintain its protected area qualities.

The tour operators provided expertise in new product development, designed guide training programmes in nature interpretation and other concepts, and are currently providing a supportive network for local landowners to adapt their facilities and services to meet the requirements the specialised western ecotourism market. The Pantanal Association for Nature Tour

Operators is now a unit working together with the Park and Association of Pousadas for connecting the local providers with parts of the international market, creating a feeling of fellowship between the Tour Operators, and creating a group-synergy around the Pantanal both as a destination and as a project, something that can further develop the local providers' products and future income.

The Pousadas have gained invaluable knowledge on not only the ecotourism market but the value as well as the limitations of their resources, as well as gaining a small but secure market that allows targeted investments.

These pousadas are receiving some tourists through tour operators that are supportive of a learning environment, and the pousadas are gaining skills such as responding to tour operator requirements, pricing, quality assurance, logistics and other elements of the incoming tour operator's job. As a result of the familiarisation trip, the new products developed in conjunction with the pousadas are high-end incentive trips for CEOs, riding holidays, jungle trips, ecotours, back packer trails, and wildlife and birdwatching tours, by Adventura AB, World Horse Riding, JungleTrekker, Worldwide EcoLodges Viventura, Saïga and Discovery Initiatives.

Developing Environmental Management Systems for Resorts: Red Sea Sustainable Tourism Initiative

The Sinai Peninsula and Red Sea Coast benefit from a USAID funded program to support Egypt's Tourism Development Authority (TDA) to plan and manage sustainably for tourism growth. The focus of the Red Sea Sustainable Tourism Initiative (RSSTI) is to highlight best practice and raise sustainable tourism awareness through awareness campaigns, and in particular to train and implement Environmental Impact Assessment and monitoring and Environmental Management Systems.

Within this program eight resorts have implemented a resort-wide Environmental Management Systems (EMS) which resulted in significant savings, as well as the development of local examples for other resorts to follow. The EMS programme covers a range of issues such as energy and water efficiency, solid waste management, landscape design and planting. To support the implementation of an EMS, the program includes training courses for hotel senior management leading to a recognised certificate, the development of practical manuals and awareness campaigns, the preparation of self-auditing checklists and the potential to access independent certification of the properties through Green Globe. The Steigenberger Golf Resort and The Oberoi Sahl Hasheesh received this certificate by amongst other actions conserving energy and water, reducing their solid waste through separation and recycling.

Production and Distribution of Food to meet the Requirements of Large Purchasers: Sandals St. Lucia

Sandals St Lucia has been working to improve their supply chain by supporting a local farmers organisation and distribution company, with support from Oxfam UK. The Caribbean islands suffer from production of only a limited range of produce which is grown locally and not well-planned in relation to market requirements.

The lack of a common Caribbean-wide market and protective national policies towards other Caribbean states, means that most goods for resorts like Sandals are in fact flown in from Miami. Oxfam UK chose to work with St. Lucia because they perceived there was a positive national government agenda, policy framework and desire to act, as well as a formalised agricultural sector, and with local food production because it could contribute to tackling poverty in ways that heritage and environmental conservation could not.

Other locations where similar work could be considered are the Dominican Republic and Mexico. Oxfam is providing support focusing on bridging the institutional gaps that exist between small farmer producers to reach potential markets. This requires linking individual farmers in groups through planned production beyond monocrops, by introducing the necessary skills and equipment.

Local producers need to focus on health and safety primarily in supplying meat and fish produce, while for most fruit and vegetables the producers need training on washing and packaging, and on quality standards set at a national level.

Common-interest Organizations

UNWTO is the Largest Tourism Organization

Originated for the International Congress of Official Traffic Associations, the World Tourism Organization is a United Nations agency that deals with tourism related issues.

As of 2005, its membership included more than 350 affiliate members, 145 countries, and 7 territories and representing educational institutions, private sector, and tourists associations. The UNWTO is located in Madrid, Spain.

Goals and Points of Concern of Air Highways Magazine

Launched in 1995, Air Highways Magazine emerged as a result of the publishing of a series of travel maps displaying diverse models of transportation.

Thousands of copies of the magazine were distributed by the company's customers Avis Rent A Car and Best Western Hotels to their clients in North America. This resulted in the assignment by Canada's Government to create a supermap of air routes, as travellers were interested in how to get to various destinations in fast and convenient manner.

Luxury and Sophistication of American Hotels

The most famous American hotels have gained their reputation and renown by hosting some important events and celebrities and providing top quality services.

Many hotels have entered into the consciousness by popular culture and are also frequented by celebrities. To these belong such famous hotels as the Beverly Hills Hotel and the Chateau Mountain in California and the Plaza Hotel and the Hotel Chelsea and many more hotels.

The Association of Hotels and Resorts-Working for the Betterment of the Tourism Industry

Created in 1987 as a Risk Purchasing Group by the management professionals and resort hotel owners, the Association of Hotels and Resorts is a non-profit insurance association, specializing in insurance programs designed specifically to face the challenges and cover risks unique to historic and luxury resorts, spas and independent destinations. It was established as a response to rates increase and insurance availability reduction by the constricted insurance market.

ATA-the Organization of the Largest US Airlines

Formed in Chicago in 1936 by a group of 14 airlines, the ATA-better known as the Air Transport Association – was the first and remains today the only organization of the largest US airlines. It is headquartered in Washington, DC. Since its foundation the company has been an important player in all major government decisions concerning aviation, including airline deregulation, the establishment of the Civil Aeronautics Board and creation of the air traffic control system.

5

Sustainable Tourism Development in Small Island

Experience Gained and Problems Encountered by Small Island Developing States in Tourism

Economic Impact

Overview of Performance: Tourism is often identified as a promising growth sector in small island developing States. It offers one of the few opportunities for economic diversification in very small islands. Tourism has many linkages with other economic sectors, and if integrated into national development plans with adequate provisions for inter sectorial linkages, it can contribute to the growth of all tourism-related activities in all of the major economic sectors-agriculture, including fishing, industry and services, including transportation. At present, the extent of tourism activities in small island developing States varies widely between geographical regions as well as between countries within regions. Likewise, the economic benefits derived from tourism are diverse. In some small island developing States, tourism has become the major contributor to the gross domestic product GDP), while in others it is still relatively undeveloped.

It is well known that in small island developing States, the scope for economic diversification and growth is limited. Their key constraints are small land areas and small populations. The relatively larger ones have the human resources potential to support a number of economic sectors viably and thus to benefit from linkages of those sectors with the tourism sector. The smaller ones, however, do not have such potential and will therefore have to be more reliant on imports to meet the material demands of the tourism sector. Other things remaining equal, the net benefits, i.e., domestic value-added per visitor, derived by the smaller islands from tourism will be relatively smaller.

The main objectives of the promotion of tourism as a growth sector are to accelerate the growth of national incomes, gainful employment, foreign exchange earnings and government tax revenues. A thorough evaluation of the contribution of tourism in small island developing States with respect to these parameters is at present hampered by the incompleteness of data. In a sample of 29 small island developing States for which data are available, gross direct receipts from tourism as a percentage of GDP ranged from a meagre 1 per cent to 88 percent on the average during the period 1989-1993. In this sample of countries, tourism and tourism-related activities have become the mainstay of the economy in Antigua and Barbuda, Aruba, Barbados, Saint Lucia, the Bahamas, Saint Kitts and Nevis and Seychelles, or mostly in the small island developing States in the Caribbean. Important exceptions apart, tourism makes the least contribution to national income in most of the African and Pacific small island developing States.

With a few exceptions, most small island developing States have realized a fast, although diverse, pace of growth of gross tourism receipts in nominal terms in recent years. During the period 1989-1993, in 24 out of 34 for which data are available, the growth of gross receipts from tourism ranged from 2 per cent to 61 per cent per annum on the average. In most, it exceeded 10 per cent and in 9 it was 15 per cent or more. Generally, but not universally, the fast pace of growth reflects low initial levels of receipts from tourism. Even among those with low initial levels, several countries did not do so well.

In view of the constraints faced by small island developing States in promoting exports of goods in an increasingly competitive and fast-changing international economy, by and large, these States are giving increasing importance to tourism as a source of raising their foreign exchange earnings. The available data show that during the period 1980-1992, for a sample of 26 small island developing States, the percentage increase in the ratio of foreign exchange earnings from tourism to total export earnings ranged from 2 per cent to 453 per cent, In 10 of them, it exceeded 50 per cent. In 1992, the contribution of tourism to total export earnings in 23 countries ranged from a meagre 2 per cent to 83 per cent; in 13 of them it exceeded 25 per cent.

The data on average daily expenditures per visitor for 10 countries ranged from US$ 41 to $304 in 1992. In 1989, average daily expenditures per visitor for 23 small island developing States ranged from $37 to $226. The diversity of performance even in these small samples is significant. It suggests that those countries that want to promote tourism as a growth sector need, in addition to adequate investments in tourism infrastructure, to make greater efforts to enhance the diversity and quality of goods and services they sell to visitors.

Countries that have relatively full employment are less interested in the employment potential of expansion of tourism than those that have substantial unemployment. The employment advantages of tourism are twofold: first, the industry is labour-intensive, and secondly, much of the employment is relatively unskilled. Consequently, investment in tourism produces a higher and faster increase in employment than equal investment in other activities. Tourism creates employment directly in the tourism industry as well as in industries providing goods and services to the tourism industry. Data on direct employment in the tourism industry is extremely scanty. It may be inferred, however, that the impact of tourism on employment in small island developing States, where tourism makes an important contribution to national income, is considerable. In 15 Caribbean tourist destinations, a total of 77,319 hotel rooms accounted for 88,697 jobs, equivalent to 1.15 jobs per room. With the recent decline in the agriculture sector, in particular sugar and bananas, the relative share of tourism in employment has risen. In the South Pacific, tourism generated 27,500 jobs in direct employment in 1991 in the 10 member countries of the Tourism Council of the South Pacific (TCSP), with a population of about 5 million. Fiji accounted for 10,340 of this amount. In the Mediterranean region, overall employment in Cyprus exhibited an upward trend during the period 1980-1992, with the fastest growth occurring in tourism and related services.

Employment in these occupations doubled from 33,000 jobs in 1980 to 64,000 in 1992. Hotels, restaurants and retail trade increased their share of employment from 17.9 per cent in 1980 to 24.3 per cent in 1992. In 1993, the total contribution of tourism to employment in Malta was roughly estimated at about 17 per cent of the labour force. In the African region, the available data for Mauritius and Seychelles indicate that during the period 1990-1994, the share of direct employment in tourism in total employment rose from 3.4 per cent to 4.8 per cent in Mauritius and remained stable at about 18 per cent in Seychelles.

While the employment objective remains important for several small island developing States, the level of wages in the tourism industry is also important. The available information indicates that most jobs created in tourism are low-paying. This is to be expected in countries with high rates of unemployment, particularly of unskilled labour. The creation of low-paying jobs in the tourism sector in countries with relatively high rates of employment is the result of the strong pull factor of the relatively less physically demanding jobs in the tourism sector from more arduous jobs in the primary sector. This process exerts pressure on producers in the primary sector to modernize and increase capital intensity so as to permit a rising level of real wages; otherwise, the sector will lose its labour force and dwindle. This could marginalize important productive activities such as agriculture and fishing, and weaken the linkages of other sectors with tourism reducing the benefits derived from the tourism industry.

Tourism is likely to play an even more important role in the growth and development of small island developing States if appropriate measures are taken to invigorate other sectors, in particular agriculture and fishing, so that they can more adequately meet tourist demand for consumer goods from domestic sources. Except for the very small ones, small island developing States can, with careful planning and provision of adequate facilities such as credit for mechanization, modernization and diversification, where necessary, support viable agricultural and fishing activities, as well as light manufacturing in addition to tourism. As inter sectorial competition raises wage rates and incomes and reduces labour supply to the tourism sector, emphasis can be shifted to up-market tourism, with reliance on a slower rate of growth but of higher-spending visitors.

Leakage of foreign exchange from gross tourism receipts (Percentage)

1.	Fiji	56
2.	Cook Islands	50
3.	Saint Lucia	45
4.	Mauritius	43
5.	Aruba	41
6.	Hong Kong	41
7.	Jamaica	40
8.	United States Virgin Islands	36
9.	Seychelles	30
10.	Sri Lanka	27
11.	Antigua and Barbuda	25
12.	Cyprus	25
13.	Kenya	22
14.	Republic of Korea	20
15.	New Zealand	12
16.	Yugoslavia	11
17.	Philippines	11

Source: Travel and Tourism Analyst No. 3

In evaluating the direct contribution of tourism to national income, gross levels of incomes or gross foreign exchange earnings are much less significant than net earnings after deductions have been made for all necessary foreign exchange expenditures of the tourism industry. The primary leakages of foreign exchange earnings from direct tourist expenditures arise from: (a) imports of materials and equipment for construction, (b) imports of consumer goods, particularly food and drink, (c) repatriation of profits earned by foreign investors, (d) overseas promotional expenditures and (e) amortization of external debt incurred in the development of hotels and resorts. The impact of these leakages varies greatly from country to country depending on the ability of countries to produce the goods and services necessary to meet the needs of the tourism industry. The estimates available for 17 countries or territories presented below show that the higher leakages pertain to small island economies.

Direct income from tourism provides only a partial picture of the contribution of tourism to national income. A complete picture would call for the estimation of tourism income multipliers in each small island developing State. Since expenditures of tourists give rise to the generation of additional incomes throughout the economy, the incomes and the associated employment thus induced can be considerable. Aside from the savings propensity of the local population, the size of the tourism income multiplier in a particular small island developing State depends on the extent of leakages of tourist expenditures overseas. The less the leakage of direct tourist expenditures, the higher the tourism income multiplier. Because of the complexities relating to the requisite data, however, the estimation of tourism income multipliers is beyond the scope of the present report.

Regional Perspectives

At the regional level, the development of the tourism industry is more advanced in the Mediterranean and Caribbean small island developing States than in those located in the Asia-Pacific and African regions. The two Mediterranean small island developing States, Cyprus and Malta, have experienced brisk expansion of tourism in the past, which is reflected by the high share of tourism in their GDP and their total foreign exchange earnings. In both of them, however, industry remains the dominant sector. The good performance of tourism in these countries is explained in part by their advantageous location in the vicinity of high-income European countries, particularly the United Kingdom of Great Britain and Northern Ireland, their main source market.

In the Caribbean, with a larger number of small island developing States, the pattern of economic performance has become closely linked to the performance of the tourism industry. The direct contribution of tourism in terms of its share in GDP and export earnings is high in most of them. In the wider Caribbean, travel and tourism is the largest relative contributor to the regional economy, at 31.5 per cent of GDP. While in some, the economic base is relatively diversified, in the majority of them most other activities have become increasingly linked to tourism, with agriculture and industry lagging behind. This is particularly the case in the smaller islands which have become essentially service economies. The development of tourism in the Caribbean has been helped by considerable amounts of foreign investments and the fact that they are located in the tropics but in proximity to high-income North America.

The level of development of tourism and its contribution to economic development is more uneven and generally much lower in small island developing States of the Asia-Pacific region than in those in the Mediterranean and Caribbean. In most of them, the level of general economic development is also much lower. Six of them-Maldives, Samoa, Vanuatu, Tuvalu, Kiribati, and Solomon Islands-are actually classified as least developed. Tourism activities are concentrated in only a few. The contribution of tourism to national income is significant only in Fiji, Vanuatu, Samoa, Cook Islands and Maldives. By and large, in small island developing States of this region, agriculture and related activities predominate. Development of tourism in the region has been slow because of low levels of development of physical infrastructures and human resources in most of them, particularly the smaller ones, isolation from the major sources of tourists, problems of communal landownership, extremely weak aviation and communication links, and heavy reliance on foreign investment, with foreign investors concentrating on the most profitable destinations.

In the African region, considerable progress has been achieved in tourism development in Seychelles and Mauritius. In the other three African small island developing States, Sao Tome and Principe, Cape Verde and the Comoros, all of which are classified as least developed, the development of tourism is still in an incipient stage. The slow pace of development of tourism in these countries is attributable to the slow pace of general economic development, and of the development of social and physical infrastructures and human resources in particular, as well as the inadequate importance attached to tourism as a growth sector in the past.

Emerging Trends

The future development of tourism in small island developing States will be affected by two principal current global trends. First, global travel and tourism is expected to grow more rapidly in the coming years, outpacing the growth of world economic output. Between 1995 and 2005, travel and tourism is projected to grow by an annual average rate of 5.5 per cent in real terms and create 12.5 million new direct and indirect jobs annually on the average.

In the wider Caribbean, travel and tourism output is projected to grow at an annual average rate of 3.6 per cent in real terms between 1995 and 2005 and to create 2.7 million jobs. For sustaining Caribbean tourism, the secretariat of the Caribbean Tourism Organization has identified a number of areas of action at the regional level, notably, maintenance of product quality, including the integrity of the natural environment; enhancement of profitability; provision of air access at competitive rates from major tourist markets; provision of a secure environment for the industry by combating crime and drugs; strengthening intersectoral linkages and creation of a regional competitive force through regional collaboration, particularly in the area of overseas marketing and promotion; and creation of social acceptability of the further expansion of tourism by the local population.

A similar trend is expected for Asia and the Pacific. The region as a whole is projected to be the fastest growing area in world tourism activities up to the year 2005. Between 1995 and 2005, the annual average real rate of growth of travel and tourism output in the region is estimated at 8.0 per cent. The South Pacific is expected to share in this growth through further growth of its traditional destinations, as well as through the gradual development of as yet untapped potentials in other islands. In most of the small island developing States of the South Pacific, the growth of tourism will require the removal of several major internal constraints, including the following: shortages of trained staff; inadequacy and infrequency of air transportation; low level and quality of supporting infrastructure-airport facilities, tour operation, restaurants; low budgets for marketing and promotion; lack of investment capital; and restriction on landownership. By far the greatest challenge for the expansion of tourism in the South Pacific small island developing States will be their ability to achieve international competitiveness.

In the African region, Mauritius and Seychelles have planned for further growth but have opted for up-market tourism. They have consequently banned charter flight operations and hope to achieve a slower rate of growth of visitors, with emphasis on higher-spending visitors on scheduled flights.

Of particular concern to these countries is the spread of drugs and of diseases such as the human immunodeficiency virus/ acquired immunodeficiency syndrome (HIV/AIDS), which can impact very severely on their small populations. The other three African small island developing States have considerable room for growth and are just beginning to develop tourism as a growth sector.

In Malta and Cyprus, the rate of growth of tourist arrivals has slowed down in the recent past. This is attributable in part to capacity constraints and in part to deliberate policies to slow down expansion in order to deal with environmental and other adverse impacts of previous rapid expansion. Both countries plan to place considerable importance on tourism as a growth sector for quite some time to come, but have opted for up-market tourism.

A second discernible trend that will shape tourism development in small island developing States in coming years is the growing interest in and demand for speciality tourism. Underlying this trend is greater environmental awareness globally, greater health consciousness, and a growing preference by travellers to experience unspoilt environmental surroundings.

In tandem with this trend, many small island developing States have embarked on a gradual policy of diversification of the tourism package emphasizing to a greater extent other natural assets than the beach and the sea. Diversification of the tourism product also reflects the realization on the part of the authorities in small island developing States of the need to innovate in order to remain competitive.

Risks of Over-reliance on Tourism

Over-reliance on tourism, especially mass tourism, carries significant risks. Economic recession in industrialized countries, their major source of tourists, and the impacts of tropical storms and cyclones to which many of them are particularly prone have devastating effects on the tourism sector and hence on tourism-based island economies. Mass tourism, unlike up-market tourism, is characterized by relatively high income elasticity of demand and is likely to fall off suddenly as a result of economic recessions in the source markets. Excessive reliance on a single major source of tourists, as in Cyprus and Malta on the United Kingdom market, is extremely risky as economic difficulties in the source country have direct adverse impacts on the receiving countries.

In small islands, there is a tendency for fast growth of tourism to be accompanied by inflationary pressures. Prices of real estate, particularly land suitable for building, which is extremely scarce, quickly rise beyond the reach of the local population. Inflationary pressures build up throughout the economy as the prices of locally produced construction materials and consumer goods rise. Although this process means higher profit margins in bottleneck sectors and could stimulate more inward investment, overly accommodating monetary policy could generalize the inflation with adverse consequences for international competitiveness and future investment.

Social and Cultural Impacts

Sudden, rapid development of tourism can cause significant social disruptions in small island States. Pressures are exerted on households and communities by the upward pressure on land prices and prices of foodstuffs and household items. Among other things, potential long-run effects could be a reduction in the living standards of high proportions of island populations and a sense of alienation brought about by their lack of access to limited land resources. Many small island populations also suffer a loss of access to beaches and important leisure areas because of exclusive rights granted to developers. This, in some cases, also translates into economic losses as fishermen and others are adversely affected by loss of access to the sea. Furthermore, excessively high visibility of foreigners can lead to anxieties on the part of the local people and a tendency to blame local problems on them, and thus to a social rejection of the growth of tourism.

An important factor in sustainable tourism development in small island States is the tourist carrying capacity of these societies, in both environmental and social terms. At peak periods, visitors are known to outnumber nationals by multiples in several of the smaller islands. In larger islands such as Jamaica or Fiji, local concentration of tourism often leads to localized problems of carrying capacity, such as overcrowding of beaches, traffic congestion, noise pollution, increased incidence of drugs and crime, and the spread of diseases brought in from outside. The ratios of tourists to local population for a number of small island developing States in 1993. While optimal carrying capacity cannot be quantified with any exactitude, it is generally contended that the population to tourists ratio, i.e., the inverse of what is shown in the table, should be kept at a level that does not exceed social tolerance limits, which may differ from country to country.

Island tourism is invariably centred on sun, sea and sand. However, to the extent that some interaction occurs with local customs and traditions, tourism is sometimes believed to exert a negative sociocultural influence on small island States. A high level of tourism can lead to commercialization, which is thought to cheapen local customs and traditions. Local arts and crafts and cultural practices are sometimes adapted to suit foreign tastes, which leads to the creation of contrived cultural products.

Some research conducted in the Asia-Pacific and Caribbean regions, however, has failed to produce much evidence of major destruction of local cultures as a result of the influence of tourists. On the contrary, the findings indicate that tourism can assist in preserving customs and cultures by providing incentives to invest in and promote them. If properly managed and promoted, local cultures can be given an impetus by the presence of tourists. It is contended, for instance, that the popularization of Jamaican reggae and carnival festivals of Trinidad and Tobago and similar cultural forms in other small island States is a direct result of the influence of tourism.

Environmental Impacts

The fragile ecosystems of small island States and their generally more limited scope for action in development alternatives make concerns for the environmental impact of tourism very acute, particularly because the sector, which is almost totally dependent on the natural environment, is viewed by many small island developing States as a fast route to social and economic development. Intensive tourism development and tourism activities often have very quick and severe impacts on their natural resources. The principal tourism-related environmental difficulties confronting small island developing States are several.

Land Resources and Terrestrial Biological Diversity

The environmental impacts of tourism are attributable to the development of tourism infrastructures and facilities and to the impacts of tourists' activities. In small islands, even more so than elsewhere, there is strong competition for the use of land between tourism and other competing uses. Rising prices of building land increase the pressure to build on agricultural land. Deforestation and intensified or unsuitable use of land cause erosion and loss of biological diversity. In many small island developing States, ecosystems are now being threatened as a result of the development of tourism, which has intensified human interference with vegetation and wildlife. This can lead to irreversible damage to their valuable ecosystems and to traditional activities such as fishing.

Waste Management

For small island developing States, treatment and disposal of liquid and solid wastes constitute a major problem. With limited physical infrastructure, the capacity of many small island States is already strained. This is exacerbated by wastes generated by tourism activities. Examples abound of damages caused by the disposal of untreated effluents into surrounding areas of land and sea. Pollution of scarce inland freshwater resources is one such example. The loss of valuable marine iife, the destruction of coral reefs and the silting and erosion of coastal beaches, on which island tourism highly depends, are others. Pollution from ship-generated wastes is also a major cause for concern for small island developing States. One dimension of this particular threat is the dumping of oily waste, sewage, garbage and cargo residues, which cause marine and beach pollution, by merchant ships plying their seas. Another dimension, particularly for the Caribbean, is the frequency of tourist cruise ships plying that region's seas and generating substantial volumes of liquid and solid wastes for disposal at the ports of call. The following factors have been cited as impeding corrective action: inadequate infrastructure; weak institutional, legislative and enforcement capacities; the absence of a regional consensus on appropriate criteria for sewage, effluents and coastal water standards; and the inability of small island developing States to require cruise ships and other vessels to comply with the provisions of the International Convention for the Prevention of Pollution from Ships regarding generation and disposal of ship wastes.

Coastal Area Degradation

Tourism as a mainly coastal development has already had a number of adverse impacts on small island developing States. In Mauritius, Seychelles, Malta, Cyprus and several islands in the Caribbean, the previously unchecked construction of tourism facilities along their coastlines resulted in the despoliation of much of the originally pristine beauty of these areas. In order to halt the degradation, the Governments of a number of these countries have, of late, taken steps through legislation to restrict and control coastal construction. Stipulations of building size, with limits on height and room capacity, and specifications of design and materials used in construction have been instituted in an effort to correct past errors and ensure better harmony with the natural environment. Beach destruction caused by intensive sand mining for tourism-related construction is also a feature of many coastal areas. This practice has recently been curtailed in Maldives, Seychelles, Mauritius, the Bahamas and Cook Islands, among other States. Beaches destroyed by sand quarrying are not being naturally replenished because of the destruction of coral reefs by sewage and other types of pollution. Erosion owing to tourism facilities and infrastructures built too close to the coast also contributes to beach destruction and coastal degradation. Another common feature of coastal area destruction in small island developing States is the removal of valuable mangrove forests, which act as nesting places for birds and other animal life in addition to their function as a natural barrier against encroachment of the sea. Indiscriminate diving, fishing and boating activities associated with tourism may further contribute to this disturbance. For a detailed discussion of coastal area issues in small island developing States, see the report of the Secretary-General on coastal area management in small island developing States.

Freshwater Resources

The problem of freshwater availability is most severe in the low-lying atolls that have the least opportunity for surface-water catchment and storage. Several other small island developing States also suffer from frequent droughts and chronic water scarcity. On the high volcanic islands, rainfall is in many cases abundant but access to freshwater is often limited by lack of adequate storage facilities and delivery systems. The supply of freshwater relative to the growing demand from agriculture, industry and households is becoming an acute problem in many small island developing States. Added to this is the growing competition of limited water resources from tourism, which is extremely water-intensive.

Climate Change and Sealevel Rise

Island tourism is a climate-sensitive industry, and being largely concentrated in coastal locations is susceptible to sealevel rise. An analysis of data by the Intergovernmental Panel on Climate Change has confirmed a trend in global warming, with increases in temperatures of 0.3 to 0.6 degrees centigrade occurring since the late nineteenth century, much of which has occurred in the past 40 years. The effect of this trend is a rise of mean sealevels at a rate of 1.5 millimetres per year. In small islands and coastal areas in general, that would cause the inundation of coastal and some inland areas, threatening sanitation systems and freshwater supplies as seawater infiltrates subterranean water tables, with possibly catastrophic consequences for island tourism. An erosion of shorelines would undoubtedly bring about severe stress and damage to both natural and built environments, the overall economic consequences of which are currently inestimable. In addition, damages from tropical storms with a possible link to changes in weather patterns have been increasing in recent years. Small island developing States that are especially vulnerable to these phenomena now experience considerable difficulty securing insurance coverage. Reliable sunshine is one of the major tourism assets of tropical islands. Potential threats of climate change, which are beginning to appear in greater health risks from direct exposure to sunlight, may undermine this asset.

Policies, Finance, Capacity-building, Technology and Infrastructure

The present section discusses some of the main policy issues in the area of sustainable development of tourism at the national, regional and international levels. Emphasis is placed on legislation, finance, capacity-building, and sustainable tourism infrastructure and policies as necessary means of implementing the provisions of the Programme of Action.

At the National Level

Development Policy Framework

Tourism development has been incorporated into the overall development plans of some small islands. Some Caribbean island authorities have established tourism master plans, with links to national development plans, and have created national sustainable development commissions or, as in the case of Saint Lucia, a National Sustainable Tourism Commission. In the South Pacific, tourism development plans and policies have been formulated in several small island developing States. However, the level of policy commitment to sustainable tourism development differs from country to country, which in turn influences the degree of action in this area. According to a study by the Economic and Social Commission for Asia and the Pacific (ESCAP), this uneven commitment in the South Pacific can serve as an impediment to the promotion of sustainability at the regional level. By and large, a long-term national policy for sustainable tourism development, with emphasis on natural resource conservation, has yet to evolve. The focus of policies generally continues to be on: (a) creating and improving conditions for attracting foreign investment in tourism;

(b) marketing and promotion of tourism to achieve maximum growth in arrivals; and (c) designing the type of legislative framework that would further those objectives. The prevalence of this situation points to the urgent need for a policy framework for sustainable tourism development in most small island developing States.

Legislative Framework

A necessary requirement for the pursuit of sustainable tourism development is an effective legislative framework. A wide range of laws have been enacted in small island developing States, in many instances since the conclusion of the United Nations Conference on Environment and Development, establishing standards for land use in tourism development, tourism facilities and investment in tourism. Despite progress in the enactment of environmental legislation, its effectiveness continues to be impaired by weaknesses in the institutional frameworks for enforcing legislation, lack of standardization of legislation and the obscurity of regulations. Consequently, the level of enforcement of regulations to ensure sustainability in tourism in many small island developing States leaves much to be desired. Regulations for coastal zone management and the creation of protected areas, both marine and land-based, present a case in point. Their enforcement, particularly in the Caribbean, remains very weak.

Investment

The majority of small island developing States suffer from a lack of local capital for bulky investments and, in many cases, the absence of a significant local entrepreneurial class. The financing required for the development of the tourism sector is therefore obtained largely through foreign investment. Special efforts are made by Governments of small island developing States to attract foreign capital through the provision of tax breaks, tax holidays, building concessions and other incentives to foreign investors. While that may well be necessary to some extent, competition among small island developing States to attract foreign capital for tourism development often leads to the provision of over-generous financial incentives to foreign investors which deprive all these States of part of the income from tourism. Moreover, since small island developing States are over-reliant on foreign capital, they are unable to impose environmental sustainability conditions on foreign investors. Both to derive the maximum benefits from tourism and to avoid environmental deterioration from tourism activities, there is a need for small island developing States to jointly adopt uniform incentive and environmental policies, at least at the regional level.

While efforts at encouraging local investment and participation in the sector have increased in many small island developing States, considerably more effort is needed. Such efforts are, in many cases, hampered by the inability of the private sector in most small island developing States to raise adequate capital.

A judicious mix of foreign and local investment, and especially the encouragement of joint ventures, would be one way of ensuring the adequacy of capital resources for sustainable tourism development and the fuller participation of nationals in the sector.

Aside from foreign direct investment in tourism, the bulk of tourism-related services are also known to be largely in the control of foreign operators in a number of small island developing States. Overseas sales and marketing, and promotion of tourism packages for most small island developing States, are undertaken by outside entities.

Several domestic operations are also handled by foreigners. In this area, there is a need for increased investments in the training of nationals for greater participation in tourism.

In order to supplement the efforts of the private sector at ensuring sustainability in the tourism sector, greater non-governmental organization/government partnerships in tourism development could be developed.

Such partnerships can be useful, especially in the restoration, development and maintenance of cultural and historical sites, while ensuring conservation and profitability. Funds for investment in such activities could be raised through mechanisms already existing in many cases, such as increases in airport taxes and airline ticket taxes, as long as they meet International Civil Aviation Organization (ICAO) stipulations, and entrance fees for tourism sites.

Human and Institutional Capacity

45. Most small island States face the persistent problem of inadequate supply of trained manpower, particularly in government agencies responsible for the implementation and monitoring of standards and environmental regulations in tourism. The shortage of skilled human resources is compounded by the dispersion in some States of roles and responsibilities among several government agencies.

To address these weaknesses, an integrated approach to tourism planning and environmental conservation, coupled with training at all levels, needs immediate attention in all small island States. A system for monitoring the implementation of sustainable tourism policies must also form part of an integrated approach to tourism planning and the building up of institutional capacity. A study by ESCAP found that national tourism organizations, important mechanisms in the development and implementation of sustainable tourism policies, are largely under-staffed and underfunded. The study also found that attempts by individual small island States to market their tourism product themselves have not been significantly effective in most cases because of the high costs involved and the lack of skilled human resources. Overall, the shortcomings of capacity could be better addressed through greater regional collaboration.

Infrastructure

The main physical infrastructural requirements for tourism development include the following: effective transportation facilities, including airports and air and/or sea carrier links; reasonably good road networks; telecommunication links; reliable energy supply systems; freshwater supply systems; accommodation facilities; restaurants and entertainment sites. For many small island developing States, the inadequacy of these infrastructures is an obstacle to the development of the sector. In some of the smaller Pacific islands in this category, efforts are being made to build new airport facilities. This is regarded as a necessary initial step to their fuller participation in tourism. In the Caribbean, where the sector is more developed, air links to long-haul markets such as Germany, Italy and France are being extended.

Many small island developing States are confronted with severe infrastructural inadequacies consequent to the growth of tourism. Many of them suffer from chronic shortages of freshwater supply for their own use, a problem that is further aggravated by the high demand of large tourist populations.

Liquid and solid waste disposal present a colossal problem to all small island developing States but especially to those that are tourism-based. Another dimension is added to this problem by the requirement of facilities to handle waste brought to their ports by cruise lines which frequent small island destinations.

The diversification of the tourism product through the development of nature and cultural tourism also necessitates additional infrastructural and environmental requirements. Some sites are remote and may require additional access routes and other infrastructures such as those for the supply of water and electricity, and new accommodation. These requirements are particularly burdensome to the archipelagic small island developing States. Generally, when developing infrastructure, the issue of the carrying capacity of the destination must also be considered.

Technology

Sector-specific technology needs of small island developing States are discussed in various reports to the Commission on Sustainable Development at its fourth session which highlight the need for the introduction or more widespread use of certain technologies by tourism enterprises and Governments of small island developing States, as appropriate.

Some examples are: (a) solar technology for cooling of hotels and for water heating; (b) environmentally sound technologies for the treatment, recycling and disposal of solid wastes generated by tourism facilities and those brought to port by cruise ships; (c) telecommunications technologies for the fuller integration of small island developing States into global telecommunications networks to enhance their marketing and promotion operations; and (d) electronic information technologies to enhance day-to-day tourism operations, such as reservations.

At the Regional Level

The need for greater collaboration among small island developing States on issues of sustainable tourism development is well recognized. Collaboration and cooperation could lead to greater long-term benefits for the environment and the economies of small island developing States, particularly in an increasingly competitive global arena. The harmonization of standards and regulations, including legislative actions to govern tourism, has been identified as a critical need in the Programme of Action for the Sustainable Development of Small Island Developing States and by some regional authorities. Integrated tourism development planning, marketing and promotion can increase both effectiveness and efficiency. Joint overseas marketing and promotion would help achieve benefits of economies of scale and increased value-added in the tourism sector. Overseas marketing and promotion by individual small island developing States entail a heavy cost to each of these States and reduce significantly their net foreign exchange earnings from tourism.

The Programme of Action provides for the pursuit of regional initiatives in: (a) the harmonization of standards and regulations to ensure that tourism and the environment are mutually supportive; (b) the promotion of cooperation in developing potential complementarities in the tourism sector; and (c) the establishment of mechanisms for information exchange and sharing of experiences, particularly through existing regional tourism organizations. The ESCAP report cited above has identified, in addition to those measures, the need for regional collaboration in: (a) integrating tourism development planning, including concerted market development and promotion; (b) strengthening and expanding the roles of national and regional tourism institutions and organs; and (c) promoting joint training and manpower development in tourism.

In recent years, attempts have been made, particularly in the two main regions-the Pacific and the Caribbean-to consolidate efforts in sustainable tourism development by forging common regional approaches for the sector. The necessary institutional framework currently exists for these regions in the form of the Tourism Council of the South Pacific and the Caribbean Tourism

Organization. These institutions have been mandated by the respective regional political forums-the South Pacific Forum and the Caribbean Community (CARICOM)-to strengthen regional cooperation in tourism development, planning and promotion. Provision for some financial support has been made for both institutions under the Caribbean and Pacific regional tourism development programmes funded by the Lome' Convention concluded between the European Community and the African, Caribbean and Pacific States.

In spite of many difficulties, the Tourism Council of the South Pacific has been successful as a regional agency in the area of marketing and promotion of the South Pacific as a tourist destination, but not in the area of strategy and planning. For the Caribbean small island developing States, the political framework was consolidated with the formation in 1995 of the Association of Caribbean States (ACS), which has identified the tourism sector as one of three areas for high-priority measures for wider regional cooperation. Regional cooperation in the area of tourism has been further strengthened by the formation of the Caribbean Coalition for Tourism, with the goal of creating the largest possible pool of resources for cooperative marketing by drawing on the resources of the widest range of players both in the public and in the private sectors. Resource constraint has been recognized as an impediment for both TCSP and CTO to adequately cover the broad range of activities that they must undertake to increase market awareness, promote sustainability, develop human resources and carry out marketing and promotion. External assistance is seen as essential to the viability of both institutions. Increased support for these bodies, aside from regional Governments, will be contingent upon increased involvement of the private sector in their work. The inadequacy of political will to cooperate meaningfully is also seen as a major impediment to effective cooperation in both regions.

In the African region, there is little evidence of meaningful effort at regional cooperation in the area of tourism development. This may be due in large part to the dispersion of the African small island developing States, three off the east coast and two off the west coast of Africa, and the considerable disparity in development and policy emphasis on tourism among these countries. Given the recognized potential for tourism development, however, there is a need to begin efforts within this region for a common approach to sustainable tourism development through an integrated subregional policy.

In the areas of joint training and manpower development, tourism research and experience-sharing efforts at regional collaboration have been made to varying extents within the regions. The pooling within each region of the limited financial and technical resources of individual small island developing States for capacity-building would be immensely beneficial to all those States. Collaboration in information exchange and research could be achieved through the strengthening of regional tourism institutions. A priority need in this respect is for training in the use of state-of-the-art information technologies at the regional level for the monitoring of environmental impacts of tourism, and for the establishment and operation of central reservation systems.

A major area for regional cooperation is air transportation. Two considerations are worthy of note in this connection. First, small island developing States cannot depend solely on foreign carriers, which must make decisions in the best interest of their owners regarding services, routes and schedules. Such decisions may not always coincide with the best interest of the countries. Besides, even a major airline serving small island developing States in a region can suddenly disappear. Secondly, small island developing States, except for a few, cannot each maintain a viable airline. An effective solution from the point of view of cost and adequacy of air transportation for the tourism industry would be regionally owned and managed carriers, with provision for regional functional cooperation. For a detailed discussion on air transport needs for small island developing States, see the report of the Secretary-General on air transport in small island developing.

Country Experiences

The economic prospects of many small island developing States depend significantly on a productive tourism sector. For the States, generally, the furtherance of sustainable tourism development is an economic as well as a socio-environmental imperative. In these countries, tourism actually provides an economic rationale for safeguarding the natural environment. Many of the policies that underpin sustainable development were recognized and elaborated in a number of small island developing States prior to the United Nations Conference on Environment and Development and were given further impetus by it and by the Barbados Conference. For instance, Maldives, concerned about sustainability in the wake of rapid tourism development, recognized the need for the establishment of a National Environment Council to address those concerns as far back as 1985. The preparation of a national environment action programme, as well as a related work programme, was completed in 1989, with provision for the systematic inclusion of environmental issues in the country's national development plan. Specific policies have been adopted to promote sustainable tourism development, particularly in the areas of waste disposal, use of coral reefs and construction in coastal sites and for the type and diversity of accommodation.

Policies aimed at the creation of national parks and the encouragement of visits to wildlife refuges, bird sanctuaries and other natural beauty spots have been put in place in Seychelles and Mauritius as a means of diversifying the tourism product with a possible spin-off benefit for the protection and conservation of these sites. The drive for product diversification and the enhancement of natural endowments is also very strong in the Caribbean. Several legislative acts have been passed in individual countries of this region with the objective of addressing environmental problems. For example, in Saint Lucia, a National Sustainable Tourism Commission was established and a National Environmental Action Plan was prepared for implementation in 1994. A Minimum Standards Act was scheduled for adoption in 1995, with a view to addressing all areas of hotel, restaurant and tourist carrying capacity. A Development Control Act has also been approved by the Saint Lucia authorities, making the conduct of environmental impact assessment and its incorporation into all decision-making processes mandatory. Jamaica recently carried out a review of existing environmental legislation. The review resulted in the passage of new legislation requiring the conduct of environmental impact assessment for all new developments. In some small island developing States where rapid tourism expansion has given rise to problems of sustainability and over-reliance on tourism as a major sector, several measures have been taken in an attempt to overcome such problems. A case in point is Cyprus, where pollution, beach erosion, physical carrying capacity and difficulties of competitive pressures on other economic sectors have been felt. Efforts have been made through the use of economic instruments and legislation to achieve sustainability and balance. Various new tax incentives have been introduced to diversify and upgrade the tourism product and a new marketing strategy focus is directed at improving tourist quality. Additionally, fiscal instruments are now being used to encourage sound land use and coastal zone practices aimed particularly at slowing down and improving coastal development and efficient allocation and use of water and other resources. Simultaneously, a policy of economic restructuring in the manufacturing and agriculture sectors have been put in place in order to improve their overall competitiveness and linkages with tourism.

Diversification within or away from tourism has been undertaken in many small island developing States, notably in Cyprus and Malta. Several constraining factors have been recognized, including a generally limited scope and capacity for novel forms of tourism development in small islands, a usually small proportion of visitors interested in other forms of activity, and more importantly, the fact that all aspects of tourism accommodation and other facilities have been geared towards traditional forms of tourism. The authorities in Mauritius and Seychelles have also adopted some policies for diversification within tourism, particularly in targeting high-spending visitors and in encouraging to some extent inland and nature tourism. In the foreseeable future, however, the need for continued mass tourism is acknowledged largely because of an existing over-capacity in tourism. A spin-off benefit of the thrust for quality has been a general upgrading of facilities and greater attention to avoiding negative impacts. Mauritius has been relatively successful in achieving some degree of economic diversification and balanced growth through the development of export processing zones and, to a lesser extent, agricultural modernization and diversification.

In the Comoros and Cape Verde, the Governments and private sector have recently demonstrated heightened interest in tourism development. The institutional groundwork has been prepared in the Comoros with the adoption in 1994 of a national environmental policy document and an environmental plan of action, and the creation in 1995 of the Association Touristique Comorienne.

The implementation of these plans, however, is subject to a number of constraints, including poor levels of infrastructure development, particularly hotels, poor air and communication links with tourist-generating areas and some degree of political instability. Recent initiatives in Cape Verde include the adoption of a tourism development plan and the establishment of a National Institute for Tourism. The main constraints identified are the following: a lack of interest by the local and foreign private sector; a lack of demonstrated support by donors for the tourism development plan; and limited domestic financial resources.

Dominica has formally launched eco-tourism as the main form of tourism development. The island is mountainous, boasts few beaches but has 60 per cent forest cover containing many endemic species of plants, animals and birds.

Two large national parks, two forest reserves and a Carib Indian reservation form the basis of eco-tourism attractions. The Government of Dominica has enacted legislation to ensure heritage and natural resource preservation, and the creation of linkages with local economic activities.

While no scientific assessment has been conducted of the impact of increased human activity on the natural environment, several negative trends have been observed, among which are the accumulation of litter and garbage around nature sites, the extraction of plants from protected areas and the effects of the use of soap by local people in rivers and natural pools. Based on the experience of Dominica, concerns have been expressed regarding issues of carrying capacity and the impact of large numbers of tourists on environmentally sensitive ecologies. Although the adoption of regulations and policy guidelines can be seen as an indication of government commitment to sustainability, weaknesses persist in the management and policing of protected areas and tourism sites. Another unique feature of the experience of Dominica is the emphasis on participation by the local population through tax exemptions for local shareholder participation in hotels and other ventures.

Experiences of Major Groups and Non-governmental Organizations

Private Sector

A survey conducted by the World Travel and Tourism Council indicates that in much of the private sector, the pursuit of sustainability measures in tourism is gradually becoming a matter of sound business practice. Little by little, recognition of the link between conservation measures on the one hand and profitability and competitiveness on the other is taking hold. Some private sector companies involved in travel and tourism have reported positive results from conservation measures, in the form of increased profitability, a rise in staff morale and an enhanced image among their clientele.

In order to develop voluntary practice approaches, tourism industry associations have emphasized the use of voluntary environmental codes of conduct and guidelines.

Through a survey and publication, the United Nations Environment Programme (UNEP)Industry and Environment Programme Activities Centre has identified more than 30 codes, among them, those prepared by main industry associations such as the World Travel and Tourism Council, the Pacific Asia Travel Association, the American Society of Travel and the International Hotels Environment Initiative.

An emerging feature among some multinational businesses, particularly in the hotel sector, is resort to voluntary measures for conservation, primarily with a view to securing strategic advantages, but also as a means of precluding more costly retrofitting that may be required by future government regulations. However, to date, most efforts have focused on energy and water conservation, waste minimization and product purchase. New tourism developments should more often incorporate improved plant designs, and improved energy-efficient features that will enable greater natural lighting, natural cooling of accommodation facilities, and waste treatment and water recycling.

Already, some progress can be noted: hotel staff are being trained to adopt energy-and water-saving, and waste-minimization measures during cleaning; and hotel guests are being encouraged to minimize water use by the reuse of towels and linens. Product purchase measures are being instituted, for example, through switching from phosphate-free cleaning products to those known to have less harmful properties.

In the Asia-Pacific region, the development of integrated resorts is setting a new trend in resort development with the key objective of exercising greater control over environmental quality as a means of providing a guarantee of quality to guests. New complexes are built with all facilities on site, with particular emphasis on water conservation and recycling, energy supply and conservation, and waste management.

Non-governmental Organization and Community Involvement

The growing trend of environmental awareness globally is accompanied by an increase in international and national environmental movements in tourism development. For instance, at the international level, the International Scientific Council for Island Development, with the support of the Government of Spain and the sponsorship of several organizations, spearheaded the convening of the World Conference on Sustainable Tourism at Lanzarote, Canary Islands, in April 1995. The Conference adopted a Charter for Sustainable Tourism which affirms, inter alia, that: (a) tourism must be sustainable and integrated with the natural, cultural and human environment; (b) the achievement of sustainability is contingent upon integrated planning and cooperation at all levels; (c) tourism development must contribute to local economic development and improve the quality of life of all people; and (d) the benefits and burdens of tourism must be more equitably distributed.

In consequence of the Conference, a follow-up committee responsible for the dissemination of the Charter and for the promotion of related studies, projects and actions was established; and the launching of a European network for sustainable tourism development in islands and coastal zones was proposed. The objective of the network is to generate and diffuse information and know-how on the promotion of environmentally sound tourism. Like industry associations, non-governmental organizations such as the Ecotourism Society and the World Wide Fund for Nature Tourism Concern have also developed codes of conduct and guidelines for tourism. At the regional level, the Caribbean Conference on Sustainable Tourism, which was held at Punta Cana, Dominican Republic, towards the end of 1995, under the sponsorship of Earthkind International and the Earth Pledge Foundation, explored a wide range of issues relating to sustainable tourism in that region. A similar conference is planned for the South Pacific in 1996.

At the local level, the involvement of non-governmental organizations, community groups and local authorities in the promotion and development of sustainable tourism policies is just beginning but a discernible trend is apparent in some small island developing States. The following are examples of recent initiatives: in Trinidad and Tobago, a project has been put in place at Matura Beach to train community youths as tour guides, with the goal of preventing poaching of leather back turtles, an endangered species; in Jamaica, resort boards, which include representatives of non-governmental organizations, the local community and business enterprises, have been established in the main tourism areas of Ocho Rios, Montego Bay, Negril and Port Antonio for overseeing all aspects of tourism policy, practice and development; in Mauritius, the authorities have published The Mauritian Code of Ethics for Tourism: For Mauritians. The Code, which focuses largely on the social and cultural aspects of tourism, presents guidelines for use by the local community in their dealings with tourists.

Activities and Experiences in International Cooperation in Sustainable Tourism Development

Organs of the United Nations System

A number of organizations and bodies of the United Nations system have reported plans and activities in the area of tourism development, in keeping with the Programme of Action. The United Nations Development Programme has reported that its programme of assistance in the South Pacific and in some small island developing States in the other regions addresses issues relating to sustainable tourism development within the overall national environmental plans of the countries concerned. The Economic Commission for Latin America and the Caribbean (ECLAC) and ESCAP have planned or recently implemented specific activities in tourism.

ECLAC has reported that proposals for environmental codes of conduct for the tourism sector, which it recently developed, are now being carried out by the Caribbean Tourism Organization. ESCAP has reported that in 1995, it convened a workshop on integrated tourism planning in Pacific island countries and published a set of studies on foreign investment in the tourism sector in Samoa and Vanuatu. The United Nations University is currently undertaking a study to examine indicators of sustainability for the tourism sector in small islands, along with a project on eco-tourism. It is expected that the results of these two undertakings will be useful to small island developing States.

In 1992-1993, the World Heritage Convention, sponsored by the United Nations Educational, Scientific and Cultural Organization (UNESCO), in collaboration with UNEP, carried out surveys on tourism management in natural and mixed heritage sites and subsequently convened an international seminar which helped formulate a set of general principles for tourism development in natural heritage sites. During 1994-1995, UNESCO collaborated with several regional initiatives on tourism in the Asia-Pacific region.

The Earth Sciences Division of UNESCO has undertaken modelling of human-induced geomorphologic change to serve as a guide to improved planning of human settlements. In addition, UNESCO has planned a world heritage promotion seminar for the Caribbean, and a pilot project on water supply problems and community attitudes in the South Pacific islands, as well as studies with reference to the Caribbean on the interrelationships between tourism, population pressures, pollution and natural hazards. In 1993, through the Pan American Health Organization Regional Office, the World Health Organization collaborated with a number of regional organizations to launch the Environmental Health and

Sustainable Tourism Development Initiative for the Caribbean and to convene the Regional Conference on Environmental Health and Sustainable Development in the Caribbean. UNEP is making efforts to promote integrated coastal zone management in small island developing States through its regional seas programme. The Mediterranean Action Plan and the Caribbean Action Plan have in particular addressed tourism issues. The Industry and Environment Office of UNEP has developed fruitful partnerships with industry associations at the international level to inform about and disseminate examples of good environmental practices, in particular on codes of conduct and environment management of hotels. The Food and Agriculture Organization of the United Nations has planned two regional workshops in 1996, one for the Caribbean and one for the South Pacific small island developing States. One of the items on the agenda of both workshops will be linkages of tourism with agriculture, forestry and fisheries.

Other Intergovernmental Bodies

In addition to the Tourism Council of the South Pacific and the Caribbean Tourism Organization, both of which are intergovernmental bodies whose activities have been discussed above, the Organization of American States (OAS) and the European Union have been active in promoting sustainable tourism development in small island developing States. OAS has assisted Caribbean small island developing States in various policy studies on sustainable tourism. The European Union has provided assistance, under ongoing cooperation arrangements, in carrying out a number of tourism development projects in African, Caribbean and Pacific small island developing States.

Main Findings

Tourism already makes an important contribution to economic growth, employment and foreign exchange earnings in the majority of small island developing States. It provides an opportunity to most of them for economic diversification and growth.

Looking to the future, there are indications that the development of tourism in small island developing States will be subject to two current global trends. First, global travel and tourism output is expected to grow more rapidly in coming years, outpacing the growth of world economic output. This trend is expected to reinforce current trends in small island developing States. Secondly, tourism development in these countries will be shaped by the growing interest in, and demand for, speciality tourism, particularly nature tourism propelled by growing environmental awareness. To these trends may be added another, namely, an apparent upward trend in global warming and sealevel rise, the persistence of which would have devastating impacts on island tourism.

From the point of view of the future course of action, the following findings on the economic, social and environmental aspects of tourism in small island developing States are worthy of note:

(a) Economic aspects. (i) Generally, the leakages through imports out of direct tourist expenditures to meet the needs of the tourism sector itself are extremely high in these countries; (ii) the daily expenditures per visitor vary from country to country but are generally low; (iii) excessive reliance on tourism carries many risks, including excessive exposure to international economic shocks and weakening of intersectoral linkages which, inter alia, reduce the potential benefits from tourism;

(b) Social aspects. Rapid development of tourism, particularly mass tourism, can have significant adverse social impacts in small islands. The following are of particular significance: (i) persistent inflationary pressures pose the danger of significantly worsening the household distribution of income; (ii) the social carrying capacity of small islands quickly reaches its limits of tolerance as the ratio of visitors to the local population rises, causing overcrowding of beaches, noise pollution and exacerbating traffic congestion; (iii) prolonged growth of mass tourism may be accompanied by increased incidence of crime, and spread of drugs and diseases, including HIV/AIDS;

(c) Environmental aspects. Intensive tourism development and tourism activities, particularly if not properly planned and managed, can very quickly cause environmental damages in small island developing States. The most notable impacts are observable in (i) land degradation and loss of terrestrial and marine biodiversity; (ii) increased levels of pollution from dumping of solid and liquid wastes generated by tourism activities on land and in the sea; (iii) coastal zone degradation through intensive sand mining, removal of mangrove forests and destruction of coral reefs, erosion and destruction of landscape owing to tourism facilities and associated infrastructures; (iv) freshwater shortages aggravated by the demand from the water-intensive tourism industry, excessive groundwater pumping and consequent lowering of water tables.

6

Sustainable Tourism Trends

Introduction

Tourism is often promoted as the world's fastest growing industry and ecotourism is quoted as the fastest growing component of this. The tourism potential to natural areas is vast. Reflecting the explosive growth in global ecotourism there has been a large number of ecotourism organisations and centres established.

Organisations include The Ecotourism Society (TES), a surrogate global ecotourism association which is based in the United States of America and The Ecotourism Association of Australia (EAA). Centres include The Institute of Ecotourism, Srinakharinwirot University, Bangkok, Thailand; the World Travel and Tourism Research Centre (WRTTERC) in Oxford, England; the International Centre for Ecotourism Research (ICER) Gold Coast, Australia; and the Centre for Ecotourism, at the University of Pretoria South Africa. Tourism, and in particular ecotourism, is growing rapidly in Indonesia, Malaysia and Thailand. Now many other South East Asian nations such as Brunei, Cambodia, Myanmar and Vietnam are poised to benefit from the emerging popularity of ecotourism.

Ecotourism has been defined as tourism and recreation that is both nature-based and sustainable (Lindberg and McKercher 1997). It is a subset of natural area tourism and may combine elements of both nature based tourism and adventure travel. However, it is also characterised by a number of other features-notably its educative element and conservation supporting practice. There are five key principles which are fundamental to ecotourism. They are that ecotourism is nature-based, ecologically sustainable, environmentally educative, locally beneficial and generates tourist satisfaction. The first three characteristics are considered to be essential for a product to be considered 'ecotourism' while the last two characteristics are viewed as being desirable for all forms of tourism.

Ecotourism has the potential to be a major market segment to be targeted for the expansion and promotion of nature based tourism resources within the countries of South East Asia. It has come to signify an attractive investment proposition especially in countries at a growing stage of development. Within developing countries it is estimated to earn US$12 billion from an overall US$55 billion in tourism earnings. Therefore ecotourism, can provide the economic basis for the conservation and protection of natural areas. Moreover, since many of the natural attractions are located away from urban areas it has the potential for regional revitalisation. An indication of the commitment to ecologically sustainable tourism within the region is shown by the fact that over 500 South East Asian companies exhibited at the 18th annual Association of South East Asian Nation's (ASEAN) forum on tourism held on the Philippine Island of Cebu in January 1998. At the conference the three ASEAN travel associations, the Tourism Association, the Federation of Travel Associations and the Hotel and Restaurant Association, met to discuss plans to improve the quality and sustainability of tourism within the region.

In addition, some South East Asian countries are to be commended for the legislation introduced in order to ensure the protection of the environment and organisations such as the Pacific Asia Travel Association (PATA) were amongst the first to develop an environmental ethic. The principles of sustainable tourism are to a large extent expressed in PATA's charter and include strategies for tourism development which benefits both the host country and population. Thus ecotourism is based on the premise espoused by PATA that environmentally responsible policies fully respect the natural and cultural identity of tourism resources. However, the development of ecotourism has not occurred without difficulties.

Frequent problems associated with the advancement of ecotourism within these countries include the lack of infrastructure development, the need for, and adequacy of, personnel training, the implementation of plans, and political instability. This paper now addresses the impacts of ecotourism operations within selected ASEAN countries, focusing on Thailand, and poses the question 'is South East Asian ecotourism environmentally appropriate?'

Ecotourism is South East Asia

Issues of ecotourism development in a range of ASEAN countries including Indonesia, Malaysia, Brunei and Vietnam is now illustrated through a series of selected vignettes.

Indonesia

Tourism is of great importance to the Indonesian economy and has been accorded progressively higher priority in the Repelites or five year plans. It is postulated that Indonesia brought ecoawareness to the South East Asian region with the 1991 PATA conference 'Enrich the Environment' being hosted in Bali. Traditionally tourism within Indonesia has been highly concentrated focusing on Bali and Jakarta. Now the country is promoting ecotourism as a major income earner with the government's current policy being to expand tourism from the nation's traditional, developed sites into remote and sometimes sensitive areas. For example, Komodo National Park in eastern Indonesia, the nation's oldest park and home of the world's largest monitor lizard, the Komodo Dragon, is keenly touting for tourists. The island is becoming increasingly popular as an ecotourism destination and the number of visitors has risen from around 3,400 per year in the late 1970s to over 12,000 per year in the early 1990s.

Unfortunately there is a tendency for investors to capitalise on the ecotourism market regardless of whether or not it is being practiced responsibly. This is illustrated by comparisons of tourism developments in Kuta Bali and Kuta Lombok. Both islands foster ecotourism but have not found an adequate balance amongst the elements of environmental, economic and social sustainability. Wall's (1996) summation of ecotourism development in the two destinations presents an interesting contrast. He concludes that tourism development has taken place rapidly, but haphazardly in Kuta, Bali in the absence of firm planning guidelines. As a result, the environment appears to be suffering many adverse consequences. In contrast the more detailed planning in Kuta, Lombok has encouraged greater environmental protection. However, he warns that there will be difficult challenges in providing an adequate water supply in the relatively remote and dry area if substantial development occurs along the southern coast of the island. Thus Indonesia is facing increased demand for ecotourism and appears to be keen to meet this demand, whatever the cost.

Malaysia

Another country which is progressively marketing ecotourism is Malaysia. As hosts of the XVI Commonwealth Games later this year Malaysia has launched a year-long global tourism promotion aimed at raising awareness of the country's new sport and leisure facilities. However, most of its attractions are nature based and ecotourism is being heavily promoted. Malaysia's tropical rainforests are amongst the oldest and most diverse ecosystems in the world. Current tourist visitation and consequent adverse environmental and social impacts are not a problem, but this is a situation which will have to be monitored especially with the government's aspiration that by the year 2000 there should be one tourist per head of population.

The Seventh Malaysian Plan is designed to boost the country's tourism industry by popularising the country's considerable natural attractions. The plan promotes ecotourism which is particularly targeted for intensive development. Eligible projects include the construction of new accommodation and recreational facilities. This strategy focuses on eight tourist destinations most of which are in natural areas. They include Langkawi, Penang, Pangkor, Taman Negara, Malacca, Sarawak and Mount Kinabalu. The plan emphasises capitalising on existing attractions and promoting the surrounding tropical hinterlands. One example occurs in Batang Ai, Sarawak. Here the development of ecotourism has created employment opportunities for the local villagers as well as helping to reduce the hunting pressure on exotic wildlife.

Tourism Malaysia is heavily promoting Sarawak and Sabah as nature and adventure tourism destinations. Recent research at Bako National Park, an established ecotourism destination in Sarawak, clearly identifies some of the negative and positive impacts of ecotourism (Chin, Moore & Dowling In Preparation). A survey of 210 visitors indicates that the more common adverse environmental impacts observed includes litter, erosion and damage to vegetation. Specific issues are litter along the beach, soil erosion and vegetation damage along walk trails, the provocation of wildlife, and a lack of enforcement of park regulations. Most visitors strongly support the management strategies of educating visitors more about conservation; providing additional directional signs and maps; limiting overall number of visitors; limiting areas of forest use; and limiting the number of people in a group. Activities participated in by most respondents include photography, hiking, sightseeing and observation of wildlife. This study indicates that adverse ecotourism impacts are apparent at Bako National Park, and visitors generally notice their occurrence. The study has important implications not only for Bako's park managers, but also for managers of other national parks in Sarawak because it represents one of the first efforts to address conservation management based on the outcomes of nature tourism.

Robert Basiuk, the managing director of the Kuching-based Borneo Adventure, feels that ecotour operators should focus on providing good guides. He suggests that there is a need to raise the minimum standard to ensure that such tours are operated in a manner commensurate with the principles of ecotourism. He suggests that the protection of the natural environment is important if products are to be promoted for the long term. A similar view is shared by David Gill from the National Park and Wildlife Office of Miri's Forest Department. He believes that Sarawak should make it the highest priority to conserve what it has, in particular the rainforest which is its greatest asset.

Sabah is also being promoted as an ecotourism destination with the recent completion of a number of new accommodation facilities. For example, last year Shangri-La opened a second, five star hotel in Sabah, located on the edge of the rainforest 40 minutes drive from the capital, Kota Kinabalu. The 330 room hotel has an 18 hole golf course and its own 64 hectare wildlife reserve Sabah's in bound operation also offers soft adventure activities such as natural history tours, including trips to the Sandakan orangutan sanctuary in the northeast of the island.

However, despite the growth of ecotourism in Malaysia concerns for its future have been voiced by Geoffrey Davison, a conservationist with the World Wide Fund for Nature, Malaysia. He states that Malaysia has about 20 ecotourism sites all of which are so over-used that new sites will have to be developed otherwise ecotourism will become unsustainable. He describes the attention given to ecotourism as slight and patchy and suggests that only a few operators have a credible ecotourism record. Operators have been slow to develop new ecotourism products mainly due to economic constraints and lack of expertise. In addition profit margins derived from ecotours in the country are slim. To minimise costs some operators have not invested in the research and development of new products.

Brunei

Tourism in Brunei is still in its infancy and it has not yet reached the level of development found in Sarawak and Sabah. However, ecotourism offers the country the promise of sustainable tourism development through its relatively low impact use of natural resources. Brunei's newly established tourism unit is currently positioning the country as the gateway to Borneo as a whole because it is considered too small to sell itself as a holiday destination in its own right. Brunei is beginning to work with its neighbouring states of Sabah and Sarawak to jointly promote Borneo and it is the only destination on the island with direct flights from Europe. The case for fostering ecotourism development in Brunei is suggested as being "particularly attractive and compelling". He states that it fits in well with the national policy of keeping the country's land covered by about 80 percent forest. These forests are gazetted for conservation purposes but have much potential for ecotourism which could also generate economic benefits for the indigenous people. These include establishing markets for their jungle produce and handicrafts and providing services as transport operators, porters and guides. In Brunei the development of ecotourism has been spearheaded by the Forestry Department and various blocks have been converted for recreation. The Batu Apoi Forest Reserve has been converted into a national park. A number of 50 metre high observation towers have been built which are linked by some of the longest aerial walkways in the world. In Brunei Bay and in the Belait District additional walkways have been built over mangrove swamps. Observation platforms have been erected in Batang Duri and the S. Liang Arboretum Forest Reserve and wooden chalets have been built at the beach park in Pantai Sri Kenangan, Tutong. The parks are small and are unable to provide a wide range of ecotourism activities thus giving credence to the argument for the establishment of large integrated nature reserves with multi-faceted facilities for visitors. However, it must be noted that to replace forest production by nature based ecotourism will not necessarily guarantee sustainability of the natural, cultural and economic environments.

Vietnam

The Socialist Republic of Vietnam has significant potential for tourism development and it is rich in natural and cultural tourism assets. Its new economic policy of 'doi moi' or 'openness' is facilitating considerable tourism development and it is anticipated that the country will attract about 1.5 million international visitors by the year 2000.

In 1991 a tourism development master plan for the Vietnam was published by the World Tourism Organisation (WTO) in collaboration with a United Nations Development Plan. The government has recognised the importance of the development of tourism by making it a priority industry for national development. This has involved preparing a new master plan focussing on infrastructure requirements, education and the marketing of tourism. Vietnam has certain advantages as an international tourism destination through its central geographical location in South East Asia combined with its ability to cater for tourists all year round. One of the new tourism concepts proposed is 'Vietnam by train'. This will disperse tourism over many regions of the country with minimal environmental impact and low infrastructure costs. In the future it is also proposed to build rail links with China and Cambodia.

Tourism development is being concentrated in and around four main economic zones. Northern Vietnam is to developed as the staging area for excursions to Ha Long Bay, with its famous scenery, beaches and ocean for cruising. The southern part of the central zone has greater potential for ecotourism. There is an abundance of natural resources favouring coastal resort development and consequent nature based activities in the terrestrial (mountain climbing and rafting) and marine (boating and recreational fishing) environments. The preservation of the environment is identified as a key issue for this area. For example, there is a need to prevent forest destruction, the pollution of the Perfume River (which flows through Hue) and the Han River (which flows through Danang) and in general the pollution of water, air and the coastline. Southern Vietnam will particularly foster ecotourism based on the central node of Ho Chi Minh City. It appears that the Vietnamese government is committed to develop tourism along sustainable guidelines. However, the achievement of this development will be difficult in light of the urgent need for Vietnam to earn foreign exchange and because of its limited resources and knowledge. The issue of sustainability therefore hinges on the political will of the government and the ability of the tourism sector to learn from other countries in the region which have developed sustainable types of tourism.

Thailand

Thailand is promoting itself as an international destination and the gateway to other Indo China countries, such as neighbouring Vietnam, Myanmar, Cambodia, Malaysia and Singapore. The government is hoping that its current 'Amazing Thailand' campaign will attract approximately 18 million visitors over the next two years. As part of the promotion cultural performances are being held across the country during 1998 and 1999. Today Thailand is at the forefront of ecotourism development within the South East Asian region with the release of its national ecotourism strategy (TAT 1995). Further enunciation of their interest is demonstrated in the holding of a large number of ecotourism conferences within the past three years. These include two international ecotourism conferences hosted by The Institute of Ecotourism Srinakharinwirot University Bangkok held in February 1995 and July 1996 and the New Zealand-Thailand Ecotourism Forum held in Bangkok July 1997. As part of the 'ecopush' the Tourism Authority of Thailand (TAT) is assisting in the design of new hotels to minimise environmental impact. Other measures already undertaken include electrifying Bangkok's tuk-tuks and installing water purification plants to clear Pattaya's beaches. The push for ecotourism development in Thailand now has the country being marketed as three distinct destination regions-mountains in the north, culture in the centre and beaches in the south. Ecotourism issues in each of the three zones is now presented followed by a specific focus on Phuket.

Northern

Lisu Lodge in northern Thailand is approximately one hour's drive from Chiang Mai. It has been upheld as an exemplar in ecotourism building design, environmental interpretation and community involvement (Muqbil 1994). Established by John Davies the lodge plays a central role in the creation of low-density, high-quality ecotours with minimal environmental impact. It promotes exotic experiences for ecotourists while providing the Lisu hill tribe people with an economic alternative to fanning as well as a renewed interest and pride in their culture. Park entrance fees have the potential to contribute directly to management expenses, but are currently channelled into the Thai government's general revenues. Doi Inthanon, a national park, world renowned for its 'birding' or 'du nok' now has a two tiered fee system, where foreigners pay a higher amount US$ 1.00 compared to $0.20 per person approximately). Recent research in the park indicates that 80% of tourists state they are willing to pay more for conservation.

Birding is a popular form of ecotourism but it has the potential to cause adverse environmental impacts. The possibility of the harassment of wildlife is a negative outcome of ecotourism development. For example, some birders attract birds by whistling or playing a tape recorded song, which brings them out into the open to confront the 'intruder'. However, when used too often, this strategy may cause birds undue stress. Other environmental issues include trampling, litter and air pollution. Attempts are being made to mitigate these, for example, through the construction of a board-walk around the summit of Dol Inthanon and through increased tourist awareness of litter and pollution. One of the key elements of ecotourism is that it should be locally beneficial. Within Doi Inthanon there are 600 villages located in the park and the residents earn their living by growing rice and cash crops and through collecting plants and fuel wood for personal use or sale. If hill tribes can benefit economically from ecotourism they may support habitat protection initiatives and depend less on unsustainable uses of park resources. However, according to Jean Michaud from Montreal University after a village has been overexposed the tour guides move onto newer, more 'authentic' territories. In a similar vein it has been suggested that ecotourism may exacerbate social and cultural impacts by intensifying the degree of contact between hosts and tourists.

Central

Today 13% of the land base of Thailand is environmentally protected. However, efficient management of the protected areas is constrained by low budgets. Attempts to alleviate this have been made by the construction of resorts within natural areas to create funds. This has not always been successful as demonstrated by occurrences at Khao Yai National Park. In the late 1980s TAT constructed a resort and golf course inside the park. The finding of dead deer in the park which had eaten golf balls, and.incidents of elephants killed by falling off steep cliffs after new roads in the park obstructed their normal feeding routes, finally led to the closing down of these projects.

One of the benefits of ecotourism is that it acts as an exemplar for tourism through the promotion of sustainable development principles, especially in the area of the 'greening' of tourism. The Thai Hotel Association is urging its members to 'turn green'. It has conducted a seminar series on the economic benefits of being 'environmentally friendly' and it has implemented a 'Green Leaf' program. The Electricity Generating Authority of Thailand has offered interest free finance to re-equip buildings with energy saving equipment. The Tourism Authority of Thailand also helps in the design of new hotels to minimise adverse environmental impacts.

The Marriott Royal Garden Riverside Bangkok and the Royal Garden Resort Hua Hin are exemplars within the field of green practices. The former has an eco code of ethics and in addition fosters environmentally friendly practices outside the immediate hotel environment. Its 'Preserve the Kingdom' environmental awareness campaign raises public awareness of some of Thailand's endangered species.

Southern

Another model in the field of ecotourism in Thailand is Sea Canoe. It is the only internationally acclaimed eco development laboratory applying innovative economic and management principles to conservation-based, locally owned rural development. Sea Canoe International began operating canoe expeditions in Phuket after years of operating open sea expeditions on the Pacific Ocean's coastlines. It has a strong environmental protection policy and the company "talks environmentalism to three publics-customers, staff and the host community". The company attributes its success to its commitment to the environment and its requirement of maintaining low tourist volumes. Another key element is Sea Canoe's desire to creatively seek out ecotourism experiences and hence business opportunities.

Siam Safari's Eco-Nature Tours was the first specialist ecotour company to be formed in Phuket. It was founded by Lerd Sun Khomkrit in 1989 and it organises 1-4 day safaris in Southern Thailand. The one-day Phuket Island Eco-Nature Safari by four-wheel drive Land Rover takes visitors off the beaten track, giving four to six people at a time a variety of insights into traditional rural life on the island. The two-day Tropical Rainforest Explorer tour encompasses Khao Sok National Park, 150 kilometres northeast of Phuket on the mainland. The trek in the rainforest with knowledgeable guides offers an opportunity to observe an environment with some of the greatest diversity of life forms on the planet. In 1996 TAT invested a large sum of money towards developing facilities at Khao Sok National Park. Despite the interest in Khao Sok National Park by the TAT concerns have been voiced over the lack of apparent control or involvement from the National Parks Division and conservation groups. There are few plans for initiating scientific research or environmental or conservation programs in the park. To date there has been very little research carried out on the flora and fauna of Khao Sok, similarly in other protected areas in Thailand. However, if we do not know and understand the resource we cannot hope to manage it effectively. In addition if the intricacies and fragile life systems of the park are not understood by scientists then it stands to reason that the ecotourist will not either. To overcome this it has been suggested that ecotourism provides a ready made vehicle for the Royal Forest Department's National Parks Division and the TAT to work together to protect the environment, increase the scientific knowledge of the area, and to work with the local community.

Phuket

The tourist destination of Phuket is a microcosm of the issues affecting tourism and the environment in Thailand. It has a history of a litany of tourism induced environmental problems but also includes some sound examples of tourism-environment symbiosis. For example, in 1992 the Laguna Beach Resort located in Phuket was awarded the International Hotel Association's Environmental Award due to its transformation of a polluted tin mine into an ecosystem of indigenous vegetation which utilizes recycled water, organic waste and treated sewage.

The International Hotel & Resorts Association 1996 Green Hotelier of the year was awarded to Peter McAlpine then manager at the Phuket Yacht Club Hotel & Beach Resort. McAlpine's efforts reached beyond the walls of the resort to the wider area of Phuket, a once pristine island threatened by overdevelopment, mismanagement and a rapid increase in tourism. His first step was to raise the environmental awareness of the Phuket Yacht Club's 245 employees, organising staff beach cleanups and tree plantings. Gradually, energy and waste reduction programs were implemented. He organised environmental workshops at the hotel and in surrounding villages. With the help of two other hoteliers, he held a Bike-A-Thon a cycling fundraiser.

Hotels in Phuket have now agreed to accept a set of minimum standards for environmental protection. To embrace the flow of ideas McAlpine hopes to implement a formal structure for ecotourism in Thailand through a system of regional councils. A further initiative is to educate primary school teachers in Phuket on environmentally friendly practices through workshops with follow up seminars . Largely due to McAlpine's efforts Phuket has agreed to accept a set of minimum standards for environmental protection and a resource management act to protect new environmental initiatives is on the government's agenda

A major survey of the tourism-environment relationship in Phuket has been undertaken in the western bays. This study indicates that increased tourism development causes adverse environmental impacts often leading to a complete alteration of the natural environment. However, the increase in tourism pressure continues. For example UK long haul specialist Silk Cut Travel has expanded its programme to the Far East with the launch of its 1998 'Hotels of Character' . Over the past two years client feedback has confirmed that the real appeal of the programme is for the character in the hotels featured combined with locational individuality, management and atmosphere. In Thailand, the operator has re-introduced its resort of Krabi, which it dropped two years ago, and has added hotels in the resorts of Phuket and Koh Samui. Phi Phi Island and northern Thailand itineraries featuring Chiang Mai, Chiang Rai and the Golden Triangle remain in the programme.

An important feature of the tourism industry in Thailand is its close association with ecosystems which have proven to be of only marginal value for other forms of economic activity. These include the mountain regions of the north as well as the coastal areas of the south. Parnwell's 1993 study of Ko Samui provides an illustration of some of the environmental pressures which have been associated with the relatively unplanned and uncontrolled growth of tourism. Although very small in size the island is estimated to host a projected 1.1 million visitors annually within two years. Ko Samui has been vigorously promoted as a major tourism destination by both private sector firms and the Tourism Authority of Thailand. As a consequence the environment is under increasing pressure from the tourism boom and the coast line has been changed dramatically. The coral reefs and their associated marine life have come under considerable pressure from scuba-diving and souvenir-hunting. This has caused considerable damage to the reefs. So has the large volume of untreated effluent which is discharged into the sea from the island. It is not tourism in itself that is destructive, but rather it is a consequence of the lack of tourism planning and management.

Discussion

The above examples indicate that Thailand's record of fostering environmentally sensitive tourism development is increasing. However, in addition to the problems cited earlier, others have been noted by Gill and Satyanarayan (1995). They state that with barely 15 to 20 percent of forest area remaining in Thailand the increasing demands on them made by ecotourism are now causing intrusions into the last few patches of 'unopened' territories. They conclude that Thailand may be treading into dangerous territory as watershed areas become exposed and polluted, natural forests are destroyed, and the remaining biodiversity of the country is lost. For example, on Ko Taen the local community has established a conservation club to 'conserve the unity of the people and to control the island's tourism to be real ecotourism'. The theme of the 7th PATA Adventure Travel and Ecotourism Conference and Mart held in Balikpapan, East Kalimantan, Indonesia from 15-18 January 1995 was Nature and Adventure Tourism: Megatrend or Niche. A key outcome was that in order for ecotourism to remain environmentally and socially responsible in future, it will be necessary to limit tour group size and frequency. Therefore, ecotourism will always remain a 'niche' market. Another major issue is the problem of 'ecopirates', that is, companies which copy existing responsible tourism products, but in a non-responsible manner. Such copies typically offer lower prices, inferior experiences, and detrimental environmental and social impacts.

The advancement of ecotourism in South East Asia has obviously had positive and negative impacts on the natural and cultural environments. From a positive perspective ecotourism fosters a better appreciation of natural environments and their intrinsic and economic worth for protection and conservation. It also provides greater exposure both for the public and governing institutions to nature and conservation and it also has the potential to motivate the designation of natural areas for conservation and protection. On the other hand pressures originating from ecotourism can and do result in degeneration of the very ecosystems on which they depend. Impacts can be particularly severe when there is visitor intrusion where there had been none previously. Another important, and often overlooked, factor is that local communities involved in the industry may not have sufficient knowledge to organise a conservation program involving visitor management techniques. Hence they may prioritise visitor satisfaction over the needs of the natural resource.

In the case of the South East Asian countries extra pressure will be brought to bear to hasten development in order to build up foreign exchange earnings particularly in the light of the current economic crises. Tourism to these countries has never been cheaper hence it is envisaged that there will be a large influx of Australian, American and European travellers. Demand could well outweigh supply and hence put unsustainable pressure on the environment.

The fostering of cruise ship tourism within the region is viewed as one way of bringing in foreign exchange earnings without the necessity of having the infrastructure in place and with minimal environmental impact. Robost growth is forecast for the cruise industry between now and the year 2000, with the Asia Pacific region rapidly gaining market share. It is the vision of the Singapore government that it become a cruise hub. From here can be generated an exciting multi-destinational ecotourism development program taking in many of the countries of South East Asia. Since the region has so much to offer naturally, historically and culturally.

Conclusion

Earlier this decade it was clear that tourism in Thailand had developed at the expense of its environment and the question was asked "is Thailand's tourism boom environmentally sustainable?". The question has as much validity today and can be widen to include the whole SE Asian region. Environmental issues in Thailand are still a pressing concern, but despite important gains such as the 1992 Environmental Act, the incapacity of provincial governmental bodies to enforce legislation against polluters and illegal builders in big resorts like Phuket Island and Pattaya is still evident.

The extent of ecotourism impacts depends on their efficient detection and identification (either through baseline monitoring of the natural resource or through indicators) and subsequent management actions. Impact identification requires some form of baseline data or indicators to determine acceptable limits of the impacts/changes to the natural environment. Resolving these impacts requires the formulation of management strategies that are able to maintain them at a level that is acceptable for both nature conservation and nature based recreation.

Tourism and the natural environment can form a symbiotic relationship. This can be achieved by developing purpose built tourist resort complexes; investment in and careful design of tourism infrastructure; and the hardening of sites to carry more tourists whilst conserving the natural environment. Thus there is a strong case for promoting 'sustainable' forms of tourism such 'ecotourism', as a way of fostering harmony between people and nature through tourism. Unfortunately, such principles would appear to be at variance with the economic arguments in favour of mass tourism

Finally, it is suggested that ecotourism development in South East Asia should not be pursued as the panacea for the economic woes caused by the 'Asian Crisis', but rather viewed as a tool for fostering the sustainable advancement of local communities, in a manner which is commensurate with sound environmental practice, cultural preservation and economic wellbeing.

In this way the development of ecotourism in South East Asia will advance tourism that is appropriate for the region when based on the principles of community participation and environmental sustainability, a philosophy advocated and pursued by the Thailand Environmental Institute (TEI 1996).

The Beauty and Danger of Ecotourism

Forward by BCN's Director Bernd Cordes

One of the benefits of working for BCN is that we sometimes have the opportunity to go to places we otherwise would never get a chance to visit. And, because of our relationships with our NGO partners and the community members, we have access to information, conversations and insights into local conditions that we would otherwise not get. That's what happened to Diane Russell, a former BCN Senior Program Officer who was based in Fiji. In 1998, she visited a BCN-funded conservation project in Makira, Solomon Islands. One part of the project there is to develop a sustainable, community-based ecotourism venture. So, she took the trip, but with a dual purpose. She went as a tourist, along for the guided ride through the forest and bringing her daughter with her. But it wasn't all play. She also went as a program officer partly responsible for the conservation and enterprise development work being done at the site. As she walked the trails and visited the villages, Diane kept notes as a tourist and as a partner in conservation, noting the good measure of success the business has had (e.g., Conde Nast travel magazine deemed this a stellar ecotourism destination and experience in the South Pacific), as well as its share of difficulties. Below are her notes, observations and experiences, which should be of interest to others doing similar work.

Trekking the Highlands of Makira Island, Solomon Islands

Ecotourism is often viewed as an ideal solution to the conservation and development dilemma: how to balance human use of biological resources with the protection of critical habitats and species. The concept is particularly attractive in the pacific islands where tourism is a dominant industry and local communities control their land. But what is the reality? What are the risks to habitats and to the local communities involved? Does ecotourism bring tangible benefits to a community? Is it truly compatible with conservation goals?

We examine these questions through the lens of my experience on a guided trek through the highlands of Makira, Solomon Islands in April 1998. Makira's Bauro communities, Conservation International (CI) and the Solomon Islands Development Trust, (SIDT), working together as the Conservation in Development (CID) Program organize this trek. The program is dedicated to conservation of the biodiversity of this unique island and the well being of the communities. In addition to the ecotour, the program also helps to manage a ngali nut *(Canarium indicum)* oil enterprise, and sponsors health, community-based monitoring and environmental education activities.

The Makira trek brings together a superb natural environment, cultural enhancement, appropriate cash benefits, and strong links to conservation. At present, it is a beautiful experience. But I encountered danger at every turn. The difficulties of setting up a sustainable enterprise in a remote location such as Makira cannot be underestimated. And community-based conservation is a process of negotiation and learning that often shreds the patience of local staff and leadership.

Background

Makira Island, also known as San Cristobal Island, is 3090 sq. km: 139 km long by 40 km wide. Mountains run like a spine down the island's centre: the highest point reaches 1040 m, then falls steeply to the sea along its southern shore. Many rivers penetrate the island in roughly parallel lines every two to five kilometres. Makira has more inland swamps—and saltwater crocodiles—than any other island in the Solomon Islands. Its coast is the only part of the Solomons where the rare olive, or Pacific Ridley, turtle is known to visit and nest. Because Makira Island was isolated for long stretches of time during periods of high sea level, a wide variety of unique plants and animals evolved. For example, 12 of its 70 resident species of birds are endemic, as are two tree species, both figs *(Ficus cristobalensis* and *Ficus illiberalis)*. This uniqueness highlights the importance of preserving Makira's forest habitat.

In 1992, the Central Bank of Solomon Islands estimated that all reserves of lowland forest would be cut down within eight to ten years. This unsustainable rate of extraction stems on the government side mainly from the desperate need to garner foreign exchange and perceived lack of alternatives. The reasons for landowner agreement to logging concessions include the desire for cash and status on the part of "big men." Many Makira communities have already succumbed to the relatively large amounts of cash that the logging companies offer people in order to cut high-grade timber on their land. To resist these threats, the CID program established Makira's first conservation area, which consists of approximately 63,000 hectares of largely undisturbed indigenous vegetation, representing the second largest protected area in the South Pacific. Since the early 1990s, the program has been working with the Bauro communities to define the area and to identify enterprises whose viability is linked to the need to conserve the area's biodiversity.

In 1995, the CID consortium of CI, SIDT and the Maruia Society received a $US347, 574 grant from the Biodiversity Conservation Network (BCN) to support these activities, particularly to assist in the enterprise and monitoring work.

Community

Makira has four main language groups. The ecotour involves people from the coast up to the highlands of central Makira, all of whom are Bauro speakers. The Bauro have been considered to be the most isolated and conservative of the Makira groups. In 1995, a CID survey found that the communities were cash poor and, though "isolated," experienced environmental problems due to more intensive use of resources. Seventy percent of households surveyed reported no cash income during the past month, and only six out of 320 households interviewed had access to salaried income. Few families (16%) had trade licenses and these involved petty trade only. The estimated 4-6% rate of population growth and use of destructive hunting and fishing techniques contribute to declining fertility of garden lands, and disappearance of river fish and some bird species.

Highlights of the Trek

On April 12, 1998, my seven-year old daughter and I joined a group of six people on a trek across the riverbeds and up the steep hills of the central Bauro highlands. Our young guides met us at the end of the road that leads from the airport — the only road on Makira. Porters took the heavy packs and started off, so that they would be there when we got to our first stop. The guides immediately put us at ease by chatting and telling us what we would expect. Their training and experience with tourists was evident. After a stop at the village of Mato, we climbed up and down two steep hills to get to a lovely bend in the western tributary of the Ravo river known as the Ravorighi, or "small Ravo." A trail from the river led to a leaf house with a raised platform that served as our home for the night. The land for this rest house, in the area called Na'ara, is owned by ecotour manager John Waihuru's family. John and his family came down to meet us, to cook food and give us information about what we would be doing in the days to come.

The following day, after climbing up and down another steep hill, we reached the entry of Hunama village. As fatigued and hungry as the group was, we became highly alert – astonished by our greeting. Upon entry into the village, which had been decorated in flowers and leaves, we were taken to a shaded reviewing stand to drink water and eat fruit. There we had our first serenade by the Hunama pan pipers, led by Dominic, one of our guides. Later, Dominic told us that he borrowed some panpipe melodies from popular and religious songs, but other melodies came from the songs of birds in the forest. We were delighted to hear about this link between the music and the forest.

Our layover day in Hunama was full of laughter, drama, music and feasting. The community had crafted a creative program designed to entertain and teach us about their culture and lifeways. We learned how, in a warrior's education, boys attempt to match their elders in the art of throwing spears. Two lively custom skits concerned the relations between humans and spirits. The village children enjoyed the show as much as the visitors did: they screamed in anticipation and hilarity at the antics of their neighbours and relatives. In contrast to the boisterous acts of the men, the women's groups singing Christian songs were shy and sweet. The visitors also introduced themselves one by one, sang a song or told a table.

We watched demonstrations of traditional arts and crafts, including carving, food preparation, fire making and basket weaving. Villagers laid out the crafts and we purchased several items. A nice touch to the whole stay in Hunama was the presentation of handmade bowls to each of the visitors to use throughout their stay. These carved bowls were identified by the name of the sculptor, and John Waihuru, who hopes to encourage and improve the local artists, marked those chosen in a book. He asked us for detailed comments on the design and construction of the bowls. Months later, when John came to my home in Fiji, he was pleased to see these crafts displayed.As night fell, we gathered in the village commons again. A few kerosene lamps were lit. Beyond the circle of the lamps, the stars blazed with intensity rarely experienced by town dwellers. Seven-year old Eva gazed at a Milky Way she had never before seen so clearly. John Waihuru announced that we would have an evening of music, dance and sharing. He wanted to focus the discussion on conservation and the experiences of the visitors to the community.

But first the dance. Eva found a girl about her age and the two of them danced and ran through the crowd all evening. This freedom of village life — to be part of the festivities that have a role for all ages, to have the run of the village with a pack of children — has all but disappeared in the "developed" world. Virtually the whole village and all the visitors soon surrounded the circle of men and boys forming the panpipe band. The dancing turned carefree and experimental, mixing some pop and local styles.

Between the dances, our talk ranged over many topics. The Hunama people were above all concerned to understand more about conservation and the visitors' experiences. They were anxious to correct any problems and to improve the quality of the tour. Because Eva was the first non-local child to visit the area, they wanted to know if the food was adequate for her. Was the climate all right? What was it like in our place? Why do people want to come to Makira — to Hunama?

We pondered the relation between conservation and health. For one, the altitude of the intact forest in the Hunama area helps prevent the spread of mosquitoes. Hunama was delightfully free of those pests, and the highland dwellers do not contract malaria as frequently as their coastal cousins do. Second, the forest provides medicines. Our guides had pointed out some medicinal plants to us during the trek. The water source flowing from the forested hilltops provides clean water, thus keeping the people relatively free of parasites and other illness. Finally, the abundance of food crops could be attributed to the health of the forest because long garden cycles allow for regeneration of the soil. On day four, we went up the hill and across to Maraone. The visitors' first experience of Maraone began long before they actually saw the village. Where the terrain became extremely rugged, the community had built steps and banisters to guide the visitors. I felt that perhaps they knew I was coming! John Waihuru was surprised and pleased at the work that went into building this infrastructure – a spontaneous innovation on the part of the community.

During our two days in Maraone, we were treated to demonstrations of custom skills, and wonderful skits that had us whooping with laughter. The view from the village, across the conservation area, was stunning. While shy, the people wanted to talk about our experience in their village, and to share stories. Maraone is the home village of some Bauro clans, a bit slower paced and more conservative than Hunama. The beauty of the place revealed itself in the details: the design of our gift beads and headdresses, the delicious ngali nut pudding, the village decorations, and the church service we were invited to attend.

Hauta was our final stop before returning to the coast. To assure a good journey, John and the guides decided to take us up across the ridge rather than down and up the ravines we had traversed to get to Maraone. We trekked through mossy forest with views of the southern "weather coast" of the island. We observed a flying fox, huge spiders perched on their webs across the path, an array of birds, flowers, caterpillars and butterflies. The talk with John and the guides was as fascinating as the forest. I was amazed to find that, unlike my experience of African forests, there are no serious hazards in the forests of Makira: no dangerous snakes, insects or plants. Fire ants, which leave a burn when they land on the skin, are the worst hazards and they are relatively recent arrivals to the highlands. It began to seem like Makira was a Garden of Eden.

In this Eden, however, I learned that there were similar social problems to those I had encountered in Africa. These problems centered on jealousy that can inhibit initiative, and the corollary of finding ways to control the greed of a few individuals that can damage the social fabric. As cash enters a society, and cash values are placed on land, labour and natural products, more aggressive people can take advantage of others to claim land, establish large plantations or overhunt valuable species. In Solomon Islands, the laws governing access to timber and minerals encourage the division of communities, as those who support companies to get access can receive large cash rewards.

Hauta, the small village that harbours John Waihuru and his late wife's vision of a primary school and clinic to serve the Highland communities, perches on a gently sloping hill. Only three families now live in Hauta: John's, Paul Wori, the headmaster of the school, and Ephrem Waraba, a "refugee" from Bagohane. The panpipes greeted us again on arrival, led by the indomitable Dominic, who quickly switched from guide clothes to loincloth. Logging and mining tempt people with large cash payments that may seem on the surface to outweigh the benefits of ecotourism.

John and I sat down to discuss the enterprise. The transparent distribution of benefits is highly important. John records every transaction and together with other community leaders decides upon wage rates and who should get training. The allocation of payments to individuals can involve over 400 transactions for each tour. John's level of involvement in the enterprise is obviously not sustainable and he is training others to take on the financial records. But for the moment, John's active participation is critical to the functioning of the enterprise. He said that even after the money is allocated, people still come to wake him up before the light to ask about money issues. The fifth and final day of the ecotour saw us trekking down from Hauta to the coast. We spent the night right near the beach at Togori rest house, which had been decorated with flowers and paper mobiles. The ecotour was over but the memories remained vivid. All those who went on the tour felt that it was unique — almost magical. This ecotour experience seemed to be ideally suited to the level of economic development of the peoples of the highlands, and had the potential to encourage conservation. In 1997, the community sent away a Malaysian logging company. Village Resource Management Planning, to begin this year, will help people to decide how best to manage their human, biological and financial resources to deal with the intensification trends.

John Waihuru has been thinking deeply about conservation in the highlands:

"In my area, it is a bit complicated because I'm trying to do conservation on customary lands. There is a link with many tribes. If I say 'I want to conserve this area', I have to get agreement first from many different landowners. Conservation is not just one specific thing. It has to do with many things: water, land and air. When you talk about the land, it is complicated. Take a small piece of land like an island. One river starts from the north to the south. All rivers link up with this river. You might get one tribe that wants to conserve the river but on the other hand the other tribe might damage the river. You might want to try to conserve an endemic bird but it flies. Others might disagree. We still have a lot to do."

Beauty

The beautiful aspects of this experience can teach others how to go about setting up a community-based ecotour:

* *A Vision for the Future: Local Ownership*-The program team has a vision and plan for local control over all aspects of the enterprise. This vision is reflected in every decision and activity. For example, local people without external assistance can maintain the infrastructure of the trek.
* *Planning and Wide Participation*-The planning that went into the tour, from the first germ of an idea, through training, testing and refining each segment, is responsible for the current success. Risks and benefits were carefully weighed, and wide participation encouraged. The community has taken the lead and not let the enterprise overwhelm them.
* *Cultural Pride*-Ecotourism has sparked a revival in local traditional knowledge, particularly by youth who now see the value of this knowledge. The pride in culture is a catalyst for conservation because of the emphasis on low-impact technology and use of forest products.

* *Appropriate Product Development and Training*-The community decided to strictly control the number of treks and tourists on each trek. The guides were given training appropriate to the type of trek and tourist. The enterprise created an important role for young people who might otherwise want to migrate.
* *Conservation Focus*-The program team has kept the focus on conservation. To help John Waihuru understand conservation and enterprise in a broader context, the program got a grant for him to visit New Zealand. His visit to conservation areas, particularly a Maori area, deeply impressed him and gave him a vision of the links between enterprise and conservation that he is transferring to the community.

Danger

This ecotour faces dangers shared by similar ventures. When these dangers are anticipated, strategies can be developed to counter them.

* Market Uncertainties-Any community-based enterprise faces challenges of selling its product unless it links up immediately with a secure market outlet. In the case of the Makira ecotour, there has been relative success in getting tourists to the site due to the diligence of the project team. But the situation is delicate in three respects. One is that the *number* of tourists coming through needs to be limited and timed to the community's needs. Second, the *type* of tourist has to be at least somewhat controlled. The expectations of tourists have to be managed so that they are comfortable with what is being offered. Finally, the non-local tour operators need to be knowledgeable about both tourism and local community needs.

Strategies Used: Diversify tour operators, use a local in bound operator with knowledge of the area, and bring operators to the community to take the tour.

* ***Misunderstandings and Conflicts***-The case of Bagohane illustrates how local misunderstandings can cut off one part of the community from participation in the enterprise.

More severe conflicts are well known in community-based enterprises, particularly those using common-property resources.

Strategies Used: Continual discussion, inclusion of all parties, wide sharing of benefits.

* *Burnout*-We saw how John Waihuru faces enormous pressures in managing the ecotour at the local level — in part because of the emphasis on participation and benefit sharing. Even the guides and porters can be overloaded, literally and figuratively.

Strategies Used: Organize local committees to streamline reporting and benefit sharing, train others to do some of the work.

* *Competition*-Other communities on Makira or other islands will certainly be attracted to the benefits from this type of enterprise. "Copy-catting" can lead to divisiveness, dilution of the quality of the product, health and safety hazards for tourists.

Strategy Used: Tourists who are not part of the ecotour are strongly discouraged on Makira, particularly in going to the highlands; the program has sought ways to complement the trek with a visit to community-based lodges elsewhere in the Solomons.

* *Inadequate Benefits to Counter Threats*-Logging and mining tempt people with large cash payments that may seem on the surface to outweigh the benefits of ecotourism. National policies foster these choices.
* *Strategy Proposed:* Village resource management planning for landowners. CID staff is also passing on information about the real benefits and risks of logging and mining.

Conclusion

Strong leadership, careful planning and a relatively undisturbed and homogenous community contribute to the beauty of the Makira ecotour. Keeping the focus on conservation is critical. But even in the best of circumstances, ecotourism is only a partial solution to the conservation and development dilemma. It is not a magic bullet. A conservation area needs a suite of viable enterprises, supported by strong institutions at the community and national levels. Communities should not be expected to face the dangers to their resources and their livelihoods alone. They need appropriate policies, markets for their products, and links to like-minded people.

For the visitors, the ecotour brings awareness of linkages between community and biodiversity. At its most profound, it is a rite of passage to a more ecologically oriented worldview. Each visitor comes away not only with an experience in a specific community, but a vision to transform global culture. In this way, ecotourism can be a powerful tool for building a more sustainable world.

Community-based Transboundary Ecotourism in the Heart of Borneo

The Kelabit Highlands of Sarawak, Malaysia, and the Kerayan (also called Krayan) Highlands of Kalimantan, Indonesia, are highland plateaus separated by the Apad Wat mountain range in the interior of the island of Borneo. This area is now known around the world as the Heart of Borneo, which references the high-profile transboundary conservation initiative led by the World Wide Fund for Nature (WWF).

These highlands offer a combination of experiences that appeal to ecotourists. Due to the altitude of just over 1000 m, the temperature year-round is cool and comfortable, thus more appealing as a trekking destination than areas in Borneo's hot and humid lowlands. Also, the remote, mountainous, and relatively 'unspoilt' (compared with other places in Borneo) forests here are the island's last places to do long-distance village-to-village trekking.

The Kelabit and Kerayan Highlands contain a number of small villages and longhouse communities that have not yet been commercialised, allowing tourists seeking remote places and exotic people to experience a more genuine cultural encounter than is possible in other places in Borneo that are promoted as tourism destinations. These tend to be heavily commercialised and, to a certain extent, 'staged'. Based on numerous discussions with tourists who visit the highlands of Borneo, it became obvious that tourists do not come here wanting to stay in hotels or resorts; they prefer to avoid artificial or contrived lodgings made especially for tourists and come with the desire to stay with local families and to trek in the jungle with local guides.

The Kelabit and Kerayan Highlands are home to several closely related ethnic groups (including Kelabit, Lun Dayeh/Lun Bawang, Berian, Lengilu, Saban, and Penan) that speak related languages and have many cross-boundary kinship ties. Shared cultural features include similar wet-rice cultivation techniques and handicrafts (such as beadwork and weaving of baskets and mats), as well as a common history of megalith-making activities.

These megaliths (erected or carved stones or large rock piles) and other cultural monuments dot the landscape surrounding the rural villages and demonstrate the cultural contiguity of these plateaus, which are a 2-3 day hike apart.

These close cultural ties between the Kelabit and Kerayan Highlands, in addition to forests that have not yet been logged or converted to large-scale agriculture development, create an ideal situation for the development of community-based transboundary ecotourism initiatives that have the potential to be both a long-term source of revenue for rural communities and a land-use option that is compatible with local, regional, national, and international goals of conservation of biodiversity and natural resources. However, there are several factors that can make implementation of this type of tourism difficult to achieve on the ground. These will be discussed later in this article, but the most obvious one is that ecotourism development is one of the several goals for development proposed by the governments for this area, and it is not necessarily compatible with other governmental proposals.

This article examines the current state of transboundary ecotourism development in the Kelabit and Kerayan Highlands, with emphasis on the Kelabit Highlands of Sarawak. It situates the promotion of ecotourism here within the rhetoric of state and national conservation and development goals, and also identifies several of the main challenges faced by the local communities in the further development of community-based transboundary ecotourism. Research for this case study was conducted primarily in the Kelabit Highlands, and it included interviews with most of the guides and homestay owners in the Kelabit Highlands 1 and with 14 tourism professionals (tour operators, members of the Sarawak Tourism Board, and employees at visitors' centres) in the main cities of Sarawak, and participation in inter-community dialogues regarding transboundary ecotourism. In addition, it analyses promotional materials (both in print and on the Internet) on ecotourism in these areas, comments in the visitors' books of lodges in the Kelabit Highlands, and tourists' websites and travel blogs. Co-written by four local guides and homestay owners in Sarawak and Kalimantan and a graduate student from the USA who has conducted 3 years of ethnographic research in the Kelabit Highlands, this case study represents a stage of introspection by people actively engaged in current ecotourism activities and seeks to chart a course forward that takes into account the specific ecological, social, cultural, and political context of this region. The process of conducting this research project helped to pinpoint some of the specific challenges of transboundary ecotourism in this area, and will form the basis for a more comprehensive ecotourism management plan for local communities on both sides of the border.

Gathering, collating, and analysing the findings of this research with local community members revealed that the main issues that need to be addressed include: (1) protection of forests and cultural sites as foci for ecotourism; (2) improved communication between villages, guides, and lodges; (3) increased promotion of transboundary trekking options; (4) village-level preparation for more tourists and more equitable distribution of income generated from ecotourism; (5) careful improvements in tourism infrastructure; (6) the negotiation of legal complications arising from international border crossings by tourists and guides; and (7) the maintenance of local control over ecotourism management and the trajectory of future tourism development. Analysis of these issues in this transboundary area will not only help maximise local benefits from ecotourism in interior Borneo but also address many themes central to the academic literature on ecotourism in other parts of the world.

Background: Ecotourism in Malaysia

Tourism, and particularly ecotourism in developing countries rich with natural and cultural capital, is often touted as a sustainable source of revenue for indigenous and rural communities, and tourism often helps to bring developing countries and even local communities into the global economy. Although it is widely recognised now that while tourism has the potential to stimulate economic growth in marginal and underdeveloped areas, it can also serve to exacerbate inequalities within and between communities, and between local communities and the larger social, economic, political context in which these communities are embedded.

Many scholars, human rights advocates, and tourism practitioners have argued that in order to address these issues of inequalities created or reinforced by tourism in rural areas, it is important that local communities are active stakeholders in tourism ventures and that such ventures are not imposed on them by outsiders who seek personal gain. However, this can be difficult and problematic on the ground, particularly when multiple communities are involved. The local communities in the Kelabit and Kerayan Highlands, both of their own initiative and with the assistance of international organisations such as WWF and the International Tropical Timber Organization (ITTO), have implemented several strategies for maintaining local control of tourism and promoting and improving community-based transboundary ecotourism.

In Malaysia, the Ministry of Tourism and Culture, established in 1987, became the Ministry of Culture, Arts, and Tourism in 1989. Now, tourism activities fall under the national jurisdiction of the Ministry of Tourism, and in the state of Sarawak, under the jurisdiction of the state Ministry of Urban Development and Tourism. In recent years, the Malaysian government has been steadily increasing its promotion of tourism, even globally advertising the year 2007 as Visit Malaysia Year. Malaysia is a popular tourist destination, and in particular, an ecotourism destination. Chin, Moore, Wallington, and Dowling notes that in the Malaysian state of Sarawak, 'tourist receipts have increased from RM 140.6 million in 1989 to RM 522.3 million in 1997'.

According to Mohamed (2002), revenues from ecotourism in Malaysia were RM 655 million, of a total of RM 14 billion generated from all types of tourism. However, Davison (1995) notes that it is difficult to obtain reliable information on the number of ecotourists to Malaysia. Tourism in Malaysia has been seen by Malaysians as a double-edged sword.

On the one hand are the positive benefits of tourism such as increased employment, infrastructure development for rural areas, the enrichment of local culture through contact with outsiders, and the revitalisation of local cultural traditions, while on the other hand are deleterious effects such as the encroachment of new (Western) values on local communities, pollution and ecological damage, haphazard development, exacerbation of inter- and intra-community tensions, economic inflation, and in some cases, even prostitution and drugs (Din, 1997). These same benefits and concerns are echoed in case studies around the world, but are particularly salient in Malaysia, which aims to be a 'fully developed country' by 2020 (as articulated in Wawasan 2020, or Vision 2020, a common reference in Malaysian development circles). Din explained what he called this 'scapegoating' of tourism: 'tourism has either been disproportionally credited with all the good effects, or has received more than its fair share of the blame for the bad effects. A balanced discussion of the subject is rarely found, if at all, in Malaysia'. Since then, there have been several focused case studies of ecotourism in national parks in Malaysia that do offer more balanced and nuanced discussions. These studies describe benefits to local communities through employment and increased protection of natural resources. They also note specific problems caused by overuse by visitors, including subsequent ecological damage and economic leakages that direct the cash flow from ecotourism away from local economies.

In the early 1990s, national discussions on tourism in Malaysia began to reflect consideration for cultural issues, such as the commercialisation of culture and the equitable distribution of benefits from tourism, as well as the linkage of sustainable development to environmental conservation in the form of new ecotourism enterprises, especially in Sarawak and Sabah. The link between ecological and cultural tourism is particularly strong in

Malaysia, and these alternative forms of tourism have been touted by governmental agencies, non-governmental organisations, tour operators, and local communities as a way to simultaneously promote conservation and non-consumptive use of natural resources, showcase unique indigenous cultures, and generate income for less-developed rural areas. The marriage of these goals is common to ecotourism endeavours around the world, but it represented an important shift in tourism goals by the Malaysian government, which previously did not thoroughly examine the effects of tourism on local communities.

Malaysia has officially adopted the World Conservation Union (IUCN)'s definition of ecotourism, and in 1997 created the National Ecotourism Plan, which outlined a set of 25 guidelines for categorising sites and ecotourism opportunities, defining carrying capacity and limits of acceptable change for each site, creating and improving national parks and forest reserves, promoting accreditation of ecotourism products and other activities necessary for ensuring compatibility between conservation and sustainable development through ecotourism. However, Abidin (1999) says that these guidelines are not specific enough, and that criteria and indicators for measuring carrying capacity, limits of acceptable change, and sustainability are lacking in this national plan, as are mechanisms for evaluating and monitoring future tourism and conservation programmes. He says: 'There are also no criteria and indicators developed for sustainable tourism management and biological diversity conservation in the protected areas of Malaysia'. Malaysia, while enthusiastically jumping on the ecotourism bandwagon, has its share of challenges and problems in ensuring such compatibility between conservation and sustainable development. An enlightening study by Lim (1999) revealed that travel agencies promoting ecotourism packages in Malaysia:

* are mostly new with 4-6 years experience;
* travel guides into ecotourism sites lack proper training and education; many have generic licenses but operate within ecotourism spots;
* only 11.9% of the agencies gave information regarding buying banned items when visiting ecotourism sites in

Malaysia. And the same percentage contributed their income towards conservation activities;

* less than 46% have close relationships with the local communities;
* over 30% have little relation with the government; another 30.8% admitted they have no relation with the government;
* 10 out of 15 agencies do not really understand the principles and concepts of ecotourism;
* Almost 80% of the activities tend to be fun-filled or adventurous but lacking in terms of getting to know the nature.

The results of this study show that Malaysia clearly can improve its ecotourism practices rather than just promoting its natural areas as ecotourism destinations.

At the Borneo Ecotourism Conference in April of 2005, Mr. Rambli Ahmad, the Manager of Planning and Development of the Sarawak Tourism Board, stated that although ecotourism had benefited the people of Sarawak, 'an adverse consequence of this business was that most of the longhouses were trying to meet the needs of foreign tourists rather than preserving their culture'. Communities around the world have faced similar challenges when tourism (including ecotourism and cultural tourism) has been introduced, particularly that of the commodification or objectification of material culture and the staging of performative culture that can lead more to the falsification or exaggeration of culture than the preservation of it.

According to Din (1997), the objective is to balance the needs of the guests and the hosts, and to allow the local communities to define their priorities. He says: 'For Malaysians, it is important that tourism will not jeopardize the societal goals that the host community defines'. In the case of the Kelabit and Kerayan Highlands, most community members agree that their main goals are conservation and development through their own local initiatives, and they see ecotourism as an important means of achieving these goals simultaneously. Community members have taken important steps to improve the quality of the ecotourism experience for visitors, to monitor and protect the natural and cultural resources in their villages, to expand the direct benefits of ecotourism to more community members, and to maintain control over the pace and course of ecotourism development. Genuine community-driven ecotourism development requires that local communities determine the type and trajectory of tourism development, not merely react to the needs and desires of foreign tourists and accept top-down implementation of tourism projects by outside agencies. Due to the remoteness of this area, so far there has been little threat of the imposition of tourism on these communities, so it has remained in the hands of the community members.

This could change in the near future, however, as the highlands become accessible by logging roads and more infrastructure development is sponsored by the government and the private sector. Concern for local autonomy has guided both local ecotourism initiatives and NGO-assisted programmes for ecotourism development in the highlands of Borneo. At the same time, communities and assisting organisations recognise the need to work with multiple stakeholders in ecotourism development. Participants elaborated on this sentiment during the Borneo Ecotourism Conference in 2005, as the conference fostered new partnerships between governmental agencies, private businesses, and local communities in ecotourism development. Both the federal government of Malaysia and the state government of Sarawak have made numerous public statements supporting the development of ecotourism, as both an income-generating activity for rural communities and as an important component of state and federal sustainable forestry policies. For example, the Deputy Chief Minister of Sarawak, Datuk Patinggi Tan Sri Dr. George Chan, said that:

> The foresight of our Chief Minister has been instrumental in moving the tourism industry here to where it is today even though funds for such developments were often hard to come by due initially to the small number of tourist arrivals which did not justify the amount spent of such facilities. However, we persevere and spending wisely we have managed to bring Sarawak into the world map of eco tourism which is envisaged as a sustainable industry for the state for a long time to come.

The Eighth Malaysia Plan (2001-2005) includes an entire section on tourism development, with a focus on nature-based tourism or ecotourism; this rhetoric supporting ecotourism development is reiterated in the Ninth Malaysia Plan (2006-2010), particularly as a means to generate income for rural communities, while simultaneously demonstrating the commitment of the government to conserve natural resources in the geographical and metaphorical Heart of Borneo.

The Heart of Borneo Conservation Initiative

Led by WWF, the Heart of Borneo is a large-scale, tri-national transboundary initiative that aims to tie ecological conservation with sustainable development in the geographical middle (or 'heart') of the island of Borneo. Following an April 2005 meeting in Brunei, the governments of Indonesia, Malaysia, and Brunei publicly committed to a cooperative conservation initiative at the Convention on Biological Diversity (CBD) meeting in Curitiba, Brazil, in March 2006, and the official Heart of Borneo Declaration was signed by representatives of these countries on 7 February 2007. The area covered by the Heart of Borneo initiative is approximately 220,000 km^2 or 2.5 million hectares, and includes the upper montane forests in highlands and watersheds that cross international boundaries (World Wide Fund for Nature [WWF] Denmark,.

The interior of Borneo is recognised internationally by scientists, researchers, and conservation organisations as being globally important, and ecologically and culturally unique. It is a repository of numerous endemic and endangered species, a source of watersheds for the entire island, and home to a number of indigenous communities who have managed this landscape sustainably for untold generations. Local livelihoods, centred on income from organic rice production and ecotourism, are dependent on intact forests and watersheds. However, government agencies and private sector companies in both Malaysia and Indonesia are planning different scenarios for this area: expansion of protected areas, continued logging, large-scale agricultural development, increased smallholder agriculture, infrastructure and ecotourism development, and creation of income opportunities for local communities. These different scenarios would have enormous impacts on the future of ecotourism in the interior highland areas of Borneo, in ways that are generally self-explanatory. The future here is uncertain, which makes long-term planning difficult for local communities, but they are pursuing ecotourism development at the moment, with the support of various government agencies. Much of the Kerayan Highlands of Indonesian Borneo is already within the boundaries of the Kayan Mentarang National Park (KMNP), encompassing over 1.3 million hectares along the border with Sarawak (WWF Denmark, 2006). On 24 March 2006, a new national park was officially gazetted in Sarawak near the border with Kalimantan. Pulong Tau National Park (PTNP), which translates to 'Our Forest' in the Kelabit language, was first requested by members of the Kelabit community in the late 1970s as a means to protect the headwaters of several major rivers in Sarawak, including the Baram, Tutoh, and Limbang Rivers. Originally, this park included 164,500 hectares, but over the years, the area was decreased incrementally to its current size of 59,817 hectares. Key landscape features were removed from the park, and all but about 2 km of the transboundary areas were also removed.

There is currently a proposal by the ITTO and the Government of Malaysia to extend the border of PTNP in Sarawak to join with KMNP in Kalimantan, thus creating a large transboundary conservation area. This ITTO project, entitled 'Transboundary Biodiversity Conservation: The Pulong Tau National Park, Sarawak State, Malaysia', is now in its second phase. During the first phase, Sarawak Forest Department employees conducted baseline ecological studies within the park, as well as socioeconomic and cultural studies on the communities in the Kelabit Highlands, areas within and bordering the proposed extension area (International Tropical Timber Organization [ITTO] and Government of Malaysia, 2003). These baseline studies were intended to inform the long-term management plan of PTNP. The second phase of the project includes implementation of the projects proposed in the first phase, the most significant of which is the actual extension of the boundaries of PTNP to create a genuine transboundary conservation area with KMNP.

A large component of the sustainable development goals of this ITTO project is to establish an infrastructure for renewable income for local communities through ecotourism, while at the same time promoting ecoregional conservation of biodiversity and watersheds.

The budget for Phase II of the ITTO project (ITTO and Government of Malaysia, 2007) includes USD 4000 for informational material on PTNP, USD 15,000 to improve and maintain jungle trails to Mount Murud, a popular trek for tourists, USD 6000 for tourist guide training and tourism information materials, and USD 2000 to propose Kelabit megalithic areas as a UNESCO World Heritage Site.

It also budgets for a total of USD 29,000 for 'cross-border socioeconomic activities among local communities', of which USD 3000 is specifically earmarked for 'cross-border ecotourism: resource development, joint promotion materials, and tourist guides training/visits'. The ecotourism potential of this area is mentioned throughout this document, and it states clearly that: 'Through transboundary cooperation, the people across the borders can work to bring their economies closer, by improving roads, promoting cross-border trade and joint ecotourism for mutual benefits'.

Ecotourism is often proposed as an economic investment in conservation; however, positive examples of ecotourism in the academic literature are still rare. Many academic articles argue that the goals of ecotourism can conflict with the goals of conservation and preservation of cultural traditions, as well as local livelihoods, and that conservation laws can conflict with local livelihoods derived from ecotourism.

A central concern with relying on ecotourism as a way to conserve natural resources is that tourism itself can bring about ecological degradation. But despite these critiques of ecotourism ventures in some areas, it is still a viable and desirable alternative in many places, so long as it is carefully planned and monitored. Malaysia is a signatory to the CBD, whose fifth Conference of the Parties (COP-5) decided that: 'tourism does present a significant potential for realising benefits in terms of the conservation of biological diversity and the sustainable use of its components'. However, it also noted that: 'Historical observation indicates that self-regulation of the tourism industry for sustainable use of biological resources has only rarely been successful'. Visitor impact assessment is vital to maintaining the health of ecosystems that are ecotourism destinations. This is particularly important in ecosystems as fragile as those found within the highland plateaus of the Heart of Borneo, and a central concern for promoting the development of ecotourism (or any type of tourism) here is minimising the negative social, cultural, and ecological effects. The most recent ITTO document says that 'with careful planning and monitoring, it is unlikely that ecotourism development will affect the sustainability of the park (PTNP)'. But what is needed in the highlands is on-the-ground monitoring of the impacts of all types of development coming to these areas. Monitoring of, and mitigation for, ecotourism presents less of a challenge in the Kelabit and Kerayan Highlands than for other types of large-scale development that are also being proposed for this area, so it is difficult to consider this in isolation from other possible futures for this complex cultural and geographic landscape.

The political landscape of this area is also complex; in addition to myriad governmental agencies and private corporations making plans for this area, there are also numerous actors involved in ecotourism efforts in the highlands of Sarawak and Kalimantan. In addition to state and national ministries and governmental agencies in Malaysia and Indonesia, a number of international conservation, development, and finance NGOs and agencies are directly and tangentially involved in the Heart of Borneo initiative: WWF, The Nature Conservancy (TNC), Conservation International (CI), the IUCN, Global Environmental Facility (GEF), Wildlife Conservation Society (WCS), ITTO, United States Agency for International Development (USAID), United Nations Development Programme (UNDP), United Nations Educational, Scientific, and Cultural Organization (UNESCO), the World Bank (WB), International Monetary Fund (IMF), Asian Development Bank (ADB), International Finance Corporation (IFC), and Association for East Asian Nations (ASEAN). Many of these organisations have attended meetings regarding the Heart of Borneo initiative, and/or have contributed financial or verbal support, but WWF is the most involved on the ground, particularly in Kalimantan. Involvement by NGOs is more limited in Sarawak, and in the Kelabit Highlands, only ITTO (working with the Sarawak Forest Department and Sarawak Forest Corporation) has been directly involved in conservation efforts.

Alongside, and to some extent in conjunction with these national and international organisations, there are several local organisations that are actively engaged in ecotourism in the Kelabit and Kerayan Highlands, including the Tourism Bureau of the Kelabit Highlands, the Bario-Ba' Kelalan Nature Guide Association, Lembaya Swadaya Masyarakat Tanah Tam ('Our Land' Indonesian NGO), and the FORMADAT (Alliance of the Indigenous People of the Highlands in the Heart of Borneo). The focus of this article is on the efforts of these community-level organisations to promote, monitor, and improve transboundary ecotourism.

Bibliography

Bolshevism, Germy: *Coping with Tourists: European Reactions to Mass Tourism*, Oxford, Berghahn Books, 1995.

Broggi, M. : *Sanfter Tourismus: Schlagwort oder Chance Für Den Alpenraum?*, Vaduz, Commission Internationale pour la protection des Regions Alpines (CIPRA), 1985.

Carl H. : *Internet Distribution of European Travel and Tourism Services*, Research Centre of Bornholm, Denmark, 1999.

Carter, John: *Chandler's Travels: A Tour of the Life of Harry Chandler*, London, Quiller Press, 1985.

Chambers, Erve: *Native Tours: The Anthropology of Travel and Tourism*, Prospect Heights, Waveland Press, 2000.

Clark, Mona: *Interpersonal Skills for Hospitality Managers*, London, Chapman Hill, 1995.

Cukier, J. : *Tourism Employment in Bali: Trends and Implications*, London: Thompson, 1996.

David L: *International Tourism Policy, New York*, Van Nostrand and Reinhold, 1990.

Donald E. : *Public Personnel Management: Contexts and Strategies*, Upper Saddle River, NJ: Prentice Hall, 1998.

Donald M.: *Customer Service in the Hospitality and Tourism Industry*, Englewood Cliffs, Prentice Hall, 1994.

Eberts, Marjorie: *Careers in Travel, Tourism, and Hospitality*, Lincolnwood, VGM Career Horizons, 1997.

Fesenmaier D., Klein, S. : *Information & Communication Technologies in Tourism*, Springer-Verlag, Wien-New York, 2000.

Foster, Douglas: *Travel and Tourism Management*, London, Macmillan Educational, 1985.

Graham M S: *Language of Tourism*, The, Wallingford, CAB International, 1996.

Harrison, Lyndon: *Tourism Means Jobs*, Chester, Lyndon Harrison, 1996.

Harrison, Lyndon: *Tourism Means Jobs*, Chester, Lyndon Harrison, 1996.

Judi Radice: *Restaurant & Food Graphics*, Glen Cove, PBC International, 1994.

Judy A: *Tourism: Management of Facilities*, London, Pitman: M & E, 1993.

Karski, A: *Urban Tourism* - A Key to Urban Regeneration?, 1990.

Kotler, Philip: *Marketing for Hospitality and Tourism*: New Jersey, Prentice-Hall, 1998.

Larkham, P J: *Building a New Heritage: Tourism, Culture & Identity in the New Europe*, London, Routledge,1994.

Leivadi, S: *Sociology of Tourism, The: Theoretical And Empirical Investigations*, London, Retailed, 1996.

Lucas, Rosemary E.: *Managing Employee Relations in the Hotel and Catering Industry*, London, Cassell, 1995.

Madhukar Manoj : *Hospitality Industries in Next Millennium*, Rajat, Delhi, 2001.

Marcussen, Carl H. : *Internet Distribution of European Travel and Tourism Services*, Research Centre of Bornholm, Denmark, 1999.

Margaret Wade: *Medieval Travellers: The Rich and Restless*, London, Hamish Hamilton, 1982.

Martin, B.S. : *The Efficacy of Growth Machine Theory in Explaining Resident Perceptions of Community Tourism Development*, Clemson University, 1996.

McNicol, B.J. : *Views of Residents, Developers and Government Planners About Tourists and Tourism Resort Developments in Canmore, Alberta*, The University of Galgary, Alberta, 1996.

Medlik, S: *Management of Tourism*, The, London, Heinemann, 1975.

Murphy, P.E. : *Tourism: A Community Approach*, London: Methuen, 1985.

Nancy, N.: *Choosing a Career in Hotels, Motels, and Resorts*, New York, Rosen Pub. Group, 1997.

Paajanen, M. : *Assessing Local Income and Employment Effects of Tourism: Experience using the Nordic model of tourism*, Wiley, 1999.

Pearce, Douglas: *Tourism Today: A Geographical Analysis*, Harlow, Longman, 1995.

Peter J.: *College & University Foodservice Management Standards*, Westport, AVI Pub. Company, 1985.

Peters, M: *International Tourism*, London, Hutchinson, 1969.

Richards, G. : *Culture, Crafts and Tourism: A Vital Relationship*, Tilburg: Atlas, 1999.

Robert C.: *Cases in Hospitality Marketing and Management*, New York, John Wiley, 1997.

Rocco, M.: *An Introduction to Hospitality Today*, Orlando, Educational Institute, 1998.

Rosenzweig, J. E.: *Organisation and Management*, New York, McGraw Hill International, 1963.

Sabharwal Rajiv : *Tourism and Hospitality Management in Liberalised Era*, Pacific, Delhi, 2011.

Scottish Tourist Board: *Visitor Attractions: A Development Guide*, Edinburgh, Scottish Tourist Board, 1991.

Sharma Sunil : *Planning and Development of Tourism and Hospitality*, Rajat Pub, Delhi, 2007.

Shrivastava Atul : *Modern Hospitality and Tourism Management*, Centrum Press, Delhi, 2010.

Slinn, Judy A: *Tourism: Management of Facilities*, London, Pitman: M & E, 1993.

Stear, L. : *Design of a Curriculum for Destination Studies*, Annals of Tourism Research, 1981.

Thomas, F.: *Introduction to Management in the Hospitality Industry*, New York, Wiley, 1995.

Timothy R.: *Cases in Hospitality Management: A Critical Incident Approach*, New York, Wiley, 1995.

Index

H

I

M

N

O

P

S

T

❑❑❑